HOMESPUN GOSPEL

HOMESPUN
GOSPEL

The Triumph of Sentimentality in
Contemporary American Evangelicalism

Todd M. Brenneman

OXFORD
UNIVERSITY PRESS

Oxford University Press is a department of the University of Oxford.
It furthers the University's objective of excellence in research, scholarship,
and education by publishing worldwide.

Oxford   New York
Auckland   Cape Town   Dar es Salaam   Hong Kong   Karachi
Kuala Lumpur   Madrid   Melbourne   Mexico City   Nairobi
New Delhi   Shanghai   Taipei   Toronto

With offices in
Argentina   Austria   Brazil   Chile   Czech Republic   France   Greece
Guatemala   Hungary   Italy   Japan   Poland   Portugal   Singapore
South Korea   Switzerland   Thailand   Turkey   Ukraine   Vietnam

Oxford is a registered trademark of Oxford University Press in the UK and certain other
countries.

Published in the United States of America by
Oxford University Press
198 Madison Avenue, New York, NY 10016

© Oxford University Press 2014

Library of Congress Cataloging-in-Publication Data
Brenneman, Todd M., 1975–
Homespun gospel : the triumph of sentimentality in contemporary American evangelicalism / Todd M.
Brenneman.
pages cm
Includes bibliographical references and index.
ISBN 978–0–19–998898–3 (alk. paper)   ISBN 978–0–19–998899–0 (ebook)
ISBN 978–0–19–998900–3 (ebook)   1. Evangelicalism—United States—History—20th century.
2. Evangelicalism—United States—History—21st century.   3. Sentimentalism.   4. Emotions—
Religious aspects—Christianity.   5. United States—Church history—20th century.
6. United States—Church history—21st century.   I. Title.
BR1642.U5B74 2013
277.3'083—dc23
2013007803

9 8 7 6 5 4 3 2
Printed in the United States of America
on acid-free paper

For my grandmother Mae March

"Precious in the eyes of the Lord is the death of his faithful ones."

Psalm 116:15

CONTENTS

ACKNOWLEDGMENTS

I have often tried to encourage my students to recognize that scholarship is a collective enterprise. Not only do we build on the works of other scholars who we may never personally meet, but also there are so many who touch our scholarship in sometimes less tangible ways. I am extremely grateful to everyone who has touched my life and my scholarship and helped me to be a better scholar of religion. There are more people to thank in the development of this project, but there are several I want to highlight publicly.

Josh Fleer has been a helpful commenter on the manuscript as well as a supporter of the work in a variety of places. He was instrumental in having the preliminary draft of this work critiqued at the Christian Scholars Conference in 2010 where Richard Hughes, Ed Harrell, and Kathy Pulley offered some generous compliments and some thoughtful insight. Other commenters including John Corrigan, Kristie Fleckenstein, Bruce Janz, Tino DiBernardo, and Vanessa Sasson, and the anonymous readers at Oxford have offered helpful suggestions in how parts of this manuscript have been conceptualized.

Amy Koehlinger has been a cheerleader for me from the first day I arrived at Florida State University. Her encouragement at various points in my career has always come at just the right time, including talking to editors about how this would be a book to publish.

Amanda Porterfield has been nothing but reassuring from the moment I decided to write my dissertation on Max Lucado. She has been a helpful conversation partner throughout the various manifestations of this project. Her grasp of religion in America and her ability to see connections and solutions is amazing.

I am very thankful to Jennifer Hammer, who saw the potential in this work even if others did not. She was very helpful with a first-time author in thinking about how to reconceptualize the project from a narrowly focused dissertation to a much broader, and hopefully more useful, manuscript. I am also grateful to Theo Calderara and Charlotte Steinhardt of Oxford University

Press for guiding me through the process of writing, revising, and publishing and aiding me in developing a better book. Any failures in the final product are, of course, mine and not theirs.

My parents provided support whenever I needed it. They have always been encouraging of whatever it is I want to do. Their belief in me and my abilities gives me strength. My in-laws have also been very supportive. They provided babysitting help and a place to get away so I could finish various stages of the manuscript. That time allowed me to focus my thoughts while pushing this work to completion.

Jeff James, sports marketing professor and (more importantly) friend, provided help with sources for the marketing chapter but also acted as surrogate advisor when I needed him to be. His insight and inspiration were extremely valuable.

Chloe is a dissertation baby and has been around throughout the development of this project. She has provided distraction from this work, slowing it down but providing it when I just needed to step back. Her beautiful smile reminded me of life outside the academy while also cheering me on to complete this work. Having her in my life provides a balance (and lots of ponies and princesses) that I know I need.

I do not have words enough to express how much Jennifer means to me and my work. She believes in me even when I do not believe in myself. I could not ask for a better partner in life who provides the kind of support I need, even when it is to ask me, "How's your book coming?" I am so grateful for everything she does. This book would not have existed without her.

And to you the reader...well, we'll get to that.

HOMESPUN GOSPEL

JUST IN CASE YOU EVER WONDER: TOWARD AN EMOTIONAL HISTORY OF EVANGELICALISM

One hundred million products. Over 25 years, best-selling evangelical minister Max Lucado has produced over 25 titles aimed at adult audiences, over 30 books for children and teens, and a variety of videos and DVDs aimed at various audiences. He is a prolific author and the minister of a sizable congregation. Oak Hills Church in San Antonio, Texas, averages around 7,000 in weekly attendance at its various campuses.[1] Based on his production numbers alone it might be reasonable to assume that he represents a large section of American Christians, not just evangelicals. *Christianity Today* ran an article on Lucado in 2004 that named him "America's Pastor."[2] *Reader's Digest* named him "America's Best Preacher" in 2005.[3] In market research done by his publisher, Lucado was second in name recognition only to Billy Graham among Christian authors. In fact, many of those surveyed listed him as their favorite Christian author.[4]

When Lucado shares his ideas, there is a similarity in how they are presented. His books read like homespun narrative. He avoids sophistication and presents his counsel straightforwardly. His prose isn't bogged down with complex ideas or difficult terminology. Perhaps that is why his words have been transferred onto products for the home and onto greeting cards. It is easy to break his writing down into a choice aphorism that encapsulates his meaning.

Lucado's message, found throughout his products, is one of a fatherly God desperately in love with his children. On the surface, it is a positive affirmation with a readily apparent appeal. It is also a concept found throughout much of evangelical popular culture. Lucado is not the only one to rely on this pronouncement and the emotionality connected with it. Other evangelicals like ministers

Rick Warren and Joel Osteen deploy similar emotionality, including comparable ideas, to great effect.

Consider some passages from the books of these ministers.

From Max Lucado's *In the Grip of Grace*:

God is *for* you. Turn to the sidelines; that's God cheering your run. Look past the finish line; that's God applauding your steps. Listen for him in the bleachers, shouting your name. Too tired to continue? He'll carry you. Too discouraged to fight? He's picking you up. God is *for* you. God is for *you*.... We know he has a tattoo, and we know what it says. "I have written your name on my hand," he declares (Isa. 49:16).[5]

From Joel Osteen's *Your Best Life Now*:

You can hold your head up high and walk with confidence knowing that God loves you unconditionally. His love for you is based on what you are, not on what you do. He created you as a unique individual— there has never been, nor will there ever be, another person exactly like you, even if you are a twin—and He sees you as His special masterpiece!... God sees you as a champion. You may not see yourself that way, but that doesn't change God's image of you one bit. God still sees you exactly as His Word describes you. You may feel unqualified, insecure, or overwhelmed by life; you may feel weak, fearful, and insignificant, but God sees you as a victor![6]

From Rick Warren's *The Purpose-Driven Life*:

God smiles when we love him supremely.... God made you to love you, and he longs for you to love him back. He says, "*I don't want your sacrifices—I want your love; I don't want your offerings—I want you to know me.*" Can you sense God's passion for you in this verse? God deeply loves you and *desires* your love in return. He *longs* for you to know him and spend time with him. This is why learning to love God and be loved by him should be the greatest objective of your life. Nothing else comes close in importance.[7]

The emotionality these preachers express in these passages is ubiquitous throughout their writings. The writers tell of a God who is infatuated with human beings and who desires to know the intimate details of an individual's existence while at the same craving the same type of affection in return. Theirs is not a habitually judgmental or wrathful God but one who is familial and loving. This is their consistent assertion in sermons and writings.

Such pastors command sizable audiences in their churches and substantial readerships both in the United States and abroad. A variety of media out-lets are often interested in their views on current spiritual crises and climates. Through these audiences these ministers are shaping contemporary evangeli-calism and guiding it to the future. It is not theologians or seminary profes-sors who are making the most impact in evangelicalism. It is these personable ministers who have cultivated publishing and product empires through their emotional appeals.[8]

Emotion has been a prominent part of American evangelicalism since its foundations. In the revivalism of the middle of the eighteenth century, Protestants found themselves on opposite sides on the question of the role of emotion in religion. While some, like New England cleric Charles Chauncy, believed that emotionality detracted from the rationality of the Christian religion, others, like Anglican revivalist George Whitefield, believed that the appropriate expression of one's commitment to God was through emotional performance. These revivalists sought ways to encourage their audiences to have experiences of feeling as the true demonstration of their conversion to Christianity.

Between Chauncy and Whitefield stood Northampton minister and theologian Jonathan Edwards. He was interested in the life of the mind and is often identified as America's greatest theologian. Yet he was also interested in aesthetics, nature, and the emotional life. Ministering through this period of religious revival, Edwards wrote and thought about the emotionality present in the revivals to affirm the authenticity of revivalism while also cautioning individuals not to equate the presence of the emotions with the validity of religious experience. Simply because one was emotional did not mean one was godly. Instead, true (or godly) emotions arose from divine operations on the heart, were excellent in themselves and not in what they brought the self, brought about a change of nature, demonstrated beautiful symmetry and proportion, and had their fruit in Christian practice. Although he believed emotion was an important component of religion, Edwards was committed to intellectual engagement with the world around him.[9]

The emotionality at the core of modern evangelicalism, however, does not represent this self-reflective attention to the role of the emotion. Instead, evangelicals have come to trust that emotion is the key to a relationship with God. It is found in evangelical sermons, evangelical music, evangelical books,

evangelical art, evangelical movies, and evangelical politics. Emotion is everywhere in contemporary evangelicalism. Yet it is a specific type of emotionality,
one best labeled *sentimental*. Those sentimental appeals encourage individuals to conceptualize themselves in certain ways, to see the world and people
around them through certain lenses, and to encounter life through emotionally charged engagement. Sentimentality is a very important and overlooked
key to interpreting modern evangelicalism.

Examining evangelicalism through emotionality calls us to reconsider
how we understand this movement in the United States. Despite evangelicalism being thought of as a religion of the heart, too often scholars have paid
attention to the mind of evangelicalism, not recognizing that most evangelicals have abandoned the life of the mind in favor of a religious life of emotion.
Since evangelical culture is so closely focused on emotion, we must stop over-
looking its importance and power in contemporary evangelicalism. Emotion
is a key component not only of how evangelicals communicate with each
other but also of how they appeal to nonevangelicals.

In focusing on the importance of emotion in evangelicalism, we will see
that evangelicals downplay the importance of doctrine. Defining evangelicalism only in terms of doctrines or beliefs, then, avoids a sizable part of evangelical practice and misses that evangelicals themselves do not prioritize the very
feature scholars point to as their essential characteristic. Evangelicals have in
fact abandoned a concern with doctrine, although the beliefs stereotypically
associated with them still shape the evangelical worldview. Emotion, however, pervades evangelicalism and provides us with a better assessment of the
vitality of the movement.

Exploring sentimentality demonstrates how powerful it is in this religion,
but the sentimentality imparted and practiced in evangelicalism might best be
considered *hypocognized*.[10] Reflecting the influence of anthropologist Robert
Levy, sentimentality and the ideas and words that convey it are hypocognized
because they participate in evangelical culture in ways that are accepted but
largely unexplored by evangelicals. Indeed, because of this unreflective acceptance of emotionality, the very sentimentality that evangelicals depend on to
convert others ends up undermining the goals they hope to achieve through
the use of that sentimental language. In deploying the emotional, evangelicals seek to bring about societal change through individual acceptance and
conversion, as they consistently have. However, their modern reliance on
sentimentality actually promotes a narcissism encouraging a belief that the
individual is the center of the world and is the focus of God's attention. They
fail to address the structures of power and inequality that exist in American

society, believing societal change will occur through individual conversion and that the inequality that exists in the world will be solved by cultivating certain kinds of emotions in oneself or acting in loving ways.

Defining Sentimentality

Sentimentality and *sentimental* are often applied in a negative or pejorative fashion in the modern United States. Whether meant to evoke images of *mawkish*, *maudlin*, or *syrupy*, sentimentality is considered a weakness. Often it is the abundance of emotionality connected with sentimentality that is disparaged. It represents too much emotion for many people. Those who attempt to create a sentimental response in an audience are also viewed adversely. To evoke sentimentality is to manipulate, to prey on the weak willed or the weak minded. While we might recognize that some agents deploy emotion to manipulate individuals, to write off sentimentality as unworthy of attention ignores the power that it often conceals.

Although it carries rhetorical baggage, the term sentimentality is a useful one. Both the literature that would qualify as sentimental and the history of critically interpreting the literature are connected to a struggle to interpret identity, to speak truth to power, and to stake a claim to the ideals of the United States. Some critics of sentimental approaches to the world have argued that individuals in power use sentimentality to maintain their authority. Others have asserted that using emotional language is a way for the powerless in society to criticize structures of authority in a form that would be palatable to audiences. Throughout the history of sentimental appeal, this seemingly innocuous literary form has been intricately entwined with other aspects of human existence like economics and gender. Sentimentality and its use do not exist outside other facets of culture.[11]

How then should we conceive of sentimentality? What constitutes the sentimental? Philosopher Robert Solomon is perhaps the foremost proponent of conceptualizing sentimentality positively and understanding its power to motivate individuals to constructive action. For him sentimentality is an "appeal to tender feelings."[12] Solomon saw feeling as a very important element in *ethical engagement* and believed that to act ethically one must encourage not just rational introspection but emotional involvement as well. Such a position, argued Solomon, had been the viewpoint of a variety of philosophers and ethicists since the time of Aristotle. While Solomon recognized that many have disparaged sentimentality from the time of the eighteenth century to the present, he argued against the immediate assumption that literature and philosophy appealing to the emotions reflect bad taste.[13]

Solomon's defense of the emotions in philosophy and ethics offers an important corrective to an easy dismissal of emotionality as a moral deficiency. It is important to remember the power of feeling to create moral action. Yet the critics of sentimentality also remind us that emotion can be deployed for other purposes. While sentiment might be used to cultivate compassion for the oppressed, it might also be employed to justify oppression through appeals to nostalgia and authority. The issue is not emotionality or even sentimentality but the consequences of the use of an emotional appeal like sentimentality. Investigating the use of emotion in the practice of evangelicalism, for example, demonstrates the dynamism sentimentality continues to have in this movement and how it is clandestinely subverting the evangelical desire to transform the United States and the world through its obfuscating power.

So what are the emotions that evangelicals rely on in their moral engagement with the society around them? In contemporary evangelicalism, those tender feelings that are appealed to could represent quite a few emotions, but in particular we will focus on the use of emotional rhetoric that appeals to or encourages certain aspects of *love*. Sentimental love primarily appears in evangelical popular culture through three key tropes: the fatherhood of God; the infancy of human beings; and the nostalgia of home and the nuclear family. These three metaphors pervade evangelicalism and form the basis for the sentimental appeal.

For evangelical sentimentalists, the love of God is a prime emotion to be deployed in discussions of what it means to be a Christian. Such evangelicals centralize the loving relationship between God and the believer as the ultimate goal of human existence. In so doing, they domesticate this love in terms of God as a father and human beings as God's children. While the contextualization of God as a father is as old as early Christianity, the fatherhood trope used by modern evangelicals has gone through romanticization in the nineteenth and twentieth centuries. The apostle Paul and other early Christian authors may have been evoking the *pater familias* of the Greco-Roman world, but modern evangelicals cast God as a loving father desperate for a relationship with his children. The modern evangelical God desires, longs, yearns, and searches for a relationship with human beings. Instead of a wrathful evangelical God, the sentimentalized modern evangelical God begins from a position of love for human beings and acts to create love for him within them.

If God is father, it makes sense that contemporary evangelicals would cast human beings as children. It is important to note, though, that the childhood of humanity is constructed as an early childhood. Human beings in the minds of evangelical sentimentalists are often *little* children. These are children who are unable to respond to God in the appropriate ways. They do not have much understanding of God's love and often reject it because they perceive it in child-like ways. Human beings need God's love and protection. Unaware that God has created them to desire such love, human beings search for things to fill that longing and turn to whatever satisfies for the moment. Those who predominantly rely on sentimentality often give the impression that human beings will always remain little children in their relationships with God. Although some popular evangelical authors and ministers call their readers to mature in their religion, most rely on the child or infant motif to describe all Christians. There is rarely a place for adult children in modern evangelicalism.

Because of the importance of the domestic realm to evangelical sentimentality, a third trope in this emotionality is nostalgia. Modern evangelicals express both nostalgia and love in terms of Victorian notions of the nuclear family. Evangelical nostalgia, however, is not just a backward-looking phenomenon. The imagined, nostalgic past is also a hope and dream for the future. This sentimental memory of times past provides a template for a future domesticity and a renewed society. Evangelical sentimentality refers to a type of appeal that intends to create emotions related to nostalgia, domesticity, and familial love. In other words, sentimental evangelical literature aims at producing an emotional response by appealing to readers' notions of familial relationships superimposed on their relationship with God.

Nostalgia often involves selecting and editing memories to present them in a form that avoids recognition of unpleasantness. This does not necessarily mean that such memories are false, although that might be the case. "Nostalgia as sentimentality is the ability to focus on or remember something pleasant in the midst of what may have in fact been tragedy and horror."[14] The remembered past and the projected future of the evangelical temperament participate in this amnesic reconstruction of both the home and society, creating a past that did not exist and positing a future that is unlikely.

Evangelical sentimentality in this context, then, refers to emotional language that depends on the tropes of familial conceptions of God, particularly God as father; impressions of human beings as children, particularly as little children; and evocations of nostalgia for the nuclear family. Although other emotions (like grief) and other appeals (like guilt) could certainly be added to an accounting of how modern evangelicals express emotion, much of the construction of sentimentality is based on love. Evangelical grief emerges out of the thwarting of God's love for human beings or out of the failure of evangelicals to be transformed by that love. Guilt is used to remind people how they have spurned God's love and turned to their own devices. Love, then, in its various forms, becomes the foundation for evangelical sentimentalists to craft their vision of the world.

By using sentimentality to construct a vision of the world, evangelicals have often employed it for political ends. Sentimentality is arguably always political. It has been employed both explicitly and implicitly for societal transformation. Authors have used sentimental devices to seek consent for their visions of society. In the eighteenth century, for example, emotional literature was a way not only for Americans to make sense of the Revolution but also for writers, particularly women, to attempt to push democracy forward. Sympathy was a tool used by people still marginalized in the wake of the promise of American Independence. They used sentimental fiction, in literature scholar Julia Stern's words, to "contemplate the possibility that the power of genuine sympathy could revivify a broadly inclusive vision of democracy."[15] Sentimental fiction, and especially the invocation of sympathy in that fiction, was "a collective mourning over the violence of the Revolution and the pre-emption of liberty in the wake of the post-Revolutionary sentiment."[16] Sentimentality was used because other political avenues were closed, and authors hoped that through it they could bring about a political change that would fulfill the egalitarian promises of the Revolution. Real political venues were unavailable, so fiction became a medium for authors to appeal to audiences for change. Although sentimental fiction did not bring resolution to marginalization, it became a repeated defense mechanism that "inevitably permeate[s] public discourse when unresolved grief lies at the heart of political society."[17]

Sentimentality was also about the creation of authority. Liberal ministers and middle-class women in the nineteenth century partnered to create a sentimental Christianity that was meant to restore both groups to power through *emotional indispensability*. Sentimentalism became a way for ministers and women to exert influence on a culture that was looking to other individuals and arenas for authority. Sentiment and the desire to shape American culture through their moral example became an avenue to justify the world around them while believing that they could change it. There was certainly more to the religious activity of women in the nineteenth century than sentimental culture. Women were involved in many reform movements including temperance and antislavery. They were also involved as missionaries at home and abroad. But sentimentality provided one way for women to craft a sphere of authority for themselves to criticize the wrongs or inequities they saw in society.[18]

The appeal to emotion was an appeal for a recreated society and for authority in crafting the vision of that hoped-for society. Sentimentality was a powerful tool for nineteenth-century authors because it located the center for understanding the world and engaging in social action in the human soul. Its usefulness rested on the tenets of the Scottish Common Sense philosophers, who asserted that proper moral action is predicated on proper moral feeling. In appealing to sentiment, authors were providing their readers with the power and impetus to enact social change. In Harriet Beecher Stowe's *Uncle Tom's Cabin*, for example, little Eva's death is not "all tears and flapdoodle"[19] but a push for action in the causes of abolition and colonization by merging her death (and later Uncle Tom's) with the vicarious sufferings of Christ and Christian mythos about sacrifice. Stowe believed that proper feeling motivated by the fictional accounts of Eva and Uncle Tom would find its expression in proper action. Because of this she attempted to create authority for herself as a motivator for changing the status quo.[20]

Sentimentality as a literary form, then, is intricately embedded in the human experience. It is linked to how people conceptualize what it means to be human and exist in the world. It draws on apparent universals. Sentimentalists believe that an appeal can be made to something common in human existence—emotion—to engage an audience in a discussion about the renewal of society. Yet those universals are themselves the result of political contestation hidden under the guise of emotional commonality. Sentimental virtues throughout their history have tended to be gendered, middle-class virtues that have obscured the political activities sentimentality is called to perform. In her study of the making of American culture through literature, religious studies scholar Tracy Fessenden noted how Christians set the boundaries of religiosity and democracy through homogenization to solidify Christian control of the nation because they sought to eliminate distinctive aspects of the racial, class, and gender differences that marked heterogeneous experiences. Emotion for Christian sentimentalists has been about universalizing experience not only to shape the destiny of the United States but also to craft all human beings as children of the Christian God.[21]

In desiring this transformation of human society through the universalization of human experience, sentimentality has often been connected to how evangelicals have conceptualized authority. In this book, we will be exploring four ways that these relationships of religion, emotion, and power have interacted in contemporary evangelicalism. The first way that we will explore the intertwining of sentimentality and authority is through therapeutic evangelical literature. Modern evangelicals who rely on sentimentality create authority for themselves through emotional rhetoric, but the authority that they create is different from the authority nineteenth-century evangelicals fashioned. In the nineteenth century, evangelicals like the Beechers crafted authority through their cultural critiques of systems like slavery. For modern evangelicals, authority comes through the rhetoric of healing and narcissism, not through critical examination of culture. Although modern evangelical sentimentalists critique culture, they ultimately focus their efforts on issues related to offering healing to their audiences.

In intertwining sentimentality, healing, narcissism, and authority, modern evangelicals give authority to those emotions themselves, the second theme we will explore. The sentimental becomes evidence and authority in a world in which most evangelicals have given up intellectual pursuits and concerns over doctrine. Essentially, sentimentality represents an abandonment of theology and critical introspection in popular evangelicalism. Instead of crafting intellectual responses to the challenges to evangelicalism, popular evangelicals appeal to the power of feeling as an authority to counteract science and criticism of the Bible. They offer their audiences the opportunity to *feel* that evangelicalism is right rather than asking them to accept the veracity of the doctrinal positions of evangelicalism.

Third, sentimentality serves as a conduit for the replication of authority in evangelicalism. In evangelical practice, the tenets of evangelicalism are expressed through emotion-laden language. The media of evangelicalism, whether music or children's popular culture, provide the opportunity to introduce or socialize individuals to evangelicalism, expressing the values of the movement in ways that seek emotional agreement. In concurring with sentimental expressions of religiosity, however, the authority of evangelicalism can be internalized. By accepting God as a God of love, emotional appeals to following God's ways can internalize the authority not only of God but also of those who claim to speak for him. When individuals stray from God's path, reminders of God's love or how they have turned from his love can serve to produce remorse for breaking the standards of the community. Sentimentality is the channel for this internal acquiescence to authority.

Finally, sentimentality and authority combine in evangelical politics. Evangelical politics is inundated with emotion and emotional appeals. Politicians seek to manipulate their constituents through feeling instead of rational exploration of the issues confronting the United States. Politicians appeal to the tropes of sentimentality—particularly the family and home—to garner support. In so doing, sentimentality provides both the authority to be involved in politics and the subjects on which to be active. The issues that primarily motivate evangelicals—abortion, school choice, homosexuality— conceptually revolve around attacks against the family or home. The sentimentalized home (conceptualized as a nuclear, heterosexual family unit) is sacred, and evangelicals should do whatever they can to protect it.

The Emotional Habits of Evangelicalism

This combination of sentimentality and authority is cultivated through certain habits in the practice of evangelicalism. The mental habits that evangelicals have adopted are largely shaped by the views of the eighteenth-century Scottish Common Sense philosophers regarding how to interpret reality and how to engage emotion for moral behavior. Philosophers and rhetorical theorists like Thomas Reid, Dugald Stewart, and George Campbell accentuated the importance of emotion in motivating people to moral action. In the words of historian John Corrigan, "Emotion lay at the very heart of the process of perception, intertwined with intellectual functions, yet adding to perception a quality that reason lacked."[22] American evangelicals committed themselves to the Common Sense theories about knowledge and truth, but they also imbibed the belief that to stimulate moral activity they must tug at the heart. This commitment to emotionally motivating action resulted in certain trends within American Protestantism. Influenced by the Scots, many Protestants became more interested in religious experience than doctrinal disputes, assumed a Common Sense approach to revivalism, and adopted Common Sense as a theology to understand experience and moral action.[23]

For American Christians, particularly evangelicals, emotionality was vital to the creation of character. Moderate evangelicals especially believed that "religious piety ought to be infused with a concern for good and virtuous behavior as well as for grace."[24] By engaging the emotions in the realm of ethics, it was believed, one could ultimately create moral habits that would lead to the construction of virtuous character. In the language of the *formation* of character or *cultivation* of moral behavior, evangelicals saw the repetitive engagement of the emotions as a vital part of making ethical living a habit that did not require conscious contemplation.[25]

Not only did evangelicalism develop an ideology that connected emotion to habit, but they also created habits of understanding and describing the world through emotional language. Anthropologist Sarah Friend Harding demonstrated the power of "Bible-based language" in conservative Christian groups like fundamentalism and also showed that fundamentalists use this language to "'speak forth' realities."[26] Ministers are especially important in evangelical language construction. They create a way of seeing the world that is repeated through *speech mimesis*. In other words evangelical preachers offer a worldview that emotionally shapes the world to the reality of the Bible and centers on the Bible and emotionality as the lens through which the world is understood. Through repetition, this approach then becomes accepted but unexamined. These language habits are obscurantist in that they do not allow most evangelicals to recognize the work being done by such mimetic practices or what is being hidden by conceptualizing reality through evangelical lenses.[27]

To claim that evangelicals engage in habitual ways of seeing the world is not to imply that there is no variation or creativity on the part of individual evangelicals or that they are the only group shaped by emotion. Some evangelicals, certainly, recognize that there are alternative worldviews and can attempt to incorporate the insights of these alternatives into their personal philosophies. Yet, in evangelical popular culture—in the realm inhabited by ministers, authors, and publishers—there is remarkable consistency in the ideology presented in the products they create for individual evangelicals to use. That consumers continue to return again and again to these producers suggests at least a partial adoption of the sentimental outlook that lies at the heart of such products.[28]

Repetitive invoking of the emotions does not carry the same ideological weight in character formation today as it did among nineteenth-century evangelicals, but in some respects it appears that such repetition has itself become a habit among evangelicals—a mental activity that is done without introspection. As noted earlier, those who employ sentimentality intentionally or unintentionally rely on the hypocognized, or accepted but unexplored, nature of sentimentality. There is generally minimal *cultural self-consciousness* about the presence and use of sentimentality in evangelicalism. Although some evangelical critics denounce the anti-intellectualism of evangelicalism that is pushing the movement toward an uncritical, emotional engagement with the world, most evangelicals are not self-critically assessing the emotionality present in their popular culture or worship practices.[29] Many emotionally internalize the sentimentality instead of investigating it. Indeed, the culture of evangelicalism works against this type of inquiry because of the historical and cultural awareness that would be required for such an exploration. In a movement that generally avoids the critiques of historical inquiry and acuity, there is no impulse to explore the origins and consequences of this approach to religiosity. In fact, many evangelicals—albeit unintentionally—actively work against such intellectual introspection.[30]

In this world of emotionality, morality, and habit, evangelicals have created what American literature scholar Lauren Berlant termed an *intimate public*. Heavily shaped by consumerist, capitalist, and political concerns, an intimate public refers to an imagined space that contains a group of people believed to have a shared historical experience:

> Its consumer participants are perceived to be marked by a commonly lived history; its narratives and things are deemed expressive of that history while also shaping its conventions of belonging; and, expressing the sensation, embodied experience of living as a certain kind of being in the word, it promises also to provide a better experience of social belonging—partly through participation in the relevant commodity culture, and partly because of its revelations about how people can live.[31]

In creating such a space, evangelicals have looked for ways to construct a sense of community among those who participate in their culture, primarily through the rhetoric of affect. Evangelicals like those examined in this work conceptualize "the social world as an affective space where people ought to be legitimated because they have feelings and because there is an intelligence in what they feel that *knows* something about the world that, if it were listened to, could make things better."[32] They live in an aesthetic world where emotion is the currency to interact not only with other human beings but also with God. They produce commodities that enable themselves to *"feel* as though it expresses what is common among them" without recognizing the differences that exist among even evangelicals about what constitutes the appropriate way to follow God's commands and expectations.[33]

Modern evangelical literature and practice appear to be outlets to habituate practitioners to a culture of simplicity that reduces the practice of religion to the creation of feeling. In such a mind-set, human beings complicate life, but God offers something more straightforward. Doctrinal division, intellectual inquiry, and elaborate constructs of religiosity all move humanity farther from God, whereas emotionality can move them closer. To paraphrase Berlant, the work of evangelical culture is to sentimentally reconstruct the details of history, biblical interpretation, and theology to craft a vague or simple version of the religion. To do so requires a lot of resourcefulness or a lot of naïveté. There is nothing simple about the history or habits of evangelicalism, a reality that sentimentality effectively (and affectively) obscures.[34]

Sentimentality, as we will see, often provides the opportunity for obfuscation, intentional or not. Some prominent evangelicals elide their commitments to elements of fundamentalist theology, such as biblical inerrancy, through a rhetoric that emotionalizes the Bible as a story meant to be felt rather than intellectually examined. That these popular evangelicals sell books measured in the hundreds of thousands and even millions of copies certainly suggests that many evangelicals accept this emotional approach, but it also demonstrates how often this emotionality is repeated in the identity formation of evangelicals. The product being sold in books, DVDs, CDs, or MP3s, wall hangings, calendars, and even wind chimes is an emotional one claiming that God considers the consumer to be special—that, in a phrase borrowed from best-selling evangelical minister Max Lucado, if God had a refrigerator the consumer's picture would be on it.

The saccharine prose of contemporary evangelicalism that tells the reader such things might seem cloying albeit innocuous. Yet here is the greatest smokescreen of sentimentality. That emotionality has had, and continues to have, real political consequences. When politicians announce to their evangelical audiences that certain policies or positions destroy the family and that action is needed to defend it, they are tapping into that sentimental reservoir and mobilizing opposition, sometimes to great effect. Furthermore sentimentality provides a fog for evangelical activists to claim an apolitical position while advocating conservative political causes.

Evangelicals are replicating a culture of emotionality—particularly sentimental emotionality—with almost every book or album they produce, implanting sentimentality in the lived experience of consumers who read the book, listen to the music, or watch the video. With this aura of emotionality, it is important to recognize evangelicalism as an aesthetic as much as a set of doctrines or beliefs. The mechanisms of evangelical popular culture—publishing houses, record labels, and evangelical celebrities—continue to rely on the same tropes for describing the world, one's place in it, and ultimately one's "relationship" with God. This sensibility, as we will see, is pervasive in evangelicalism.

But the sentimentality of the late twentieth and twenty-first centuries is also distinct from the sentimentality that motivated evangelicals in the nineteenth century. The sentimental appeal of modern evangelicals predominantly relies on narcissism rather than notions of common feeling. While

Harriet Beecher Stowe might encourage her readers to "feel right" to get rid of slavery,[35] contemporary evangelicals call their readers to "feel right" about their relationship with God. The center of the focus is on the reader and not the common experience of all human beings. While American literature scholar Ann Douglas is probably right that some of the sentimentalists in the nineteenth century relied on an uncritical narcissism and self-absorption, twenty-first-century evangelicalism is more heavily dependent on this narcissism to be successful.

As Douglas also noted, there is quite a bit of obfuscation in sentimentality, and this is especially true in contemporary evangelicalism. Sentimentality obscures the deeper ideologies at work in evangelical emotional rhetoric and conceals certain aspects of human experience, such as structural inequalities from the evangelical gaze. Ultimately the narcissism of the sentimental appeal works against clear engagement with the difficulties of human life, focusing instead on the glorification of the individual. Yet this individualistic approach is false. The stuff of evangelical sentimentality is mass-produced. Evangelical publishing houses do not create just one copy of a book that is specifically marketed to an individual. They print hundreds of thousands of copies and hope to sell them all and sell the next book and the next one, and so on. Whether or not God values each individual as a special creation and child, evangelical publishers advance the idea that he does so that they can continue to market more products to their consumers. The sentimentality of such works obscures the facts that the author does not really know the reader, that the individually addressed book is read by multitudes of people, and that the transformational vision of the author—whether godly or not—is also motivated by economic interests. Publishers produce books to sell them.

The narcissism of evangelical sentimentality also works counter to evangelical interests in other ways as well. One of the central concerns of Reformed Protestant Christianity—including evangelicalism—is the transformation of human society into the kingdom of God, but this trajectory of sentimentality does not provide a path for this transformation. Contemporary sentimentality relies too heavily on intricately marketed, politicized, narcissistic forms of emotionality that actually undercut what evangelicals are trying to accomplish in the world. It trends not toward communal transformation but to solipsism. The hoped-for communal transformation of eighteenth-century evangelicalism has been replaced by a focus on individual transformation that advocates—explicitly or implicitly—self-absorption. With this shift evangelicals have perhaps sown the seeds of the failure of their own ideology.

Defining Evangelicalism

If sentimentality is so important in contemporary evangelicalism, why is it largely unexplored and why do definitions of evangelicalism not include some recognition of this emotionality? Two considerations appear to be at play here. First, for scholars with evangelical commitments, much of their work has been focused on demonstrating the contributions evangelicals have made to American culture. While certainly not shying away from bringing the problems of evangelical history to light, most of these scholars have attempted to present the intellectuality of evangelicalism to challenge the assumption that evangelicals have always been or must be anti-intellectual. In a sense, their commitment to intellectual forms of the movement and their desire to subvert the anti-intellectualism of sentimentality and other components of evangelicalism are probably behind the push to define evangelicalism according to its doctrines.

The second consideration for why definitions of evangelicalism tend to focus on belief is possibly the historiographical context for much of the recent works on evangelicalism. Not only have prominent evangelical historians shaped the field and the questions for debate, but also their writings and the works of other scholars have arisen in the context of the advance of conservative evangelicals publicly engaged in political life. Much of this political historiography has focused on determining what evangelicals believe to construct what their political vision was for American society. But certainly there is more to conservative evangelicalism than the activities of the Religious Right. Although we cannot strip the political from the religious, especially in the context of evangelicalism in the United States, focusing only on issues related to the rise of politically active conservative evangelicals gives us a myopic view of what makes evangelicalism so vibrant as a religious movement.

One of the purposes of this study is to expand current definitions of evangelicalism into broader classifications of what makes up this movement. In so doing, consider the following definition of what constitutes something (or someone) being evangelical:

> "Evangelical" refers to an aesthetical worldview fashioned by belief in the truthfulness of the Bible, by experience of new birth into the

Christian community, by emotional relationship between individuals and God through Christ, by concern to share the message of Christ with others, and by interest in shaping human society into the kingdom of God.

Instead of solely defining *evangelical* in the context of belief, we should see it as an aesthetic formulated not only on belief but also by affective and experiential concerns. It is an aesthetical approach to evangelicalism that grounds this work. Like most definitions of evangelicalism, it is necessarily broad to suggest conceptual unity while allowing for actual diversity. Various evangelicals would emphasize any of these characteristics, but they tend to mark all evangelicals from the most sentimental to the most rational, and describing evangelical as an aesthetic would allow scholars to consider both evangelical beliefs and practice, evangelical theology and emotion. Claiming that evangelicals believe the Bible is true, for example, does not limit scholars to only evangelicals who believe in biblical inerrancy. Broadly noting that evangelicals experience new birth does not require us to ascertain differences between, for example, Baptists and Pentecostals. Most evangelicals would affirm that one must have a relationship with God, and the language suggested here allows for openness to both rational connections to the deity as well as sentimental ones. Concern for shaping human society into the kingdom of God keeps open the opportunity to label individuals both on the Religious Right and the Religious Left as evangelical. We will explicitly return to the question of definition in the conclusion, but the rationale for it comes throughout the work.

The Scope of This Study

This book investigates sentimentality in white, middle-class conservative evangelical Protestantism. The main focus will revolve around a small sample of evangelical ministers who offer the best representatives of the emotional trends in evangelicalism. These individuals are consummate ones because of their popularity both as ministers and the number of books they have sold. Though the volume employs the work of these preachers as case studies, they are not alone in adopting this approach. Moreover, sentimentality is not absent from other forms of evangelical Protestantism. In some places throughout the text, we will consider emotional trends in non-white or non-male evangelical sources, but in general the same kinds of themes abide in evangelical Protestantism across the board due to shared histories and over-lapping worship and practice cultures.

We will primarily focus on the writings of ministers Max Lucado, Rick Warren, and Joel Osteen. They provide the clearest examples of how prevalent sentimentality is in evangelicalism and show us how it has developed, especially in the latter twentieth century. Although we will mainly explore the written works of these authors, the same types of emotional appeals prevail in their sermons as well. As such we will refer to them throughout as ministers more often than authors because they position themselves as *pastors* or *ministers* as their primary identities to emphasize their service to a variety of communities, both local and national/international, real and imagined.[36]

All three of these individuals have parleyed their charismatic personalities and folksy preaching styles into ecclesiological success, but they have become best-selling authors as well. They have sold tens of millions of copies of their books and are recognizable luminaries in evangelical circles. They are staples on talk shows that seek to incorporate a religious perspective on momentous issues, and they appear always ready to discuss God's love. Their prominence in evangelical spheres combined with the prevalence of emotional language in their works makes these three ministers excellent specimens for discussing the role sentimentality plays in modern evangelicalism. Certainly this produces a limited sample, but it is one that provides us good data to explore the power of sentimentality.

Sentimentality, however, is not just limited to white, middle-class, conservative, Protestant, male ministers. It is pervasive throughout evangelicalism in its various forms. While we will not explore the variations of sentimental appeal as it differs by race or by gender, we will touch on its use by non-white and non-male evangelicals. For example, Bishop T. D. Jakes, the prominent African American minister who started the Potter's House ministry and is also a best-selling author, evidences the same kind of emotionality, albeit at times to a lesser degree. Female authors such as popular author and television minister Joyce Meyer also employ these tropes. These additional examples and others we will encounter in the text demonstrate the pervasiveness of sentimentality and the work it is called to do in evangelicalism. Certainly sentimentality differs in its expression in various communities, but evangelicals call upon it for very similar functions.[37]

Throughout this work, we will examine the works of the ministers and other evangelicals to especially explore the relationships between sentimentality and authority. Chapter 1 focuses on tracing out the contours of what constitutes evangelical sentimentality by examining its presence in therapeutic culture. Therapeutic evangelical texts provide the best examples of thinking about what evangelical sentimentality is as well as its prevalence because therapeutic evangelical ministers rely so heavily on sentimental tropes in their offerings. These works bring out in relief the components of evangelical sentimentality because these ministers are so dependent upon them.

Building off Chapter 1, the next chapter focuses on understanding how sentimentality provides a way to avoid intellectual challenges to evangelicalism. It also investigates the anti-intellectual stance presented by evangelicals who use sentimental tropes as justification for avoiding or discounting intellectual approaches to religion. An examination of how the idea of hell is presented in the works of Max Lucado and popular pastor Rob Bell provides a concrete example of the work sentimentality does in the absence of intellectual approaches.

Chapter 3 looks at how sentimentality is instantiated in evangelicalism through the products of evangelical popular culture that are connected to religious practice. Children's literature and media and contemporary Christian music will provide the material from which to examine the connections between sentimentality and practice while marketing and market interests are also explored.

Chapter 4 investigates the role of sentimentality in evangelical politics. The language of sentimentality provides the foundation from which to build an evangelical platform, but those sentimental notions are often deeply connected to a religion of fear. Contemporary evangelical fear is deeply entrenched in sentimentality and is often deployed for sentimental ends. Evangelical emotionality also provides a way for individual evangelicals to claim an apolitical stance while offering a political vision. Importantly, we will see that sentimentality offers a foundation for social action, but the emphasis on individualism prevents a strong critique of unjust systems of power. This chapter also demonstrates not only the pervasiveness of sentimental tropes in evangelicalism but also how useful sentimentality becomes in the political sphere.

What are the ramifications of evangelicals' extensive reliance on sentimentality? Their dependence on emotion—especially sentimentality—as the sine qua non of religion renders them unable to answer the intellectual challenges that evangelicalism faces in the contemporary period. Many of those challenges—both scientific questions about the origins of human beings and historical and critical challenges to the inspiration of the Bible—rely on intellectual critiques. These challenges question whether the doctrines of evangelicalism can meet a certain burden of proof to be honored in the public square.

In addition, reliance on sentimentality has provided a foundation to change evangelical doctrine. We will see this especially in Chapter 2, but downplaying doctrine in favor of emotion has allowed evangelicals to questions traditional beliefs. Whether it is reinterpreting biblical texts, openness to denying the eternality of hell, or amenability to same-sex marriage, there are a variety of changes occurring in evangelicalism, many of which can be connected to the emotionology of the movement.

Yet opponents should not herald the demise of evangelicalism. Although much of popular evangelicalism cannot intellectually meet the analyses that call it into question as a viable explanation for human origins and destiny, for most evangelicals it does not need to. Because of the transition from comprehending their religion as a set of doctrines to conceptualizing their religion as an emotional relationship with God, evangelicals have actually made their religion more resilient to intellectual challenges. Calling into question evangelicalism's intellectual foundation ultimately does not undermine the religion because for many evangelicals their adherence was never about those foundations anyway. Evangelicalism becomes true because it *feels* true. Modern evangelicalism has largely transitioned to a new form of truth, one based not on intellectual assent to propositions but on emotional connections.

The history of evangelicalism cannot be best understood now solely in the terms of Jonathan Edwards (or even George Whitefield). Instead, evangelicalism has undergone its own conversion. Evangelicals have left Edwards's angry God for a domestic one who is busy cataloging mementoes of his children. Modern evangelicals no longer carry the burdens of intellectuality or doctrine; instead, they have abandoned them and are traveling light.

1 GOD'S IN THE BUSINESS OF GIVING MULLIGANS: SENTIMENTALITY AND THERAPEUTIC CULTURE

The background of the cover of the book is mostly white. On the upper two-thirds, underneath the author's name, two hands reach for each other. One is the hand of an adult male. It takes up nearly this entire section. You can see from the tip of the middle finger to the wrist. The other hand is that of a young child, no more than five. It reaches toward the other hand, perhaps to compare size, perhaps to have the larger hand encase it. Whose hands are these?

Below the hands in royal purple the title *God Came Near* is emblazoned. While one may not be able to judge a book by its cover, could this book's title help us judge the meaning of the cover? Is the adult hand meant to be God's hand? Maybe. If so, whose hand is the child's? Is it meant to represent a human being who is but a child when compared with God the Father? Is it the child Jesus' hand? Is it meant to represent that God became a child and recognized God as father so that all human children can recognize God as father? In any case, the photo most likely represents a father and a child reaching toward each other across some spatial division. Furthermore, the conclusion seems to be that it is the father's hand to which the child is trying to measure up. The title *God Came Near*, however, suggests that it is the father who has had to come close for the child to reach.[1]

The cover for this book, Lucado's third, says much about its author and his approach. Since its publication in 1987, Lucado has published over 80 books and has created several series of children's DVDs. Despite the differences in media and presentation, however, one element has remained constant throughout Lucado's publishing career. He uses sentimentality to present his version of evangelical Christianity.

Lucado is not alone among evangelical ministers in relying on sentimentality to connect with his audience. Other popular Christian ministers like Rick Warren and Joel Osteen appeal to their audiences through this type of emotionality. The works of ministers like these are often referred to as *inspirational*, but we can also understand them as demonstrating a concern with using evangelical methods for therapeutic ends. Therapeutic evangelicalism, in this context, refers to a religiosity that addresses psychological concerns in a pop psychological manner (e.g., self-help books). Some of the most successful evangelical inspirational books fall into this category. Therapeutic evangelicalism is evangelical in the sense that evangelicalism provides the religious framework for understanding psychological concerns.

Therapeutic evangelicalism depends on sentimentality because the framework used to address psychological concerns in inspirational titles draws on sentimental tropes related to the emotions of readers. This approach has emphasized the importance of spiritual answers to individual psychological problems, but promoters have done so with a narcissistic appeal that accentuates the individual's problems as God's grand concern. Ultimately this encourages readers to conceptualize their relationship with God as something apart from a larger community of faith. In addition, inspirational ministers implicitly encourage their readers to be consumed with emotion and adopt an aesthetical worldview.

The emotionality of therapeutic evangelicalism also offers the opportunity for ministers to position themselves as authorities in the community. By connecting to their audiences through sentimentality, these ministers take on healing roles that require individuals to follow the paths that these ministers lay out. Instead of creating authority based on logical argument or commitment to doctrinal tenets of evangelicalism, they seek the assent of their various audiences based on the feelings produced by sentimental messages.

The Rise of Therapeutic Culture in Evangelicalism

Evangelical Christianity, as any religious system, has served a variety of functions for its participants. Its tenets have offered an explanation of the world to make life understandable to evangelicals, and it has provided a description of who God is and how one can become acceptable to God. Evangelicalism has also offered a way for evangelicals to deal with the psychological, physical, and emotional struggles of life and to find meaning in them or work to change them, giving rise to a therapeutic approach to religion.

Many scholars would identify *therapeutic culture* or the *self-help movement* as a twentieth-century phenomenon, despite nineteenth-century antecedents.

They might point to the development of Alcoholics Anonymous in the 1930s as an important early progenitor. Others would also point to the rise of Freudian and post-Freudian psychology as an explanatory force in society as an additional part of the transformation of American society to a therapeutic culture.[2]

Conservative evangelicals, and later fundamentalists, often were antagonistic to both the nineteenth-century mind-cure movements like New Thought, which tended to promote styles of healing dependent on fostering appropriate mental states instead of appealing to God, and to the field of psychology in the early part of the twentieth century. Opposition to these therapeutic schools of thought gradually disappeared, and evangelicals became more interested in framing their message in therapeutic terms. The Keswick movement—based in an annual conference that featured various speakers and times of prayer—was an especially important nineteenth-century contribution to the creation of this contemporary evangelical therapeutic culture because of its emphasis on the practicality of the Christian message. The Keswick teachings developed in Britain but found resonances with Holiness teachings in the United States, particularly the concept of perfectionism, the idea that one could lead a perfect life free from sin. Although many evangelicals with a Calvinist background did not accept the validity of perfectionism, the Keswick teachings allowed Calvinists to believe that human beings could eliminate the tendency to sin without actually losing the ability to sin. Along with this freedom from sin, participants in the Keswick movement also emphasized the "higher life" that individuals would experience when free from sin.[3]

The Keswick movement inspired the beginnings of another theological creation in twentieth-century America. Called the Victorious Life, it emphasized a higher life–type experience that connected a supernatural component, the power of the Holy Spirit, with a practical outcome, freedom from worry, fear, anxiety. The Victorious Life was a response to the instability and uncertainty of late nineteenth-century shifts in American culture that brought industrialization, urbanization, (im)migration, and other changes that were disconcerting to many Americans. This theology was not simply a theological concept about sin in the believer's life; it was also about how individuals could live everyday lives. In some sense, Victorious Life was mind-cure in evangelical clothes and justified by evangelical rhetoric. Yet believers did not see it that way. Instead it made perfect Christian sense that if Christ or the Spirit lived in the believer, that believer should have a life free from emotional distress. Because of the Keswick movement, more evangelicals became interested in framing their gospel as a therapeutic and practical one. Late nineteenth-century revivalist Dwight Moody's adoption of Keswick teachings was an especially important combination of an evangelical gospel with a message of practical piety.[4]

Progressive Era revivalist Billy Sunday was not concerned about emotional distress, but he too believed the gospel of Jesus Christ could have practical effects. While Sunday did not preach that Christianity would make people happy or unafraid, he did preach that conversion would help men and women shape the systems of power in the United States and bring about a utopia. As historian Douglas Frank noted, Sunday's message was "that if enough people were good and strong, politics would be purified, insanity and poverty would disappear, families would be made whole, young people would grow up to be solid citizens, and, in general, America would be saved."[5]

Like other optimists of his time, Sunday preached a message of societal transformation through individual conversion. Society would be just when its members followed Jesus Christ. Although Sunday had a myopic view of what constituted societal justice, he preached a gospel of practical piety from inward transformation. Sunday's sermons "were also lessons in his version of applied Christianity rather than mere discourses in a fundamentalist theology or emotional appeals for repentance."[6] Although much of the discussion of Sunday's message has focused on his *masculine* approach, which deprecated liberal Christianity as feminine and advocated manly virtues like patriotism, he believed and preached that acceptance of the Christian message would lead to practical outcomes.[7]

The 1950s and 1960s were particularly important for the rise of modern therapeutic evangelicalism. Scholars have pointed to economic changes, migration patterns, and the decline in the power of religious institutions as impulses for the shift to a therapeutic or psychologized approach to religion that emphasized the importance of the individual and the primacy of emotional healing as the goal of religiosity.[8] Additionally sociologist Wade Clark Roof noted that baby boomers grew up in a culture immersed in language that elevated the possibilities of human potential, language that became the self-help or recovery movements of the 1970s and 1980s.[9] As self-help and self-improvement literature continued to grow, so too did an impulse to conceptualize religion as a private, individual, interior experience. Evangelicalism was not immune to either of these impulses and joined the fray.

Popular mid-twentieth-century minister Norman Vincent Peale was one of the first to introduce this popular new therapeutic evangelicalism. Peale presented a practical Christianity that relied on a supernatural power to achieve desired results. His 1952 book *The Power of Positive Thinking* was a culmination of several threads in the history of American evangelicalism.[10] It demonstrated the impact of a strand of evangelicalism that conflated Christianity and mind-cure approaches to healing. For its time, it was the pinnacle of a transition of practical Christianity to therapeutic Christianity that would influence later thinkers and authors.[11]

In *The Power of Positive Thinking,* Peale combined evangelical Christianity with New Thought and mind-cure to create a work that was aimed at the problems he perceived to afflict his audience. The book consisted mostly of anecdotes about individuals who had various problems. Instead of an in-depth examination of these issues, Peale offered a treatment schema that rested in the power of the individual and her or his mind. Although critics panned him for many things—including his theology—audiences received the book well. It became a very popular best seller and went through several reprints over three decades.[12] With the publication of *The Power of Positive Thinking,* therapeutic evangelicalism burst onto the publishing scene in a way that had not been seen before. Although other inspirational books had been written by evangelicals and other religious individuals, this was the inauguration of the best-selling evangelical self-help book, a genre focused on therapeutic concerns framed by a conservative Protestant approach.[13]

By the 1980s, self-help or therapeutic culture was a fully entrenched part of American life. When sociologist Robert Bellah and his coauthors wrote *Habits of the Heart*, a sociological study of individualism in the United States originally published in 1985, they frequently noted—and often bemoaned—the ubiquity of therapeutic culture, observing that "[a]lmost the only groups that are growing are the support groups...oriented primarily to the needs of individuals."[14] While Bellah and his fellow investigators perceived the prevalence of a therapeutic mind-set in many aspects of American life, it had even become a part of religion. Drawing inspiration from sociologist Philip Rieff, who was one of the first to study the impact of Freudian psychology in the United States, the authors claimed that the privatization of religion in American culture had led to the rise of an American therapeutic culture. They also introduced an informant named Larry Beckett, pastor of a California evangelical church, as an example of how even evangelicals were integrating psychological concepts of *self-worth* into evangelicalism. The message of Beckett's church was one of "Jesus as the friend who helps us find happiness and self-fulfillment."[15]

As the evangelical self-help, or inspirational, genre developed, it possessed an important difference from the general self-help books that filled bookstore shelves. Nonevangelical self-help authors combined a popular approach to psychology with a nebulous spirituality that appealed to the power within the reader, or a Higher Power, that existed outside the reader but whose main purpose was the emotional well-being of the reader. While evangelical inspirational literature demonstrates some psychologizing of the individual's problems, most inspirational Christian books are still very evidently evangelical. One has a relationship with God (not a generic Higher Power), and it is only through Jesus Christ. Though evangelical inspirational books are like other self-help books in many ways, evangelical sentimentality becomes the key to how the writings of popular evangelical ministers are distinctly evangelical. For Lucado, Warren, Osteen, and other authors like them, the answer to the readers' problems lies with God, not with the reader—although the inspirational God is intensely interested in what is going on in the reader's life.[16]

The latter part of the twentieth century continued this trend of uniting evangelicalism with therapeutic concerns. Roof's study of baby boomers in the mid-1990s noted that "the psychologically oriented culture in which we now live is far more influential than either theology or ecclesial tradition."[17] The captivation with the therapeutic (among other forces) had caused a change in how not only the general American public but also evangelicals viewed the self; with the self in transition, therapeutic evangelicalism exploded onto bookshelves in both Christian bookstores and general market retailers. Though largely shaped by a psychologically obsessed culture, it promoted an emotionality with a long evangelical pedigree: sentimentality.

Case Studies in Therapeutic Evangelicalism

In exploring the presence of therapeutic concerns and sentimentality in evangelicalism, we will be using three ministers as premier case studies. Focusing on only three ministers does mean that this is a limited sample, which is more suggestive than comprehensive, but they represent not only the most explicit demonstrations of the utility of sentimentality in evangelicalism but also how popular it is. All of them have sizable congregations, are frequently called upon to participate in the new media as examples of Christian voices on issues, and have sold copies of books and other products that number in the millions. Other evangelicals like Bruce Wilkinson and Joyce Meyer will be included to demonstrate the prevalence of sentimentality and therapeutic evangelicalism, but these three predominate throughout.

Max Lucado started his writing career in 1985 with the publication of his first book, *On the Anvil*.[18] Since that time, Lucado has balanced his writing with his work serving as a minister at the Oak Hills Church in San Antonio, Texas. He cut back on his ministry service in 2009 due to a heart condition but continues to preach intermittently in addition to writing. He has averaged at least one published title a year since *On the Anvil*, winning awards from Christian publishing associations and appearing on Christian and general market best-seller lists. Lucado has also written several children's books and expanded his product line to children's DVDs, greeting cards, and materials for the home such as calendars and wind chimes. He has also appeared on national television programs, usually in response to major tragedies like September 11th, the 2003 *Columbia* explosion, and the beginning of the Iraq War. The Republican National Committee invited him to offer a prayer at the 2004 convention, and he has participated in the National Prayer Breakfast (1999) and was the honorary chairperson of the National Day of Prayer (2005).[19]

Although not as prolific as Lucado, minister Rick Warren has also balanced a writing career and ministry. Warren's early writing was directed toward evangelicals interested in growing their churches and ministries. His book *The Purpose-Driven Church* (1995) encouraged ministers to be oriented to those in a community who did not affiliate with a religious group.[20] Trained at Fuller Seminary, an educational institution of evangelical higher education, Warren combined his evangelical background with marketing savvy to create Saddleback Church, a megachurch in California that has helped ministers throughout the world to develop evangelical marketing strategies to gain adherents. What brought Warren to widespread attention, however, was his book *The Purpose-Driven Life*. Released in 2002, the volume has sold tens of millions of copies and was on general-market best-seller lists like the *New York Times*' for over a year.[21]

Pastor of the largest church in the United States—Lakewood Church in Houston, Texas—Joel Osteen has quickly risen to national prominence based in part on his boyish appearance, everyman personality, and constant smile. He became the pastor of Lakewood Church when his father died in 1999 and has managed to grow the congregation from the 8,000 members when his father died to over 40,000. The church grew so much that it eventually acquired a 30-year lease to the Compaq Center after the NBA's Houston Rockets moved. Osteen has written best-selling books including *Your Best Life Now* (2004) and *Become a Better You* (2007), has a large television audience, and has amassed a substantial amount of wealth—he received an eight-figure book deal for his second book.[22] His charismatic evangelicalism and his market-savvy business skills have made Osteen a very successful minister.[23]

The Tropes of Therapeutic Evangelical Sentimentality

All three of these ministers represent the conflation of therapeutic evangelicalism and sentimentality. Because therapeutic evangelicalism draws on sentimentality, it would make sense that it draws on the themes that are central to sentimental appeal. Nineteenth-century sentimental authors were often concerned about issues related to social order, with the home as a prime arena for fostering that order. Like other romantics with whom they shared an ideological pedigree, sentimentalists often expressed feelings of nostalgia and loss, but they often entrenched these feelings in anxieties about family life and the encroaching marketplace. The family and the need for protecting the domestic sphere were frequent topics that formed the foundation for authors and ministers to make appeals to their audiences. These concepts continued to be important in conservative Protestantism, especially revivalism, and are still a significant part of evangelical rhetoric. In examining contemporary therapeutic evangelicalism, there are three main motifs that connect this type of religiosity with its nineteenth-century progenitors: God as father; human beings as God's children; and nostalgia for home and the nuclear family.[24]

The image of God as a father in Christianity is as old as the New Testament. In the nineteenth century, however, this notion of the fatherhood of God took on sentimental connotations that persist to this day. In Lucado's works, for example, he emotionally appeals to his readers to enter into a relationship with God or to deepen such a relationship. Of particular utility is the image of God as a *desperate* father concerned about a relationship with all human beings. This trope appears in nearly all of Lucado's works, but it can be seen most prominently in his work *The Great House of God*, his exposition of the Lord's Prayer.[25]

Lucado breaks the prayer into separate lines, associating each one with a room in God's house. Moving through the prayer, Lucado takes his readers on a tour of the house: for example, the phrase "thy kingdom come" is connected to God's "throne room;"[26] the phrase "give us this day our daily bread" prompts a tour through God's "kitchen."[27] Through 15 chapters, Lucado travels through all the "rooms" in God's "house" to show his readers that: "God wants you to move in out of the cold and live...with him. Under his roof there is space available. At his table a plate is set. . . . And he'd like you to take up residence in his house. Why would he want you to share his home? Simple, he's your Father."[28] Lucado's use of the fatherhood of God as a trope is not primarily a theological concept but an emotional one. He uses the concept of God as father to pull at the emotions of his readers. If God were a physical being with a physical house, it would be cluttered with all the mementos of his children that he would amass. Not only would God have photos and scrapbooks, but also, according to Lucado—in his book *In the Grip of Grace*—"had he a calendar, your birthday would be circled. If he drove a car, your name would be on his bumper. If there's a tree in heaven, he's carved your name on the bark."[29]

Joel Osteen's popular book *Your Best Life Now* frames the loving fatherhood of God in terms of abundance. For Osteen the concept of abundance is related to God's attention to detail in a person's life. According to Osteen, God wants everyone to experience a blessed life. Many people do not experience those blessings because they do not believe that God can change their life. "The good news is," writes Osteen, "God wants to show you His incredible favor."[30] He goes on to tell his readers, "God has so much more in store for you."[31] Too many people, argues Osteen, have a "small view" of God, which limits how much he can bless them. "[God's] dream for your life is so much bigger and better than you can even imagine."[32] It is this encouragement to have a large view of a God that is ready to incredibly bless readers with great jobs, a large house, and general happiness that connects Osteen to a sentimental evangelical view of God.[33]

People have a right to expect these giant blessings because they are Christians, which for Osteen means they are children of God the father. Osteen, who has experienced great prosperity in his own life, encourages his readers to adopt his attitude to receive great blessings: "My attitude is: I'm a child of the Most High God. My Father created the whole universe. He has crowned me with favor, [sic] therefore, I can expect preferential treatment."[34] This attitude is the key to Osteen's theory on blessings and prosperity. Because Christians are children of a loving God who wants to bless them, they should expect blessings: "It doesn't matter what the circumstances look like in your life. Regardless of how many people tell you that what you're attempting can't be done, if you'll persevere, declaring the favor of God and staying in an attitude of faith, God will open doors for you and change circumstances on your behalf."[35]

In *The Purpose-Driven Life*, Rick Warren shares Osteen's belief that God wants to provide abundance in the life of a human being, but that abundance for Warren's audience is to be found in fulfilling their God-given purpose. The ultimate goal of one's purpose-driven life is the object that God—the ever-loving father—created one for. "You are not an accident," Warren tells his readers.[36] God had specifically created them and planned them, long before their parents conceived them: "He thought of you first."[37] God's special creation of each of Warren's readers is meant to make them feel unique and loved. This creation was also very detailed: "God prescribed every single detail of your body. He deliberately chose your race, the color of your skin, your hair, and every other feature. He custom-made your body just the way he wanted it. He also determined the natural talents you would possess and the uniqueness of your personality."[38]

The details of God's planning for the reader do not end there. God decided when the reader would be born, where the reader would be born, and how the reader would be born. "Many children are unplanned by their parents, but they are not unplanned by God.... God never does anything accidentally, and he never makes mistakes."[39] Warren invites the reader to believe that she or he is vitally important to God by suggesting that "God was thinking of you even *before* he made the world. In fact, that's why he created it!... This is how much God loves and values you."[40] Warren assures them that God highly values them: "You were created as a special object of God's love! God made you so he could love you. This is a truth to build your life on."[41]

The theme of God as father is also a prominent one in *The Prayer of Jabez* (2000), the best-selling work (selling 20 million copies worldwide) of prolific author and minister Bruce Wilkinson.[42] God is a loving father who wants to bless his children, but there are some blessings he will give only if explicitly asked: "In the same way that a father is honored to have a child beg for his blessing, your Father is delighted to respond generously when His blessing is what you covet most."[43] Wilkinson never clarifies why God would withhold blessings unless human beings specifically ask for them, but that is the entire premise of his book—there are blessings to be had, but only if one prays the prayer of Jabez found in 1 Chronicles 4:10. Wilkinson relies on the reader's belief that God is fatherly and willing to lovingly provide good things to his children: "The very nature of God is to have goodness in so much abundance that it overflows into our unworthy lives.... God's bounty is limited only by us, not by His resources, power, or willingness to give."[44]

To demonstrate his belief in the truth of this point, Wilkinson uses a narrative about a visit to a playground with his young children. There were three slides of varying heights in this park, and Wilkinson's five-year-old son David was enamored with them and began playing on them. Wilkinson's wife suggests that he go with David, but he does not, saying, "Let's wait and see what happens."[45] David plays on the small slide for some time before moving on to the medium slide. Wilkinson's wife again encourages him to go to David, but he again refuses. After sliding down the medium-sized slide several times, David approaches the largest slide. Wilkinson and his wife discuss the situation and agree that David should not go down the large slide by himself. When David calls for his father, however, Wilkinson ignores him and pretends that he cannot hear him. David finally musters the courage to climb the slide's ladder but gets only part of the way up before he is too afraid to continue. He again calls out for his father, who comes to him this time. When David finally admits that the slide is too tall for him to go alone, Wilkinson agrees to slide down with him. Why Wilkinson needed David to explicitly say that he could not climb without him is unclear; perhaps he believes that David needed to assert his inadequacy. His point in telling the story, however, is clear. Human beings must declare that they are unable to achieve success. They must recognize that they have referred agency—they have the ability to accomplish certain activities only through their identity as God's children: "That is what your Father's hand is like. You tell him, 'Father, please do this in me because I can't do it alone! It's too big for me!'"[46] By recognizing God as father, the readers are expected to proclaim that they cannot shape their own destiny—they need someone else.

The usefulness of God as father in the works of these ministers is not to make philosophical points about the characteristics of God. While these pastors incorporate traditional concepts of God's omnipotence, omniscience, and omnipresence into their writing, they are not using these theological concepts to craft an intellectual defense of God's existence. It appears in their writings that they assume God's existence but use concepts of God being all powerful, all knowing, and all present to create a context for emotionality. God being omnipotent becomes *God can do anything*. God being omniscient becomes *God knows everything*. God being omnipresent becomes *God is everywhere*. This popularizing of theological terms is not just simplification of concepts for an audience that might not be educated in theology. It is also part of the narcissism of therapeutic evangelicalism. The claim is not just God can do anything but God can do anything *for you*, God knows everything *about you*, God is everywhere *to help you*. While all of these ministers might claim that God is the father of all human beings, the rhetoric of therapeutic evangelicalism centralizes God as father of the individual reader. Lucado might claim that if God had a refrigerator the picture of everyone would be on it, but in the actualization of this concept it is the individual reader who confronts a God who cares about him or her in a fatherly way. The same could be said about how Osteen, Warren, and Wilkinson present God. God has big dreams for those looking for their best life now, a distinct purpose for each of those who go through *The Purpose-Driven Life*, and special blessings reserved for each of Wilkinson's readers.

Although Lucado titled one of his books *It's Not about Me* and Rick Warren's first line in *The Purpose-Driven Life* is "It's not about you," the picture that they paint of God is different from these claims.[47] Both Lucado and Warren especially want to claim that human beings exist to serve God's purposes, but all the authors discussed here offer a God who is consumed with affection for human beings. It is certainly plausible to read these texts narcissistically despite what the ministers intend. How else should one understand a God who hoards mementos of an individual's life, is at an individual's beck and call, planned out all the aspects of an individual's life, and bestows special favor on an individual, if it cannot be understood at least partially as a narcissistic appeal?

The narcissism of therapeutic evangelicalism carries over to a second sentimental device: the individual is a *child* of God. Here again, the idea of Christians being children of God draws on New Testament language. The writers of the Gospels present Jesus as saying favorable things about children and urging his disciples to emulate children. In Matthew 18:3, Jesus tells his disciples, "Truly I tell you, unless you change and become like children, you will never enter the kingdom of heaven." He later tells them, "Let the little children come to me, and do not stop them; for it is to such as these that the kingdom of heaven belongs" (Matt. 19:14). When modern evangelicals describe their readers as children, however, they demonstrate the influence of a romanticizing of childhood that would not necessarily have been a part of New Testament usage of the phrase *children of God*. In addition, the modern usage of this comparison again reflects a narcissistic appeal. While many evangelical authors would most likely claim that all human beings are God's children,[48] the way they write emphasizes to the reader how special a child she or he is.

Because conceptualizing God as father is a vital part of the contemporary evangelical worldview, it is reasonable to assume that depicting human beings as his children would also be an important motif of evangelical sentimentality. Yet the nature of human beings as God's children is understood in a distinctive way. Frequently in therapeutic evangelicalism the naming of the readers as children infantilizes them. In Lucado's writings, for example, he urges his readers to become like children and accept the sentimental expressions of love from their father: "If I know that one of the privileges of a father is to comfort a child, then why am I so reluctant to let my heavenly Father comfort me?"[49] He wants his readers to believe that despite narratives that discuss God's wrath and justice, in essence God is a Father who wants to relate only sentimentally to his children: "When I am criticized, injured, or afraid, there is a Father who is ready to comfort me. There is a Father who will hold me until I'm better, help me until I can live with the hurt, and who won't go to sleep when I'm afraid of waking up and seeing the dark. Ever. And that's enough."[50]

Although in *Romancing God*, a book about evangelical romance novels, religious studies scholar Lynn Neal hesitated to allow critics to identify the evangelical theology of her informants and their novels as childish,[51] Lucado's theology is self-consciously childish in the sense that he expects his readers to identify with children and become children to be in a relationship with God the father. In describing a trip to Jerusalem with one of his daughters, for example, Lucado notices a lost daughter calling for her father using the word *abba*, a Hebrew word meaning "father." Since both Jesus and the apostle Paul encouraged Christians to refer to God as their Abba, Lucado watches how the father of this daughter would respond. The father finds his daughter, takes her hand, and leads her across a busy street. Lucado rhapsodizes, "Isn't that what we all need? An *abba* who will hear when we call? Who will take our hand when we're weak? Who will guide us through the hectic intersections of life? Don't we all need an *abba* who will swing us up into his arms and carry us home? We all need a father."[52]

Although Warren does not infantilize his readers to the extent that Lucado does, he still frequently uses the image of reader as child throughout *The Purpose-Driven Life*. As already mentioned, Warren expresses to his readers that God created them for specific purposes. He continues this theme throughout the book, emphasizing that this purpose is related to one's purpose as a child of God. In a chapter titled "You Were Formed for God's Family," for example, he tells the reader, "God wants a family, and he created you to be a part of it."[53] The believer as child receives many benefits when one becomes part of God's family. As a child the believer gets "the family name, the family likeness, family privileges, family intimate access, and the family inheritance! . . . As children of God we get to share in the family fortune."[54]

Sharing in the family fortune is an idea that resonates with how Wilkinson and Osteen deploy the child trope in their writings. Both pastors suggest to their readers that as a child in God's family they have access to great blessings. Osteen, for example, encourages his readers to recognize that they "have the DNA of Almighty God."[55] The reader's value as a person "is based solely on the fact that you are a child of the Most High God."[56] The reader, as a child of God, is "an original."[57] Because of this, Osteen says, "Quit being negative and critical toward yourself and start enjoying yourself as the unique creation of God."[58]

By putting their readers in the position of *children* in connection to God as father, ministers like Lucado, Wilkinson, Warren, and Osteen are not relying solely on Christian theology. They are psychologizing it. In the context of therapeutic evangelicalism, being a child suggests something about the state the individual reader is in. The reader needs something or someone outside of himself or herself. The reader is a dependent being. For these ministers, what the reader needs is God. Positioning the reader as a child is also useful to locate the reader as being worthy and valuable; the reader is a *special* child to God—another tactic that has the potential to breed narcissism. As a special child, the reader is entitled to special privileges as God's child. Such blessings do not come to everyone, but they do come to the child of God. So childhood also provides assurance that God is concerned and will act on the behalf of the reader.

Given how prevalent the Christian as child motif is in evangelicalism, it suggests much about the self-image that authors like these want their readers to adopt. In his 1989 book *Mine Eyes Have Seen the Glory*, historian Randall Balmer noted that evangelicals had latched on to the image of the fetus in antiabortion activity because of how their perceived experience of marginalization in American culture resonated with the perceived vulnerability of the fetus.[59] In much the same way, images of evangelicals as children in evangelical popular culture appear to play on an emotional need for protection and inclusiveness. In contrast to a public sphere that does not privilege evangelical concerns or positions, God considers evangelicals special. In contrast to a political atmosphere where evangelicals perceive their way of life as being under attack, God offers protection and provision. The narcissism that evangelical ministers offer provides an opportunity for evangelicals to resolve the psychological tensions that contemporary life creates. Unlike the world around them, God is deeply focused on the plight of the individual. At times, it seems as if evangelicals assert that such is God's only concern.

The collective nature of all human beings—or at the very least all evangelicals—as God's children is often downplayed in the interest of emotionally appealing to the reader to trust in God's goodness and fatherhood in light of the unique nature of the individual reader. That is not to suggest that collective identity is completely lost in these ministers' writings and sermons. Warren is emphatic that being God's child means being a part of a *family* and that each child has certain responsibilities to the family that reinforce the collective aspects of the Christian experience. However, even when collectiveness is discussed, these ministers accentuate the importance of the individual in the collective. In other words, God has many children, but the individual reader means something special to God.

Nostalgia for home provides a third theme in therapeutic evangelicalism. Frequently nostalgia is intricately tied to sentimentality. Nostalgia is conceptualized as a *sentimental* longing for certain aspects of the past, not just a longing for the past. Whether or not nostalgia can be understood only sentimentally, this longing for the past to return is a vital part of therapeutic evangelicalism. Sentimental evangelical ministers and authors seem particularly interested in generating nostalgia for a traditional nuclear family or traditional ways of life. Frequently, they cultivate nostalgia through imaginative reconstructions of the past. One might look on the past in a way that looks back on bad memories as the antithesis of what should have been. Alternatively, a minister might use nostalgia in a forward-looking way. Instead of building on positive memories of the past, the pastor promises fond memories to be made in the future. Finally, these pastors might evoke nostalgia for family by asking readers to conceptualize themselves as orphans. While there are certainly other ways to use nostalgia, these three rhetorical techniques demonstrate the utility of nostalgia in therapeutic evangelicalism.

In *The Purpose-Driven Life,* Warren uses rhetoric meant to evoke nostalgia by painting the reader's past as a time of pain. When he discusses becoming a part of God's family, he asserts, "Your spiritual family is even more important than your physical family because it will last forever. Our families on earth are wonderful gifts from God, but they are temporary and fragile."[60] By introducing the fragility of human families, Warren locates his readers as the product of families that are "often broken by divorce, distance, growing old, and inevitably, death."[61] Instead of evoking a family life of beauty and wholeness—traditionally the stuff of nostalgia—Warren invokes an antinostalgia that suggests that physical families cannot compete with what can be found in the spiritual family of God: "It is a much stronger union, a more permanent bond, than blood relationships."[62]

Unlike Warren's rhetoric depicting the past as a time of brokenness, Osteen often looks back to his familial experience—especially his relationship with his father—as a positive one. But he also encourages a forward-looking nostalgia that promises good memories to come. In other words, he assures his readers of a certain point in the future when they will be able to look back nostalgically. "God is working in your life," writes Osteen.[63] "Right now, God is arranging things in your favor."[64] Acting behind the scenes, God arranges the parts of one's life for one's good. "He is doing things that are going to thrust you to a whole new level. You may not see the culmination of it for years, so you must learn to trust Him."[65] Ultimately a believer can accept this, says Osteen, because "if the curtain were pulled back so you could peer into the unseen realm...you'd find your heavenly Father getting everything arranged in your favor."[66]

Lucado's use of nostalgic appeal also takes various forms, but one prominent one is situating the reader as an orphan about to be adopted. The seed for the adoption metaphor comes from the biblical text. Paul used adoption to refer to the relationship between God and new Christians. He told the Roman Christians, "You have received a spirit of adoption. When we cry, 'Abba! Father!' it is that very Spirit bearing witness with our spirit that we are children of God" (Rom. 8:15–16). Paul also wrote to the Galatians that "God sent his Son...so that we might receive adoption as children" (Gal. 4:4–5).

The biblical symbol of adoption serves as a foundation for emotional exploitation in contemporary evangelicalism. In his book *God Came Near,* Lucado relates the story of a Brazilian woman named Carmelita attending her adopted mother's funeral. After the funeral, Carmelita, the orphaned child of a prostitute and unknown father, stood at her adoptive mother's casket weeping, saying thank you over and over in Portuguese. In his book Lucado reflects, "Driving home that day, I thought how we, in many ways, are like Carmelita. We too were frightened orphans. We too were without tenderness or acceptance. And we too were rescued by a compassionate visitor, a generous parent who offered us a home and a name."[67] Furthermore, Lucado reasons that we should exhibit Carmelita's response: "We, too, should stand in the quiet company of him who saved us, and weep tears of gratitude and offer words of thankfulness."[68] In *Come Thirsty*, he tells another story of an orphan who was adopted. In this case, some of Lucado's friends adopted Carinette, a Haitian orphan.[69] In this narrative, the reader observes Carinette in a Haitian orphanage prior to the finalization of her adoption and travel to the United States. She is waiting for her parents to return: "Carinette's situation mirrors ours. Our Father paid us a visit too. Have we not been claimed? Adopted?...Before you knew you needed adopting, he'd already filed the papers and selected the wallpaper for your room."[70]

Lucado's use of adoption evokes nostalgia for a nuclear family through situating the reader in the place of an orphan. The reader is unwanted and alone. Then God found and adopted the reader (or is preparing to do so). The reader now finds love, compassion, and belonging. The reader has found a home. God, the doting father, made the choice to bring the reader into his family. Lucado combines the tropes of fatherhood and childhood with adoption to produce a feeling of nostalgia for home and family by telling readers what awaits them.

These three examples of the efficacy of nostalgia are representative of its usefulness in evoking an emotional response. Instead of critically engaging the past, these evangelicals urge their readers to romanticize the past as a time of either wonderful memories or painful experiences. They put the physical past into service to emotionally create a present or future where spiritual life will be as good as the physical was or the spiritual will better than the physical was. Frequently that past involves the experience of family. The fatherhood of God and the childlike nature of the reader combine to produce feelings of desire for belonging. The appeal is for their readers to desire familial relationships that resonate with sentimentalized notions of the traditional nuclear family.

These particular ministers represent the various ways that evangelicals use sentimentality. Some, like Lucado, rely heavily on it. Their writings and sermons drip with it. It is their prime method of making an appeal to their audiences. Others, like Wilkinson, subsume it to other concerns—like convincing their readers that praying a specific prayer will offer great rewards in their lives. The books and sermons of ministers like Warren and Osteen fall in between these two poles, with Warren using these tropes more often than Osteen. Sentimentality, then, is prevalent across a large section of evangelical literature in various measures. The fatherhood of God, the childhood of the reader, and the pull of nostalgia are frequent devices, but despite the familial rhetoric that evangelicals like these employ sentimentality operates in a narcissistic individualism that stresses the importance of the reader. All of these ministers claim that involvement with a larger community of believers is a vital component of the Christian life, but the bulk of what they present to their audiences centers the individual reader as uniquely valuable to God. They then take this impression and use it for therapeutic goals. Because God cares about his children, he will heal them of their maladies. The purveyors of therapeutic evangelical works postulate that there is something "wrong" not only in the universe but also in the lives of human beings. Human beings suffer. But for evangelicals, God has the answer for that suffering, and the ministers of evangelical sentimentality claim to know what that answer is. Through emotionality, they guide their audiences along a path of healing, staking out positions of authority through their emotional language.

Healing and Therapeutic Evangelical Sentimentality

In using these sentimental tropes to heal their readers, therapeutic evangelicals depend on the power of their writing and the power of emotion. Two methods that they use to facilitate the possibility of healing are the construction of their personas and the modeling of successful experiences of healing. These ministers attempt to make connections to their audiences by creating a common or everyman persona that relates to the reader by claiming that they are just like the reader. In addition, they show their readers through their own lives or through the examples of others that the reader can achieve healing through their methods.

In his book *Persuasion and Healing,* psychiatrist Jerome Frank observes that psychotherapies are constructed to put the healer and the patient in a relationship where the patient draws healing from the way the therapist produces emotional responses through the clarification of symptoms, the inspiration of hope, and the facilitation of experiences of success or mastery.[71] The inspiration of hope is particularly important in Frank's study: "Hopelessness can retard recovery or even hasten death, while the mobilization of hope plays an important part in many forms of healing in both nonindustrialized societies and our own."[72] Part of the healer's success is based on how well she or he can instill hope in their patients that they will be cured of their illness. To have this hope instilled, patients must have hope in the healer.[73]

Frank discusses the placebo effect as a demonstration of how expectations of help and trust in the healer can drastically improve the patient's response and healing rate. A placebo is "a pharmacologically inert substance that the doctor administers to a patient to relieve distress when, for one reason or another, the doctor does not wish to use an active medication."[74] There is nothing in the placebo itself that can bring about healing—any healing that comes from the ingestion of a placebo comes from the mind of the patient, particularly the trust the patient has for the healer. "Placebos exert their effects primarily through symbolization of the physician's healing powers."[75] The placebo works when the patient believes in the power of the healer and the healer's statement that the unidentified placebo will affect healing.[76]

The belief or expectation of help is a very important component for healing to take place in nearly any type of healing situation. In some ways, then, the placebo effect is part of all types of healing, even when pharmacologically active drugs are used. The successful healer is one who recognizes that the effects of the placebo part of healing are dependent "primarily on interactions between the patient's momentary state and aspects of the immediate situation, including especially the attention and interest of the healer."[77]

This concern with healing is the therapeutic part of therapeutic evangelicalism. Therapeutic evangelicals position themselves as healers, and as such they depend on the placebo effect, whether consciously or unconsciously. All healers use the placebo effect in their healing, even if that effect is connected only to their societal recognition as healer. Even the symbolic connotations connected to *doctor*, for example, draw on the placebo response. As Frank notes, part of the healer's role in the use of the placebo effect is the creation or massaging of trust in the healer's power. The patient must believe that the healer not only is *able* to heal the patient but also is *interested* in healing the patient. In the case of these ministers, this is expressed in the creation of their persona. Part of the placebo effect is the way each presents himself as interested in his readers and concerned about their emotional, psychological, and—above all—spiritual welfare.[78]

One way that evangelical ministers attempt to cultivate an image of interest is through the epistolary format of their writings. Although the use of the letter as a mode for Christian instruction dates back to the time of the apostle Paul, modern evangelical epistolarity reflects the influence of sentimental and Victorian influences. Modern evangelical sentimentalists will frequently address their works directly to their audiences, using *you* in a conversational style that makes the book appear as a letter addressed to the reader or as a long chat between author and reader. Because authors have adopted epistolarity in sentimental writing since the eighteenth century, it should be no surprise that contemporary sentimental evangelicals would still find it suitable to their writings. Epistolarity serves to blur the boundaries between author and reader. In the eighteenth century, authors frequently used female narrators in their novels, even when the authors were male. Epistolarity blurred other lines as well. Textuality, performance, and vocality merged together as narrators spoke directly to their readers. Public and private also blurred because the novel was in the form of a letter but publishers produced these works for a sizable audience; epistolarity created the opportunity for the individual readers to believe they were each participating in the correspondence with the author–narrator. The epistolary form also served to enact power relations. The epistolary novel could be, in American studies scholar Julia Stern's words, "a conduit for equal and open exchange or a guise for vocal tyranny."[79]

The epistolarity of modern evangelical writings works similarly in creating relationships and generating correspondences. The conflation of text and voice, public and private, are features of the kinds of works we have been examining. For example, many of Lucado's adult titles come from sermon series that are performed vocally. Lucado recreates those sermons into text, but the texts often bear the imprint of vocality. Blurring also occurs in the conversational style of a therapeutic book. The use of literary devices that imagine the response of the reader—phrases like "I know what you are thinking"—further clouds the distance between the minister and the reader. Therapeutic evangelicals also muddle public and private through their conversational style. The reading of a book suggests an often private activity, but the works examined here are available for a broad audience. Readers may feel like the minister is speaking to them individually, but in fact these ministers and their publishers hope that a large audience will read the book—the thoughts of which are part of the public sphere of commerce.

Lucado serves as a prime exemplar of how a pastor can use epistolarity to attempt to create a relationship with his readers. One of the places he does this is in the Acknowledgment section of his books. Although he does not do it in all of his books, Lucado recognizes the reader for taking the time to read his book. Sometimes the reference is simply one of thanks: "*And to the readers* . . . You are so gracious to invite me into your home. I'll do my best not to overstay my welcome."[80] At other times Lucado tells his readers that in preparing the book he has prayed for them. For example, he opens *In the Grip of Grace* with, "And to you the reader: I've prayed for you. Long before you held this book, I asked God to prepare your heart. May I ask that you pray for me? Would you offer the prayer of Colossians 4:4 on my behalf? Thank you. I'm honored that you would read these pages."[81] Some are written are in the plural (readers), but most are singular (reader).

In other works, Lucado might have an extended "conversation" with his reader: "You've been on my mind as I've been writing. I've thought of you often. I honestly have. Over the years I've gotten to know some of you folks well. I've read your letters, shaken your hands, and watched you eyes. I think I know you."[82] In this one-sided conversation, he lays before his readers the conditions he believes they have. In establishing this relationship, Lucado constructs his readers as people with emotional, relationship, and spiritual problems: "You're busy. . . . You're anxious. . . . Your spouse cheated. . . . You've made mistakes."[83] He constructs his book as providing the solution: "And so as I wrote, I thought about you. All of you. You aren't malicious. You aren't evil. You aren't hardhearted (hardheaded occasionally, but not hardhearted). You really want to do what is right. . . . I sought to give a repertoire of chapters that recite well the lyrics of grace and sing well the melody of joy. For you are the guest of the Maestro, and he is preparing a concert you'll never forget."[84]

When the readers' lives "turn south," they can pick up a Lucado book—whose author has prayed for them, spoken to God for them—and allow the minister to remind them that "God knows your name."[85] Lucado writes as if he is speaking to the person holding the book and not to a large community of readers numbering in the millions across the globe.

Connecting with her readers is also an important part of best-selling author and television minister Joyce Meyer's approach to bring about healing. Throughout her book *Beauty for Ashes* (1994), Meyer use epistolarity and the sharing of her own experience to bond with her audience.[86] She assures her readers that not only she but also God understands their experiences. In fact, it was God who had encouraged Meyer to write and later expand the book. In the 2003 introduction, she writes, "Years ago, God inspired me to share these truths in order to help set free other people who are in similar positions.... Recently the Lord encouraged me to expand the teaching in this book to further develop a solid foundation for people who are ready...to move on to the beautiful life God wants them to enjoy."[87] In other words, the reader picked up a Meyer book, but it is God's message that they will be reading. Meyer and her message become a trustworthy vessel for the love of God.

Like Lucado and Meyer, Warren asserts the divine character of the message in *The Purpose-Drive Life*. He is a friend to the reader, interested in helping them through life. The connection between Warren and the reader is not just a personal one, however; it is one that has divine significance. Instead of dedicating the book to a family member, personal friend, or even a deity, Warren dedicates the book to his readers: "This book is dedicated to you. Before you were born, God planned *this moment* in your life. It is no accident that you are holding this book. God *longs* for you to discover the life he created you to live—here on earth, and forever in eternity...I thank God and you for the privilege of sharing them with you."[88] Whether we should understand such a statement as arrogance or providence, from the very beginning of the book Warren seeks to establish the truthfulness of his message (God has planned the reader's reading of this book), the importance of it (God has great desire for the reader to know what is contained in the book), and the trustworthiness of the minister in proclaiming the message (God has given Warren the privilege of writing this book).

Another method for cultivating relationship between minster and audience is to create an everyman persona. The minister appears as a common individual who shares the everyday experiences of the reader. The emphasis of the quotidian nature of the pastor is to suggest either that minister and reader are the same or that the minster is someone with whom the reader can relate. In profiles on Lucado in *Christianity Today* and *Publishers Weekly*, for example, journalist Cindy Crosby notes that people put their trust in the Max Lucado who seems like a good neighbor or favorite relative. They cling to a Max who appears fun, authentic, and humble but is also like all of us. Max Lucado is a nice guy who is approachable. He is Max, not Reverend Lucado or even Mr. Lucado. He is real. He is plain and simple in his approach to people and his use of words.[89] Warren and Osteen present similar personas in their writings and public appearances. They prefer to be called by their first names, Rick (or sometimes Pastor Rick) or Joel, and present themselves as the friend of the reader or listener. They are common individuals whom the readers can connect to and trust.[90]

Not only do therapeutic evangelicals attempt to bring healing through the cultivation of personal relationships, but they also offer examples of successful healings to bolster their readers' faith in God and the minister. They model the types of behavior or thinking the reader needs to engage in to achieve their desires. In modeling, says Frank, "patients enter into emotionally charged interactions with a therapist on whom they depend for guidance or advice."[91] In this atmosphere, modeling becomes a way that patients "imitate the therapist's way of approaching problems or adopt aspects of the therapist's values."[92] In the context of therapeutic evangelicalism, the connections the ministers attempt to make are meant to heal through the reader adopting the minister's values and outlook on religion.

Part of the reason that modeling is successful is in the construction of the healing context. As Frank notes, the expectations of the therapist affect the success of healing in the patient. Specifically, Frank argues, "The kind of improvement patients report tends to confirm their therapists' theories."[93] To expect their readers to experience spiritual healing, these ministers have to make that connection to the reader where they feel like the minister actually cares about them and expects that they can have a better relationship with God through reading his or her words.[94]

There are many ways therapeutic evangelical ministers engage in modeling. They might specifically list out how to solve the problems the reader faces. They might offer specific examples from contemporary, historical, or biblical figures. They might stress that their message is beneficial to everyone while claiming that it worked for the "ordinary" minister. Whatever method is used, the pastor accentuates to readers that if they follow the outlined path they will achieve the result of healing and wholeness.

Throughout *Beauty for Ashes*, for example, Joyce Meyer emphasizes not only that she is a common person but also that the path she is offering was the very path she took to recovery. She was abused like many of her readers were abused. Yet she found the path to recovery through her relationship to God and promises her readers the same opportunity: "God will do for you what He has done for me.... He will, Himself, be your reward and will recompense you for what you have lost."[95] The reader can trust in this truth because it is rooted in God's love. Because God is love, "what He does for one person, He will do for another, if it is a promise found in His word."[96] By accepting that love, healing can occur because "God has an individual, personalized plan for each of us."[97]

By guiding his readers through a series of 40 devotionals, Warren also provides specific steps for his readers to follow. Because *The Purpose-Driven Life* is meant to help readers find their God-given purposes, Warren offers a method that guides readers to discovering that purpose. Although Warren might claim that there are commonalities among human beings, *The Purpose-Driven Life* is not about finding a universal purpose that is applicable to everyone. Instead, Warren encourages his readers to discover their individual purpose and then to develop a personal life purpose statement. To do this he instructs them to be introspective and discover God's purpose for their lives by asking specific questions that he outlines at the end of the book.[98]

Lucado employs modeling in several ways, but one common technique that he uses is to highlight specific individuals in the biblical text. Many of these narratives are about a biblical character's interaction with Jesus, which usually results in some sort of healing of the character. The reader is then put in the place of the character—similarities are emphasized—you, the reader, are like this character. If Jesus healed the character, so the reasoning goes, will he not also heal the reader? Lucado's emotionalizing may alter the meaning of the biblical narrative in its context, but for his purposes this presentation of biblical tales is a common tactic in using modeling. His approach to these narratives reiterates the same theme, intending to create the same emotions. Lucado is attempting to produce a way for his readers to see themselves and the world through the repetition of biblical accounts, sentimental rhetoric, and narcissistic allure. The Woman at the Well story in John 4 can serve as an example of Lucado's therapeutic approach to the biblical text and his use of modeling.

The woman in the context of John 4 is from a region called Samaria. Samaritans and Jews had an antagonistic relationship, and they often avoided one another. Jesus, a Jew, stops at a well in the middle of the day. The Samaritan woman comes to the well to draw water, and Jesus asks her for a drink. After her initial hesitation, she and Jesus begin discussing religious topics like the proper place of worship. She returns to town and convinces a sizable group to go with her to listen to Jesus' teaching. The point of the text seems to be either the universal audience of Jesus' message or a condemnation of the Jewish people for rejecting Jesus. It also appears to function as a narrative injunction against racial prejudice in early Christianity.

Lucado focuses not on any of these aspects but instead on the Samaritan woman's marital situation. During their conversation, Jesus tells the woman, "Go, call your husband, and come back." She replies, "I have no husband." He responds, "You are right in saying, 'I have no husband'; for you have had five husbands, and the one you have now is not your husband. What you have said is true!" (John 4:16–18). The woman takes this as a sign Jesus is a prophet. In Lucado's narrative, this interaction demonstrates that this woman has had a hard life. According to Lucado, this woman has failed "not at work but at marriage. Her first one failed. So did her second. By the collapse of the third, she knew the names of the court clerk's grandkids. If her fourth trip to divorce court didn't convince her, the fifth removed all doubt. She is destined for marital flops."[99] In Lucado's version the woman comes to the well with "half a dozen kids, each one looking like a different daddy."[100] Jesus can tell she has had difficulties. "Her life story was written in the wrinkles on her face. The wounds of five broken romances were gaping and festered."[101] Lucado's Jesus understands her pain, and "silently the Divine Surgeon reached into his kit and pulled out a needle of faith and a thread of hope. In the shade of Jacob's well he stitched her wounded soul back together."[102]

In *A Love Worth Giving,* Lucado emphasizes that Jesus knew everything about this woman and her marital problems, "and he loved [her] anyway."[103] If Jesus could do that for Samaria's down and out, he argues, "see if God's love doesn't do for you what it did for the woman in Samaria."[104] The reader is juxtaposed with the Samaritan woman to create a sympathetic bond that, in turn, leads to a sympathetic resolution of the reader's problems: Jesus took care of her; he'll take care of you[105] The work of modernizing the narrative, assimilating the reader and biblical character, and resolving emotional tension is all done to create a reiterative approach to the Bible that invites the reader to participate in this emotional performance. Lucado models the kinds of attitudes and approach the reader needs to take. No matter what kinds of problems beset the reader's life, encountering Jesus like the Samaritan woman did can lead to healing.

Although he bases his entire book on a biblical person, Wilkinson also frequently applies personal narratives throughout *The Prayer of Jabez* to demonstrate his principles. These narratives are his evidence that praying Jabez's prayer brings results and his attempt to convince readers that if it worked for the minister it will work for them. Throughout the book, he claims that God has great blessings in store, even for "someone as ordinary as I."[106] The trope of ordinariness is an attempt to claim that his message is appropriate for everyone: rhetorically this is not a book for a certain group. God loves everyone and as such wants to bless everyone. Wilkinson uses himself (or his son, as we have seen) to model the appropriate steps to find healing and success, assuring his reader based on his own personal experience.

In all of these methods, therapeutic evangelicals stress the emotional and not the intellectual. There is a glaze of intellectual encouragement—be it introspection or an examination of biblical passages—but at the core of the healing process is an emotional experience. In the types of modeling drawn from both Lucado and Wilkinson, for example, understanding the biblical text is accented: Here is this story from John 4, or here is this prayer made by a man named Jabez. The ministers do not encourage intellectual engagement with the text, however. They emphasize an experience of the text that is therapeutic and emotional. This approach is an encouragement to find the emotional and therapeutic in scripture by creating a groove of how to read the Bible to find these elements. As ethnographer Susan Harding notes about fundamentalist minister Jerry Falwell, therapeutic ministers create a set of interpretive practices that not only produce a habitual way of seeing the Bible as real but also craft authority for the ministers through the relationships they seek to produce and the modeling they offer.[107]

Creating relationships and using modeling are two methods therapeutic evangelicals use to claim the reality of the healing they offer. This healing is grounded in the sentimental tropes introduced earlier. Ultimately, healing will occur because the reader is a child of father God who desires to transform the reader's situation. The problems these ministers seek to heal, though, often feed back into the general narcissism of therapeutic evangelicalism. The therapeutic rhetoric often promotes a culture of victimhood that elevates even the smallest of problems to grand proportions. Lucado, for example, will create lists of "ailments" and lump together simplistic and complex problems without distinguishing between them. In a list in the book *Facing Your Giants*, Lucado lists "Debt. Disaster. Dialysis. Danger. Deceit. Disease. Depression" as Goliaths that affect our world.[108] There are differences between the experiences of debt, dialysis, and depression, but Lucado fuses them together as problems for which his writing can provide the solution. Wilkinson's appeal, in contrast, would be most successful among an audience who feels alienated from a culture of success. The message of unclaimed or untapped blessings would be attractive to those who feel marginalized from the valorization of celebrity and wealth in American society. That such blessings are available for even the most ordinary of people is a useful rhetorical metaphor to fascinate readers of the potential of Jabez's prayer. And, given Wilkinson's enormous financial success from the book, it has clearly charmed an enormous audience. For these ministers, the ultimate claim, based on the tropes of evangelical sentimentality, is that God will heal the lives of their readers if they follow the steps outlined in the book, situating the minister as an authority based on emotion and healing, not doctrine or logical argument.

Additionally, the primary focus in much of evangelicalism is on the problems of the individual. Little attention is given in the works of ministers like these to the ills of society. While all our case studies express the need to think about the problems of society, their best-selling works are those that individualize suffering. Here too is where narcissism has the potential to undercut the goal of societal transformation. While evangelicals might explicitly conceptualize the world and its power structures as being inherently broken, the methods and messages they offer for healing are primarily individual. The message appears to be that societal transformation can occur only if readers intensely focus on themselves. The ending of injustice, oppression, and social crises and ills will occur as enough people are individually transformed through a self-centered focus on one's relationship with God and the practical benefits that relationship provides.

Become a Better You: The Practicality of Therapeutic Evangelicalism

Not only do these ministers assert that their books offer a path to healing, but they also frequently maintain explicitly or implicitly that following their plan will produce practical results in a person's life that are not just related to healing. For these creators of sentimental therapeutic evangelicalism, their messages have real effects. These evangelicals provide a practical piety that alleges that being a Christian will produce certain positive changes that come directly from the reader's relationship with God. Here, too, narcissism comes to the fore as the ministers profess that God wants to make the reader's life better.

Lucado and his publishers especially have centered the Lucado brand on a practical piety that minimizes theological speculation and emphasizes how the Christian message can change everyday lives for the better. There is some discussion in his books about Christian doctrine, but he uses this discussion for the larger purpose of convincing his readers that the practicality of Christianity is more important for them. Lucado's books are about how his readers can have better marriages, better relationships, better jobs. The books are also about day-to-day problems people have: loneliness, failed marriages, lost jobs. Evangelical beliefs and the importance of conversion are still prominent in his works, but the sentimental practicality of evangelicalism is also emphasized. His *Cure for the Common Life* is perhaps the clearest and most extended examination of the practical piety of Christianity.[109]

Subtitled *Living in Your Sweet Spot,* the book is about how individuals can find the divine spark within themselves. The book reads as part Lucado inspirational title and part career counseling book. Although Lucado wants to emphasize his belief that "God endows us with gifts so we can make him known," the book is not like his other works.[110] Not only does Lucado discuss the spiritual vocations of Christians, but he also intends to help readers find their vocations in the world: "Look at you. Your uncanny ease with numbers. Your quenchless curiosity about chemistry. Others stare at blueprints and yawn; you read them and drool. 'I was made to do this,' you say."[111] Readers should put all their efforts into finding their calling and using it to glorify God. As Lucado puts it, "Whether you work at home or in the marketplace, your work matters to God. And your work matters to society. We need you! Cities need plumbers. Nations need soldiers. Stoplights break. Bones break. We need people to repair the first and set the second. Someone has to raise kids, raise cane, and manage the kids who raise Cain."[112] Ultimately, Lucado emphasizes that the vocation that God created one for is based on the familial relationship between the reader and God: "God planned and packed you on purpose for his purposes.... And since you are God's idea, you are a good idea.... Set apart for a special work.... How do you explain such quirks of skill? God.... And *his design defines your destiny.*[113]

Cure for the Common Life ties Lucado's religious vision with his belief in the practicality of Christianity. Not only does God want to save humanity, but he also cares about what jobs human beings do, at least according to Lucado: "God does big things with small deeds."[114] The emphasis on the fatherly love of God provides the framework to join Lucado's piety with his practicality. If Lucado's God is intimately concerned about every individual, it would make sense that part of that concern would be how those individuals live their everyday lives.

Even more than Lucado's works, Osteen's books express a piety that emphasizes the utility of spirituality in everyday life. Because God cares about individuals, he wants them to have their best life now. Because God is involved in the ordinary, according to Osteen, Christians should expect that following God will produce practical results: "You can dare to start believing Him for a better marriage. Start believing Him for better health. Believe for joy and peace and happiness. Start believing for increase and abundance."[115] This practical piety is intricately interwoven with an evangelical childish theology. As God's children, God wants evangelicals to have good finances, good health, good businesses, and good children. Osteen also argues that Christianity has the answer to all sorts of problems: "Alcoholism, drug addiction, poverty, depression, anger, low self-esteem, whatever the problem, the good news is that you have the opportunity to break the negative cycle."[116] A sentimental outlook allows Osteen, like Lucado, to connect alcoholism and low self-esteem in such a way to create the impression that his approach is broad enough to be all-inclusive while also maximizing his appeal to a culture of victimhood by aligning low self-esteem with alcoholism and drug addiction.

Unlike Lucado or Osteen, Warren downplays the practical effects of Christianity in *The Purpose-Driven Life* in favor of the transformation of his readers' character. He denounces the view (that would appear in the works of someone like Osteen) that Christianity produces your best life now: "Many Christians misinterpret Jesus' promise of the 'abundant life' to mean perfect health, a comfortable lifestyle, constant happiness, full realization of your dreams, and instant relief from problems through faith and prayer. In a word, they expect the Christian life to be easy."[117] The very focus of the work, however, suggests that the message of the book has a practical benefit. Warren's overarching concern is that his readers find their purpose in life that will give their lives meaning. And while it may not bring them riches or health, knowing one's purpose, claims Warren, "will reduce your stress, simplify your decisions, increase your satisfaction, and, most important, prepare you for eternity."[118]

In all of this the focus is on the individual reader. The ministers of therapeutic evangelicalism ask their readers to practice a narcissism that accepts that God is desperately concerned even about their menial, quotidian problems. Whether it is finding the meaning in one's life or simply finding a parking space, God loves the individual reader so much that he is waiting to help her or him with whatever problems come up in life. While each of these ministers has declared in other works or sermons that there are bigger problems in the world than finding a parking space or having a better job, they frequently suggest the opposite: that the universe revolves around the practical problems of day-to-day life. The combination of sentimentality and therapeutic concerns leads to an individualistic gospel that encourages readers of works like these to consider that God has nothing better to do than make sure he fills his children's lives with blessings.

Conclusion

The development of a therapeutic bent to evangelicalism has highlighted the consequences of accentuating certain religious tenets—the power of the individual, the value of an emotional approach to spirituality. In the therapeutic works of these evangelicals—which are a small but very popular segment of the entire catalog of therapeutic evangelical works—we see how much American culture and pop psychology have infiltrated into the religious expressions of evangelicals. Sociologist James Davison Hunter pointed to this assimilation as early as 1983 with his examination of evangelicalism and its subjectivism. Even at that time he was highlighting an evangelicalism that had been domesticated in modern culture and that was developing a softness on traditional doctrines. In other words, by capitulating to American culture including American therapeutic culture, the strong intolerance and brashness of nineteenth-century evangelicalism was being displaced by an evangelicalism that tempered the drawing of rigid boundaries and gave rise to a narcissistic impulse.[119]

At its core therapeutic evangelicalism draws on the long tradition of emotion in evangelicalism. Moreover, this type of religiosity molds the power of those emotions into a narcissistic mold creating the evangelical individual as the center of God's desire. While evangelicalism has been individualistic since it began in the eighteenth century, the current individualism of evangelicalism is heavily shaped by the therapeutic culture and pop psychology of the United States. The individual in evangelicalism has become a self-important obsession. What therapeutic evangelicalism brings out in relief are ideological changes in evangelicalism about who evangelicals are. Instead of encouraging their audience to think about themselves as individuals with responsibilities to a larger community, the purveyors of therapeutic evangelicalism ask evangelicals to think about themselves as individuals who are loved by a God who wants a personal relationship with them.[120]

Seeking or fostering language about *a personal relationship with God* is ubiquitous in evangelical literature, especially of the therapeutic variety we have examined here. What does this suggest about evangelicalism? First, it demonstrates the influence of popular psychology on evangelical emotionality. It also implies how much psychological concerns dominate how evangelicals think about themselves, based on how popular certain titles are and how many new therapeutic titles flood the Christian market. Finally, it would also be sensible to hypothesize that emphasis on a *personal relationship* with a deity would lead to less engagement in transforming the world through the adoption of a set of doctrines. Although evangelicals have been involved in social action since the beginning, the rise and proliferation of therapeutic evangelicalism indicates a culture of emotion present in the movement. This culture of emotion downplays reasoned argument or defensible doctrine in favor of how the message of evangelicalism makes one feel.

The evangelical reliance on emotion also means that evangelicals can be shaped by the emotional currents of the time or of a particular charismatic individual. This would suggest why evangelicalism in recent decades has evidenced such *cults of personality*, to use Balmer's phrase.[121] Magnetic leaders can manipulate the emotions of congregants, sometimes to their detriment. Even where the leaders' intentions are positive and sincere, they draw their audiences through emotional constructions of religiosity, not through doctrinal positions. In the case of Osteen especially, sometimes those audiences are quite sizable. But all of the ministers focused on here have sold millions of books and various other products. Readers respect them as authorities, returning again and again to each new formulaic and often repetitive book that comes out. This following must come from the emotional import of the works since the messages of the books are not based on logical assent to propositional truths. Emotion provides evangelicals like these with authority over their audiences.

If emotion is so prominent and doctrine so subsumed in the practice of evangelicalism, why then do we who study evangelicals continue to frame their identity solely through the intellectual categories of belief? The rise of therapeutic culture and the influence of sentimentality place emotion in the center of the evangelical experience, a feature of evangelicalism that current definitions do not address. Continuing to rely on the doctrines and beliefs of evangelicals misses what evangelicals are incorporating into their daily lives and why the movement remains a vibrant one in the early twenty-first century.

2 YOU ARE SPECIAL: THE ANTI-INTELLECTUALISM OF SENTIMENTAL EVANGELICALISM

In the fiftieth anniversary issue of the evangelical magazine *Christianity Today* (October 2006), the editors selected the top 50 books they believed had shaped evangelicals the most. These were "landmark titles that changed the way we think, talk, witness, worship, and live." Included in the list were titles by C. S. Lewis, evangelical theologian J. I. Packer, and Rick Warren as well as fiction titles like *This Present Darkness* by Frank Peretti (about spiritual warfare) and *Left Behind* by Tim LaHaye and Jerry Jenkins (about the end times).[1] At number 45 was Mark Noll's *The Scandal of the Evangelical Mind* (1994).[2] In this work he argues that despite having a strong intellectual heritage evangelicals are by and large anti-intellectual, or at least non-intellectual. Noll's scandal of the evangelical mind encompassed three categories: cultural, institutional, and theological. Culturally "the evangelical ethos is activistic, populist, pragmatic, and utilitarian," leading away from cultivating a life of the mind.[3] Institutionally there were no strong intellectual evangelical journals, nor did evangelical educational institutions foster intellectual pursuits. Theologically evangelicalism was stunted because of its lack of intellectual rumination, leading Noll to remark, "For an entire Christian community to neglect, generation after generation, serious attention to the mind, nature, society, the arts—all spheres created by God and sustained for his own glory—may be, in fact, sinful."[4] In citing Noll's book as the forty-fifth most influential book in shaping modern evangelicalism, the editors of *Christianity Today* noted, "Few people have accused evangelicalism of being an intellectual movement—but now we feel bad about it, at least."[5]

Whether or not evangelicals as a group actually feel bad about anti-intellectualism, it is certainly a feature of modern evangelicalism in the United States. Given the amount of attention previous generations of evangelicals have given to theological precision, comprehensiveness, and investigation, it is curious that anti-intellectualism should color modern evangelical counterparts.[6] Attention to evangelical intellectual history, so important to many scholars, reveals the ways evangelicals have made this transition, allowing individuals like those introduced in the previous chapter to play upon the intellectual emphases of evangelicalism for emotional ends.

Shifts within evangelical scientific and religious thought have created an ideological situation that sentimental expressions of piety exploit. When Protestants adopted an understanding of biblical revelation that was shaped by a Baconian approach to nature that insisted that the natural world was best understood by searching for facts and inductively determining general truths, it committed conservative Protestants to a specific intellectual path. Because in the nineteenth century they had so thoroughly embraced Scottish Common Sense philosophy, which asserted that people could directly and intuitively understand the world as it really is through the senses, conservative evangelicals encountered intellectual challenges in the late 1800s. Questions about the authorship and dating of biblical documents provided a test for the veracity of Christianity. Darwinian science, which emphasized developing hypotheses and then searching for verification or falsification, moved conservative evangelicals from the scientific and philosophical mainstream in the United States. Although liberal evangelicals tried to accommodate both biblical criticism and Darwinian evolution, conservatives responded based on Baconian Common Sense, which was becoming an outmoded approach to the world. The inadequacy of evangelicals' worldview to understand and respond to Darwin's scientific method and theories led them as a group to retreat from the U.S. public sphere. Yet many remained committed to a vestigial combination of a Baconian approach to truth and a Common Sense worldview. Other evangelicals, however, turned to sentimentality as a way to avoid intellectual challenges to Christianity.

Those who employ sentimentality take advantage of these shifts—intentionally or not—to present a Christianity in which God loves individuals as individuals without concern about most of their doctrinal positions. Sentimental ministers often downplay doctrine intentionally since the vision of Christianity that they offer is bounded by sentimentality and open to individual preference and conscience. Max Lucado and others have created a simplistic message that operates in place of a well-reasoned, intellectual approach to spirituality. They employ sentimentality as a motivation to minimize doctrine, sacralizing the ordinary and experience. A culture of anti-intellectualism in evangelicalism has participated in fostering this sentimental shift.

When exploring evangelical anti-intellectualism, it becomes clear that evangelicals use sentimentality for additional purposes. Earlier we noted how sentimentality can work as a tool for crafting authority. Emotional messages in the context of healing provide ministers the opportunity to gain the confidence of readers and situate themselves as healing experts with divine insight. In the absence of a climate of the mind, sentimentality and emotion become the authority. Purveyors position the emotions as being more reliable than the intellect and as a trustworthier source of truth.

The Rise and Fall of Baconian Science and the Evangelical Intellect

Many people would probably say that a majority of evangelicals eschew intellectuality, especially in matters of faith. Although certainly evangelical intellectuals exist, they are a much smaller portion of the population and do not reflect popular evangelicalism as a whole. Why has contemporary evangelicalism gained this moniker of anti-intellectual when certain expressions of nineteenth-century evangelicalism are frequently considered the opposite? The answer partly lies in the ideological strand that runs through both nineteenth-century and contemporary evangelicalism. Much of evangelical thought over the past two centuries has been dependent upon a Baconian view of science. Francis Bacon, a late sixteenth-century philosopher and politician, set out to create a great renewal of learning through the promulgation of a new method to approaching nature. Bacon's new process stood in contrast to the previous accepted method of deductive examination, which sought to expand and detail long-held theories about the world or a specific part of nature. Instead of deductive reasoning, Bacon emphasized the importance of inductive reasoning based on observation and experimentation. Baconian science started from gathering facts and then formulated theories about the world. Scientists—or natural philosophers according to the parlance—would create theories from facts instead of creating theories and then finding facts to support the theories.[7]

Bacon's approach to the world offered a new model of science, but it also influenced how Reformed Protestants understood the Bible and the world around them. While Bacon may not have wanted to look to scripture for scientific principles, Protestants used his method to do this. The Puritans, for example, assimilated Bacon's worldview and regarded his writing almost on a par with biblical writings. Bacon's approach to science and technology pervaded other aspects of Puritan thought, including economics and politics. Historian Charles Webster referred to Baconianism as "the key to Puritan sensibilities."[8] As an ideology, Baconianism led to a search of the biblical text to support advances in learning, improvement of nature, advances in arts, and even trade increases. Puritans even incorporated Baconian ideas about utopia through scientific advancement into their notions of the Kingdom of God. As Webster noted, "The Puritans genuinely thought that each step in the conquest of nature represented a move towards the millennial condition, and that each extension of the power of parliament reflected the special providential status of their nation."[9] Bacon provided precision and systematization that made the Puritans amenable to his philosophy of science and reality, especially since "Bacon's philosophy was explicitly conceived in the biblical and millenarian framework which was so congenial to the Puritans."[10]

Bacon's ideas also significantly impacted the development of Scottish Common Sense Realism. Thomas Reid and Dugald Stewart, two influential Scottish philosophers, used Bacon's inductive scientific method as a foundation for their approach to understanding reality and morality, which allowed for an emphasis on the rational order of nature. In their extrapolation of Bacon, Reid and Stewart emphasized the importance of the collection of "facts" from which one could inductively draw conclusions instead of hypotheses and theories. The Scots also emphasized that "abstract concepts not immediately forged from observed data have no place in scientific explanation."[11]

Baconian science and philosophy, which interpreted Bacon through the Scottish Common Sense philosophers, "took America by storm in the first half of the nineteenth century."[12] The Puritans had looked to Bacon for the ways science could bring about the Millennium, but American thinkers in the nineteenth century committed themselves to the empiricism of Baconian philosophy. Although different denominations were variously committed to the Scottish philosophy, nearly all evangelical denominations became dependent on this philosophy for understanding the world and the Bible. Obviously the belief that the Bible is true was not new to evangelicals or Christianity, but the fusion of Baconianism and Common Sense created a certain way the Bible was true. The Bible was seen as a storehouse of facts. The Baconian inductive method was a way to examine those facts and create a theology around this examination. Inductive reasoning from facts brought "truth"; deductive reasoning from previously conceived theories brought speculation or one's prejudices to scripture. "Evangelicals assumed that when they applied scientific Common Sense to Scripture and God-given experience more generally, they could derive a fixed, universally valid theology" much like Isaac Newton's laws.[13]

In the mid-nineteenth century, new developments and discoveries challenged both Baconian science and the Baconian Common Sense approach to the Bible. The acceptance of Darwin's theory of natural selection, and of organic evolution in general, among academics, scientists, and some Protestants was a challenge to literal interpretations of biblical accounts of the creation of the world. While many Protestants accepted evolution and believed it to be compatible with a belief in Christianity and Christianity's God, others were more hesitant about the impact of these scientific developments. These conservative evangelicals were also concerned about liberal theologies, coming mainly from Germany, that questioned the historicity and composition of the Bible. *Higher criticism*, as biblical scholars called it, postulated multiple sources for the first five books of the Hebrew Bible (Christian Old Testament), which many had previously believed that Moses wrote. Higher criticism also questioned the authorship of the book of Isaiah and the New Testament Gospels.[14]

Conservatives believed that evolution and higher criticism were detrimental to Christianity and could destroy the faith of many and lead America away from God. Evolution especially challenged the intellectual foundations of nineteenth-century evangelicalism. Although Darwin identified himself as following Bacon's method, his discoveries challenged the welding of Christianity, Baconianism, and Common Sense.[15] In an attempt to intellectually answer the problem of Darwinism, however, evangelicals continued to rely on Baconian Common Sense.

One of the first responses to Darwin and higher criticism was the creation of fundamentalism. Although many today consider it as anti-intellectual, early fundamentalism was an attempt to intellectually reply to the challenges of new modes of thinking about the Bible and reality. Additionally, fundamentalists answered the challenge of *modernism* by asserting what they saw as ancient beliefs. Among others, a belief in the inerrancy of scripture and the special creation of the world by God stood as a bastion for fundamentalists of what it meant to be a Christian and how the world operated. Modernists, as fundamentalists identified those who accepted liberal theology, were a danger to Christianity with their new, hence erroneous, understandings of the world and the Bible.[16]

Two examples demonstrate the intellectual response by proto-fundamentalists to the challenges of the nineteenth and twentieth centuries. The creation of the Princeton theology, a strict conservative

Presbyterian ideology developed at Princeton Theological Seminary, and the publication of *The Fundamentals*, a journal series of 12 volumes that conservative evangelicals wrote between 1910 and 1915, evidence a reliance on Baconian Common Sense as an intellectual framework that conservatives were committed to despite the weakening of both a Baconian approach to science and a Common Sense approach to reality and scripture. Presbyterian theologian and professor Charles Hodge, and later Hodge's student conservative theologian Benjamin Warfield, relied heavily on Common Sense in crafting a theology at Princeton. Although parts of it developed prior to the rise of Darwinian science, the Princetonians met their downfall in Darwin, partly due to their reliance on Common Sense. Hodge, Warfield, and other Princetonians assumed that "basic truths are much the same for all persons in all times and places."[17] The Bible contained these truths, and conservatives believed it was best understood through Common Sense principles. In a particularly useful image, historian George Marsden compared the Common Sense–influenced Princeton theology and the developing modernist view to differences between the Ptolemaic and Copernican understandings of the universe. Princeton theology, like the Ptolemaic version, was concerned with a "fixed truth that could be known objectively, while around it revolved all sorts of errors, speculations, prejudices, and subjective opinions."[18] Competing modern worldviews were more Copernican in that they saw truth "in motion—caught in historical processes. Rather than seeing truth as objectively existing at one fixed point, they have viewed knowledge at least to a considerable degree relative to a person's time and point of view."[19]

Written to combat Darwinism and other modernistic impulses in Christianity, *The Fundamentals* further demonstrate a reliance on Baconian Common Sense. Subtitled *A Testimony to the Truth*, this work included over 90 articles that presented arguments in a straightforward manner as appeals to average Christians. The articles of *The Fundamentals* were largely apologetic in nature as the authors attempted to respond to the challenges of modernism by presenting what they saw as timeless, unchanging truths. Inspired by a Baconian approach to science, the authors argued that *true science* and historical-critical approaches toward scripture did not contradict traditional, biblical views of the world. True science followed the Baconian method—reasoning inductively from facts that observers gathered. The competing science of modernism relied, according to conservatives, on games of the mind—creating speculations, hypotheses, and theories. That the response of *The Fundamentals* was an intellectual attempt can be seen in the authors' credentials. Many of the authors chosen to write the articles had some sort of advanced degree—qualification enough, it was believed, to attack and question the scientific findings of the modern age. That they relied on the vestiges of Common Sense in writing those articles is evident in the off-handed way they critiqued higher criticism especially. The Princeton theology and *The Fundamentals* were two intellectual sources providing the foundation for fundamentalism.[20]

Fundamentalism as an intellectual phenomenon was short-lived, however. Many observers—both academic and not—would point to the 1925 Scopes Trial as the downfall of fundamentalist intellectuality. Although in theory the trial was about whether or not John Scopes had broken the Butler Act of the state of Tennessee—a law that prohibited the teaching of evolution in public schools—it came to represent a contest between differing explanations for the origin of the universe and human beings. When defense attorney Clarence Darrow called prosecuting attorney William Jennings Bryan as a witness, Darrow was challenging not only the law and the power of fundamentalism but also the validity of Baconian Common Sense as an accurate approach to science. Fundamentalist Baconian Common Sense failed the test. Darrow challenged the law and Bryan on the literalness of the Bible, and Bryan's only defense was a Common Sense one. "Evolution is not truth," wrote Bryan in his closing argument; "it is millions of guesses strung together."[21] Bryan relied, as did many other anti-evolutionist fundamentalists, on the Baconian-induced belief that the hypothesis-experiment model of modern science was inaccurate because it was speculation—not based on truths that observers inductively drew from facts. Darrow managed to demonstrate the inadequacy and weakness of Bryan's knowledge of both science and the Bible, allowing commentators like journalist H. L. Mencken to ridicule fundamentalist intellectuality. In response to the prevailing pressures and ridicule, fundamentalists withdrew from American life to create a thriving subculture, but fundamentalist intellectuality suffered a crippling blow.[22]

Fundamentalism was not the only way conservative evangelicals have attempted to counteract the intellectual failings of Baconian Common Sense. Scholars have often pointed to the creation of an educational system centered on Bible colleges as part of the reason for the survival of fundamentalism after the Scopes trial. According to historian Randall Balmer, Bible colleges and institutes provided "islands of refuge" for fundamentalists wary of higher criticism, evolution, and their impact on religion.[23] Fundamentalist-evangelical colleges also provided at least the appearance of intellectual validity. The awarding of advanced degrees allowed ministers and educators to claim respectability alongside scientists and philosophers from secular schools. After all, these fundamentalists were also doctors. These schools, however, continued to be mired in the Common Sense philosophy and a Baconian worldview. The illusion was that fundamentalist schools taught ancient approaches to scripture and the "proper" approach to science. Although they attempted to shore up intellectual responses to evolution and higher criticism, fundamentalist educational institutions further separated fundamentalists from the intellectual mainstream of American culture. Once again fundamentalists failed to intellectually respond to their opponents.[24]

The attempt to legitimate creationism as a scientific field of inquiry able to be taught in public schools is a third example of the failure of Baconian Common Sense to achieve and retain intellectual legitimacy. Although the history of the relationship between evolution and conservative Protestantism is a complex one, conservative evangelicalism became united with an antievolution stance. When evolution gained acceptance in the scientific community and public schools, conservatives in the late twentieth century attacked it on Baconian grounds. The battles with evolution for most of the early twentieth century were amorphous, focusing on what were seen as loopholes in evolutionary theory or challenging it as acceptable science. In the mid-twentieth century, however, conservatives fashioned *creation science,* or *scientific creationism,* as an answer to evolution. The foundations of creation science date back to the late nineteenth century, but as a cohesive unit creation science is a late twentieth-century product.[25]

The formation of the Creation-Science Research Center and the Institute of Creation Research in the 1970s was an attempt to prove the scientific validity of the biblical accounts of the creation of the world in such a way that creationism could be taught in public schools. They did achieve some short-lived success. The legislature of the state of Arkansas, for example, passed a law requiring educators to present creation science alongside evolutionary theory. In the late 1980s the Supreme Court determined that creation science was an attempt to slip religion into schools as a subversion of the separation of church and state. The failure of creation science to gain entrance into academic spheres, however, did not end the attempt to validate evangelical intellectuality. Creationism appeared again in the 1990s in another form—intelligent design (ID).[26]

ID was an attempt to self-consciously present creationism without its religious underpinnings. The coalition behind ID was broader than evangelicalism or even Christianity and included individuals from a variety of fields. Its proponents also differed widely over who the designer was, how the designer acted, and the timetable for design. However, the philosopyhy was popular among many evangelicals because it seemed a way to integrate an alternative explanation for the universe and life into the evolution-controlled public schools. Advocates of intelligent design achieved some success in places like Wisconsin and Kansas, where school boards redefined science standards to allow for the teaching of intelligent design due to the so-called theoretical nature of evolution. Unsurprisingly, scientists and other advocates of evolution challenged the acceptance of intelligent design, claiming that it was pseudo-science and inherently philosophical, not scientific. Either track led to the same conclusion: intelligent design belonged in philosophy classes, if it belonged in curricula at all. Ultimately, intelligent design fared the same as creation science.[27]

Creation science and intelligent design may have acquired advocates outside of evangelicalism and Christianity, but the impact of Bacon and Common Sense is just as important for their evangelical adherents. In his book *Creation and the Modern Christian*, Henry Morris, one of the founders of creation science, argued that "science once was recognized as the organized body of known truth, or at least as a *search* for truth. It dealt with *facts*, demonstrated facts."[28] While Morris allowed that the scientific method should involve "factual predictions which could be tested and at least in principle, either falsified or confirmed by measurement,"[29] he further demonstrated the influence of Baconian Common Sense when he told Christians how to respond to those who questioned the validity of a creation science:

> If Christians will simply keep these distinctions [about the definition of science] in mind, they need never be intimidated by naturalistic scientists or other skeptics. Whenever someone says that science has proved evolution, simply ask him to cite *and document* one scientific *proof* of evolution, reminding him that "science" means *knowledge*, not theory or assumption or speculation.[30]

If evolution was theory and speculation for Morris, the Bible contained facts: "many of the Biblical statements of scientific fact preceded their confirmation by scientists by thousands of years. Such facts can be cited and explained both as evidence of Biblical inspiration. Real science will always be found to support creation and the Bible."[31] Despite allowing for the use of hypotheses and experimentation in science, Morris argued that real science was about the discovery of facts that lead to conclusions—a Baconian approach.[32]

Evangelical supporters of ID also evidence the influence of Baconian Common Sense when discussing intelligent design as an alternative to evolution. Popular evangelical voice Charles Colson is representative of the thought of many supporters of ID. In an April 2005 article in *Christianity Today* Colson claimed that the burden of proof regarding the origins of life rested with those who believe in evolution not those who supported intelligent design. In answer to a question he rhetorically posed about whether scientists have empirically proven Darwinian evolution, Colson responded, "Wrong. Sure, there's evidence that evolution takes place within a species— but the fossil record has not yielded evidence of one species becoming another, as Darwin confidently predicted."[33] Since Christianity is "a historical religion that deals in facts and events," the facts should predominate in questions about the origins of life.[34] Intelligent design, then, should be present in public schools as an alternative to evolution. Claiming that "the evidence for Intelligent Design has become so persuasive," Colson stated that "any objective observer must conclude that belief in either the biblical or the naturalistic worldview demands faith. The issue is not science versus faith, but science (evolution) versus science (Intelligent Design)."[35] Colson concluded by saying he would like to argue the case of evolution versus intelligent design in the Supreme Court: "pitting the common consensus against the Darwinist establishment."[36] Although intelligent design and evangelicalism have both moved beyond an explicit reliance on Bacon and Common Sense, the influence is still present. The appeal to facts and the disdain for theories and speculation demonstrate that influence. In some respect Colson is right. The issue between ID and scientists is one of science versus science. One of those models of science, however, is outdated. The evolutionary-Darwinian approach to science has superseded the Baconian one; evangelical attempts at intellectual respectability, however, have not adapted to this change.

One could add other examples of the reliance and impact of Baconian Common Sense within evangelicalism, but these examples demonstrate how the uniting of Bacon, Common Sense, and evangelicalism in the nineteenth century has shaped the path of evangelical intellectuality in the twentieth and into the twenty-first centuries. Bacon and Common Sense have failed evangelicals when they need it most—in historical moments where they might have shaped the intellectual climate of American culture. In the vacuum of a strong intellectual culture, sentimentality has taken root.

Beginning in the late nineteenth century, some evangelicals specifically chose to downplay intellectual questions in favor an emotionally driven religiosity. These evangelicals also evidence the influence of Scottish Common Sense. As noted in the introduction, the Scots emphasized the importance of emotion to motivate people to moral action. Many evangelicals turned to sentimentality as the key to moral engagement. Dwight Moody incorporated Victorian sentimentality into his revivalistic appeal. He supported the theological positions of conservative evangelicals but focused on appealing to the emotions in his sermons through evoking narratives meant to elicit a response from the affections, not the intellect. Because his concern was conversions, Moody also simplified his message and presented sermons that focused on a limited number of topics, contained a message that would have broad appeal to Protestants of diverse theological backgrounds, and avoided the controversial attitude of proto-fundamentalists. Billy Sunday employed many of the same techniques, although he rhetorically deprecated a sentimental approach to Christianity. Sunday's sermons demonstrated his reliance on the domestic typology of the Victorian period and the sentimentality that went along with it. He valorized the piety of women, especially mothers, and emphasized the importance of the sanctity of the home to the success of the nation. In promoting a *masculine* Christianity, Sunday encouraged men to take their rightful place as strong leaders of the home. While he offered memorable and fanciful statements deploring *feminized* Christianity, he employed some of the same tropes in his messages. Like Moody, Sunday offered a simplified message aimed at the conversion of people in his audience.

Theological controversy had no place in a Sunday revival unless it was as a foil to the type of Christianity that Sunday promoted. The use of a simple, sentimental message that avoided intellectual topics also marked the careers of prominent evangelicals in the middle of the twentieth century. Historian Joel Carpenter records an event in Billy Graham's life that demonstrates this abdication of intellectual rigor among popular evangelicals. Early in his career, before his widespread success, Graham experienced serious doubts about the inerrancy of scripture and the validity of the fundamentalist viewpoint. Liberal theology and modern scholarship challenged Graham, and he was conflicted. Graham, however, eventually resolved his conflict without resolving the intellectual challenges. He decided to simply trust that the Bible was God's word. His career reflected this evasion of the intellectual problems of Christianity for sentimental simplification.[37]

The use of sentimentality allows many people to remain committed to evangelicalism without questioning the Baconian Common Sense foundations that create an antipathy to evolution and liberal theologies about the Bible. Sentiment allows for greater receptivity of the evangelical message because it promotes feeling and relationship and, explicitly or not, an anti-intellectualism that elides the intellectual difficulties evangelicalism faces. Popular evangelicals have used this to their advantage. Sentimentality is strategically employed to avoid exploring the intellectual foundations of evangelicalism and to disregard the intellectual stability of either evolution or higher criticism. Emotionality becomes an authority greater than knowledge gained through the intellect, particularly if that knowledge is antagonistic to religious truths.

Yet sentimentality must be a flexible tool to sidestep intellectual challenges. Particularly it must be used to convince individuals that the questions and challenges directed toward evangelical Christianity are insignificant compared with the emotional connection available between the individual and God. The goal is to make people feel good, not necessarily to convince them that Christianity is ideologically true. Sentimentalists—especially those entrenched in the therapeutic evangelicalism discussed in Chapter 1—appear to assume, and expect their readers to as well, that Christianity is true based on feeling and not on intellect. Although intellectual defense is usually not their intent, there are places in their writings where they deploy sentimentality to counteract intellectual examination. Sometimes this elision occurs with a tongue-in-cheek expression that encourages the reader to recognize that intellectual challenges to evangelicalism are not worth either the minister's or the audience's time.

In his book *In the Grip of* Grace, for example, Max Lucado uses a parable about crickets to downplay the impact scientific hypotheses have had on the origins of the universe and life. According to the narrative, he happens to notice a cricket under his pew one Sunday as he was about to take Communion. Although he is not a bug lover, the presence of the cricket allows Lucado to rhapsodize about the similarities between himself, his audience, and this cricket. "We have something in common, you, me, and the cricket. Limited vision."[38] According to Lucado, the auditorium is the only universe the cricket knew. The cricket has no lofty aspirations and a minimal understanding of the world around it. Lucado also wonders whom the cricket worships. "Does he acknowledge that there was a hand behind the building? Or does he choose to worship the building itself? Or perhaps a place in the building? Does he assume that since he has never seen the builder there *was* no builder?"[39] Lucado then postulates about a cricket philosophy that would ignore the importance of a builder if crickets could understand how everything in the room works. In this scenario these crickets have understood electricity, air conditioners, and speakers and determined there was no life beyond the room:

> Would we let the crickets get by with that? Of course not! "Just because you understand the system," we'd tell them, "that doesn't deny the presence of someone outside the system. After all, who built it? Who installed the switch? Who diagrammed the compressor and engineered the generator?" But don't we make the same mistake? We understand how storms are created. We map solar systems and transplant hearts. We measure the depths of the oceans and send signals to distant planets. We crickets have studied the system and are learning how it works. And, for some, the loss of mystery has led to the loss majesty. The more we know, the less we believe. Strange, don't you think? Knowledge of the workings shouldn't negate wonder. Knowledge should stir wonder.[40]

Lucado fails to engage the intellectual questions about the origins of life and dismisses them sentimentally: if someone understands the universe scientifically but doubts God's existence, then he is like a cricket, thinking he understands an auditorium. There is no real engagement of science or evolution; there is only smoke and mirrors. Because the sentimental message is an anti-intellectual one, Lucado can strategically deploy sentimentality to create a simple, well-honed message that appeals to a large audience.

A similar tactic to avoid intellectual challenges by appealing to emotions can be seen in Rick Warren's *The Purpose-Driven Life*. According to Warren, "if there was no God, we would be 'accidents,' the result of astronomical random chance in the universe."[41] Instead of deconstructing evolutionary theory or attempting to refute scientific evidence, Warren appeals to a narcissistic sense of value. He asserts, "God never does anything accidentally, and he never makes mistakes."[42] Such a contention means that the individual reader is not an accident but someone whose life has "profound meaning!"[43] In fact, God had created the world because of his love for human beings: "God designed this planet's environment just so we could live in it. We are the focus of his love and the most valuable of all his creation.... This is how much God loves and values you!"[44] Instead of addressing an argument that life exists on this planet because this planet was able to support life, Warren contends that the reader should believe that God has a tremendous plan for the reader's life and that this is the reason God created the planet to support life. Warren maneuvers around intellectual challenges to the Christian cosmogony by trying to make his readers feel loved by God.[45]

Although Warren has a doctorate of ministry from Fuller Seminary, he encourages his audience to focus on the experiential aspects of religion instead of the intellectual ones. For Warren, experience trumps intellect, especially when it comes to spreading the message of Christianity. In this case Warren is much more explicit about his anti-intellectualism than Max Lucado is. In a chapter of *The Purpose-Driven Life* titled "Sharing Your Life Message," Warren tells his readers that God expects them to share their testimony about what God has done in their lives. The conveying of personal experience, argues Warren, is a better tactic to spread Christianity than intellectual arguments:

> You may not be a Bible scholar, but you *are* the authority on your life, and it's hard to argue with personal experience. Actually, your personal testimony is more effective than a sermon, because unbelievers see pastors as professional salesmen, but see you as a "satisfied customer," so they give you more credibility. Personal stories are also easier to relate to than principles, and people love to hear them. They capture our attention, and we remember them longer. Unbelievers would probably lose interest if you started quoting theologians, but they have a natural curiosity about experiences they've never had. Shared stories build a relational bridge that Jesus can walk across from your heart to theirs. Another value of your testimony is that it bypasses intellectual defenses. Many people who won't accept the authority of the Bible will listen to a humble, personal story.[46]

Warren is not addressing external challenges to the veracity of Christianity. Instead, he is weighing the differences between an intellectual presentation of Christianity and an experiential one. The effect, however, is the same: emotionality and experience become the methods to bypass the intellectual difficulties of a view of scriptural inerrancy by appealing to the emotions and experience. Warren does not lay out a procedure for proving the veracity of the Bible. Instead, he urges people to show others that God loves them and Christianity is true because of what they have personally experienced. As Warren states, "It's hard to argue with personal experience."[47]

What we see in these popular ministers—and others as well—is an evangelical elision meant to avoid the intellectual challenges confronting evangelical Christianity in the contemporary period. How does one respond to scientific evidence and theories questioning not only that God created the universe but also that God even exists? Tell a story about how foolish it would be for crickets to argue that an auditorium developed out of nothing. How does one explain one's commitment to Christianity in a time when

Christianity is derided for its anti-intellectual stance? Focus on one's personal experience and avoid intellectual questions. That is supposedly what people want to hear. Instead of addressing the intellect, these evangelicals, and others like them, appeal to their audiences' emotions by making the implicit—and sometimes explicit—claim that the emotions provide a greater understanding of God and reality than the intellect does.

Anti-intellectualism, based on the elevation of the individual and usually associated with anti-elitism, has allowed sentimentality a space to blossom. Systematic theology and intellectual contemplation are frequently conceptualized as the province of the elites; it is no surprise that it would be denigrated in the context of antiauthoritarianism. Emotionality has always been a strand within evangelicalism, but in the contemporary period it has flourished in the wake of the stigmatization of intellectual pursuits. In place of even a cursory life of the mind is the power of the emotions to provide meaning, even in the ordinary aspects of life.[48]

Sacralizing the Ordinary

From the days of the Reformation, Protestants have sacralized the ordinary aspects of life. The concept of the *priesthood of all believers* and the importance of fulfilling one's calling rhetorically leveled Protestants and made even the most mundane events possibilities for holiness. Although these ideas have a long provenance in evangelicalism, they are emotionalized through modern evangelicals. The ordinary, the sentimental, and the anti-intellectual are combined to remove authority away from a life of the mind to the emotions evoked by everyday life.

Lucado uses narratives, which feature prominently in his books and which some have pointed to as a key feature of his writing, to accomplish this sacralization of the quotidian.[49] His use of narrative further removes evangelicalism from an appeal to the intellect because the messages of his stories are meant to create a responsive feeling in his readers. In these narratives the ordinariness of both the characters and events become holy and sacred when understood through sentimental eyes.

Although Lucado crafts his own fictional parables for his works, he frequently uses "real-life" examples in his books. These are narratives that Lucado has encountered in other sources including newspapers or magazines. He appropriates the events to make a sentimental spiritual point. The narrative is most likely truncated, and only details that are useful for sentimentalizing are included in the abstraction. These types of narratives are ubiquitous throughout Lucado's works. His inspirational titles usually include at least three or more narratives that Lucado has drawn from history books, news articles, or some other source presenting real life occurrences. These events and people range from notable Christians like Mother Teresa, Billy Graham, and writers of famous hymns like John Newton and George Matheson to historical individuals like Dwight Eisenhower, the brother of John Wilkes Booth (who unknowingly saved Robert Todd Lincoln from being hit by a train in the late nineteenth century), George Washington Carver, and Alfred Hitchcock. These narratives might be about a garbage barge that continues to travel the seas because it cannot find port, a woman suffering from fibrodysplasia ossificans progressiva (a disease where the entire body becomes solid bone), or a doctor performing an appendectomy on himself. They might be about men in a life raft saved by a seagull or about a man convicted of manslaughter who, according to a wrongful death suit, had to send a check for $1.00 every week for 936 weeks to the family of the woman he killed. Whatever the narrative and its original context, Lucado abstracts and emotionalizes it to make it into a story about spirituality.[50]

Such a romanticizing occurs in a story in his book *Come Thirsty*. Lucado tells of a 17-year-old boy named Jake Porter who went to school at Northwest High in McDermott, Ohio. Porter suffered from chromosomal fragile X syndrome, a condition connected to a variety of intellectual and behavioral challenges, but he loved sports. He went to all the practices for a variety of sports, but he never played due to his condition. When his high school football team was playing a team from Waverly, Ohio, however, he got the opportunity to play. Northwest High was down 42–0 in the final seconds of the game. The Northwest coach called timeout and crossed over to the Waverly coach to ask him to allow Porter into the game to take a knee and end out the game. The Waverly coach agreed to allow Porter in the game only if Porter would be allowed to score. Porter entered the game, thinking he would take a knee. When handed the ball, his teammates prevented him from taking a knee and told him to run. The defense allowed Porter to pass through and score a touchdown. Lucado's version of this story is used to introduce a chapter titled "Angels Watching over You." Lucado notes, "What Jake's team did for him, the Lord of the universe does for you every day of your life. And you ought to see the team he coaches."[51]

The *Sports Illustrated* article "The Play of the Year," which serves as the source for this story, contains some sentimentality, as one might expect considering the subject matter.[52] There is more, however, to the source material than makes it into Lucado's *Come Thirsty*. Not only did the play raise a national debate from some commentators concerning the role of those who are disabled in athletics (like whether Porter and others with mental challenges should be allowed to play football), but there were racial issues surrounding the play as well. Waverly's coach Derek Dewitt—the first African American coach in the conference—features just as prominently as Porter does. Rick Reilly, the author of the article, mentions racial slurs and other difficulties Dewitt had faced because of his race. Reilly also noted that, at least apparently, relationships between the towns of McDermott and Waverly seemed better than it had been before the game. The collective impact of Porter's touchdown and its overtones concerning race and disability, a prominent aspect of the *Sports Illustrated* article, is lost in Lucado's sentimentalizing of the individual.[53]

In his sacralizing of the normal events of everyday life, Lucado's characters are generally common individuals who become important through his construction of the narrative. Because Lucado presents them as nondescript, he attempts to convince his readers that they are in a similar position, that they can respond similarly, or that they relate to the supernatural in the same way. In some respects Lucado chooses narratives that are similar to the parables of the Gospels. The parables of Jesus featured common elements of contemporary Jewish life—farming, fishing, merchandizing. The Gospel parables also contain emotional appeals, although those that do are very few. Lucado's narratives, however, are dependent on emotional appeal. They may evoke heart-rending feelings or may be cutesy in their presentation, but the purpose is not to make individuals examine the validity of the story but to make them feel loved by God. The power comes not from the words or the message itself but from an uncritical acceptance of Lucado's narrative. The plain and familiar style invites readers to come with a hermeneutic of faith, not a hermeneutic of suspicion. The operation of a hermeneutic of faith, however, lends a measure of control to Lucado that his audience is unaware of relinquishing.[54]

Although Joel Osteen uses narratives in his books, his sacralization of the ordinary occurs in other ways as well. As might be expected, Osteen encourages his readers to see the importance of the ordinary in prosperity. According to Osteen, God's blessings for his children appear even in the mundane acts of everyday life: "at the grocery store, at the ball field, the mall, at work, or at home."[55] God will even open up a lane for them in traffic. He will find them a parking spot or a shorter checkout line at the store. God might even arrange a meeting with someone they want to do business with. All of this is God's favor and is something children of God should not just dream about but also should expect—due to Osteen's sentimental understanding of God as father.[56]

Osteen also elevates career choice as a divine benefit. Like Warren, Osteen claims that everyone has a purpose in life—although he prefers the term *destiny*, which includes a person's job. God intended each of us to have a certain type of employment and created each of us with desires and abilities that are only fully activated when that destiny is discovered. In fact, when we find the destiny God intended, "it shouldn't surprise [them] that [it] will involve something [they] enjoy."[57] Destiny, especially in one's career, provides the opportunity for holiness because people are doing what God created them for. No matter what that is, once it is found individuals should fulfill it to the best of their ability: "if you are called to be a stay-at-home mom and raise your children, do it to the best of your ability. Don't allow society to pressure you into some career simply because your friends are doing it. Recognize your purpose and do it well. If you are gifted in the area of sales, don't sit behind a desk all day long in a room by yourself.... If you're going to fulfill your destiny, you must do what God hardwired you to do."[58] In fact, for Osteen, when we fulfill our destiny—find the job God made us for—is to honor God. The very ordinary activities of our life become sacred moments because of the divine imprimatur placed on the quotidian.[59]

Although we could expect part of the purpose of a purpose-driven life to be finding our God-given career, Rick Warren also stresses that even our flaws are given—or at least allowed—by God. Whether it is "financial or relational limitations" or "a handicap," "trauma scar," "personality quirk, or a hereditary disposition," God can take advantage of these situations for his glory.[60] Citing biblical figures who had some sort of "weakness," he tells the reader to "be content with your weaknesses."[61] God will ultimately take our weaknesses and transform them. The ordinary difficulties of life become opportunity for divine–human interactions as God supernaturally works in the struggles to demonstrate great things.[62]

Chapter 1 outlined how Bruce Wilkinson uses the theme of ordinariness to make a connection between himself and the reader. He also uses this rhetoric as the core of his message. Jabez was ordinary, according to Wilkinson, and God is looking to bless ordinary people today. Indeed, *The Prayer of Jabez* "is about what happens when ordinary Christians decide to reach for an extraordinary life—which, as it turns out, is exactly the kind God promises."[63] Even Jesus' apostles were ordinary believers until Jesus "filled them with His miraculous power."[64] Although Lucado, Osteen, and Warren sacralize the ordinary, suggesting that there is something important in the actual ordinariness of life,

Wilkinson suggests that it is more a base level for greatness. Because we are ordinary, God can do great things. Indeed the blessing will be so great that it will be obvious that it came from God and not through our skill. Ordinariness is still potentially sacred because it ultimately reveals that human beings are dependent upon God, and "for the Christian, dependence is just another word for power."[65]

The theme of God being involved in the ordinariness of life is not limited to white conservative evangelicals. In his book *From the Cross to Pentecost*, for example, minister and businessperson Bishop T. D. Jakes claims that God wants us to see his presence in every aspect of the ordinariness of life and not just moments designated religious. According to Jakes, God and Jesus say to people:

> You know that job you got? That was me! And when your credit was messed up, I was the one who opened the doors so you got that car anyway. And when they set a trap for you and tried to destroy you, but someone intervened and helped you just in the nick of time—that was Me! Because I fight battles for you; I open doors for you. I made a way for you. When you didn't even have a jove, I fed you![66]

Because the audience is interpreted sentimentally as individually important to father God, even the most ordinary aspects of an individual's life take on greater purpose. As Warren suggests—and Lucado, Osteen, Wilkinson, and Jakes would probably echo—each individual has a God-given purpose; fulfilling that purpose in living our life is an expression of holiness. The ordinary becomes sacred.

Sacralizing the ordinary participates in the spread of sentimentality because it communicates a view that the mundane events in life contain divine significance. Here too is the narcissistic appeal of modern sentimentality. Everything about each of our lives—our jobs, character flaws, search for the perfect parking spot—are all moments with the potential for God to reach down and impart holiness. Although Wilkinson would suggest that God wants to move people beyond the ordinary, Lucado, Warren, Osteen, and others claim that God honors the commonness of the life of the individual. Father God blesses all the occasions of his child's life so that every instant is a gift from God. These ministers invite the reader to accept this view and see the individual's world as the province of the divine: God is concerned about all the aspects of readers' lives; that's how important they are to God. The proliferation of this view discourages intellectual questioning or exploration. It is the mundane that is holy; the intellectual distracts because it tends to over-think or overexamine and misses the operation of God. Authority is centered on emotion. Sentimentality becomes a viable source of knowledge about God and the word, trumping the mental acumen. The proliferation of such litera-ture participates in both the spread of evangelical anti-intellectualism and the expansion of the authority of evangelical sentimentality.

Downplaying Doctrinal Differences and Attacking "Religion"

Evangelical sentimentality and anti-intellectualism combine in another prominent feature of modern popular evangelicalism: the downplaying of doctrine and the differences between denominations. Sentimentality allows prominent evangelicals like the ones we have been examining to present themselves as beyond denominations, despite often having strong denomi-national connections. Rick Warren's Saddleback Church, for example, is a Southern Baptist church, an attribute not given much prominence by either Saddleback or Warren. Perhaps he believes that softening doctrinal commit-ments will allow him and his church to reach a broader audience and stand apart from denominational conflict.

In many respects this sentimentalizing of doctrinal differences is meant to counteract denominational competition like what historian Philip Mulder saw in the eighteenth-century awakenings in the South around the time of the Revolution. In Mulder's study, Presbyterians, Methodists, and Baptists emphasized their doctrinal distinctiveness in an attempt to gain adherents. Even as they responded to each other and became closer in beliefs and prac-tice, these groups emphasized distinction and not commonality. "The awak-eners strove to make clear their differences with other awakeners and to identify precisely who was on the path toward heaven."[67] Distinction was a mark of identity. Mulder further argued that the separation present in the eighteenth century was still animating denominations in the twentieth and twenty-first centuries. Despite the language of ecumenism, the actual expe-rience of congregations was quite different. Groups attempting to practice unity have organized themselves into structures that create distinction sim-ply through their organization—delineating what a group believes cre-ates distinctions against groups and individuals who believe differently. As Mulder wrote, "Ecumenicity among Protestant groups remains as elusive an ideal today as it was when it was created in awakening fervor. Individual denominational concerns and debates continue to make headlines with strife over civil rights, women's participation, and homosexuality."[68] Focusing on emotionality, however, allows for at least the appearance of ecumenicity, and the moderating tendencies can offer readers the impression that the minister is above such petty conflicts that run contrary to the image of Christianity that he promotes.

Lucado denounces Christian infighting and promotes diminishing doctrinal distinctiveness in his parable "Life Aboard the Fellow-Ship" from *In the Grip of Grace*. "God has enlisted us in his navy and placed us on his ship," writes Lucado.[69] God's ship is a battleship. Those who have signed on the ship have different responsibilities. Some watch the waters to snatch people who are drowning. Some arm cannons because they are concerned about the enemy. Others feed and train the crew. "Though different," continues Lucado, "we are the same. Each can tell of a personal encounter with the captain, for each has received a personal call."[70] Each individual, however, has different interests and concerns and tends to cluster with others who share those interests. This clustering has led to disharmony among the crew. Of particular concern to Lucado is "the plethora of opinions."[71] Some believe in the need for serious study, rigorous discipline, and "somber expressions."[72] They can be found in the stern. Some emphasize prayer by kneeling. They are found in the bow. Some claim that only real wine should be used in Communion. "You'll find them on the port side."[73] Other opinions are even more distinctive:

> Some think once you're on the boat, you can't get off. Others say you'd be foolish to go overboard, but the choice is yours. Some believe you volunteer for service; others believe you were destined for the service before the ship was even built. Some predict a storm of great tribulation will strike before we dock; others say it won't hit until we are safely ashore. There are those who speak to the captain in a personal language. There are those who think such languages are extinct. There are those who think the officers should wear robes, there are those who think there should be no officers at all, and there are those who think we are all officers and should all wear robes. And, oh, how we tend to cluster.[74]

Lucado continues to describe how clustering occurs around worship practices before appealing to Jesus' prayer for unity among his followers (John 17). The fellow-ship, however, is a "rocky boat" that has lost opportunities because "some adrift at sea have chosen not to board the boat because of the quarreling of the sailors."[75]

Lucado downplays denominational differences through his ecumenical view of Christianity. The dissension aboard the fellow-ship resulting from apparent doctrinal commitments is really a matter of personal preference. The clustering of individuals around certain preferences is not the problem for Lucado. The judgment of one cluster over another is. Lucado's exposition makes his ecumenical point clear. Unity comes from accepting fellow Christians in spite of their personal doctrines. Lucado offers the example of his own life as a model for this sentimental ecumenism. Although raised in the West Texas Church of Christ, he "found encouragement in other state-rooms" on God's ship.[76] Presbyterians, Anglicans, Baptists, Pentecostals, and Catholics provided Lucado with different perspectives on spiritual themes, and he encourages other Christians to be as eclectic. He writes, "I'm a better husband because I read James Dobson and a better preacher because I listened to Chuck Swindoll and Bill Hybels."[77]

By naming prominent evangelicals Dobson, Swindoll, and Hybels as important teachers, Lucado is placing himself among an ecumenical group of evangelicals who attempt to elevate elements of Christianity that are intentionally noncontroversial about matters of Christian doctrine. In her study of gender and James Dobson's *Focus on the Family*, historian Colleen McDannell observed that Dobson's organization avoids theological speculation in favor of doctrinally nondivisive approaches to family guidance—although it often supports controversial political positions. Instead of staking out a doctrinal stance, Dobson's ecumenical approach to family issues is an approach that does not require "an analytical response" but one that attempts to create a foundation where most people would find common ground.[78] In many ways this is the same tactic used by Lucado, especially in parables like "Life Aboard the Fellow-ship." Lucado appears to believe that most Christians would accept that their distinctive doctrines are small compared with the element that unites them—belief in the saving work of Jesus Christ. There is no search for intellectual validity or viability in examining the different doctrines—Lucado accepts that the doctrines he is referring to are matters of personal preference that may inhibit the sentimental connection between the individual and the deity.

Warren also shares Lucado's tendency to downplay doctrinal distinctiveness. Although he is a Southern Baptist, in *The Purpose-Driven Life* he takes an antidenominational stance and promotes a relationship with Jesus instead of religion. Like Lucado this is an attempt to create as broad an audience as possible and to target people dissatisfied with or alienated from institutional religion. At the end of time, argues Warren, "God won't ask about your religious background or doctrinal views. The only thing that will matter is, did you accept what Jesus did for you and did you learn to love and trust him?"[79] Furthermore Warren argues that "Christianity is not a religion or a philosophy, but a relationship and a lifestyle."[80] In describing churches, Warren states that "as believers we share one Lord, one body, one purpose, one Father, one Spirit, one hope, one faith, one baptism, and one love.... These are the issues, not our personal differences, that we should concentrate on. We must remember that it was God who chose to give us different personalities, backgrounds, races, and preferences, so we should value and enjoy those differences, not merely tolerate them."[81] Despite the variety of differing Christian beliefs about these nine things, Warren ignores the theological problems by asserting that more is shared among Christians than separates them (although differences in Christology alone are often polar opposites—how is Jesus the Son of God; how does his death affect the forgiveness of sins; if, when, and how will he return to Earth). The minimalizing of doctrine, however, makes the acceptance of an affective approach to God much easier to promote.

In previous generations—and still in some quarters—theologians would sometimes proffer a systematic theology that laid out their views about what the Bible taught regarding a variety of subjects. The intent appears to be to offer the audience a well-reasoned work that should provide doctrinal answers to a variety of questions. By their very makeup, such works tend to be polemical in nature. Although such an author might take an irenic tone, by laying out the doctrinal exploration with a definitive answer she or he would be denying the validity of other competing answers. When explored through a sentimental worldview, however, the doctrinal is diluted in favor of the experiential and emotional. In this framework someone doesn't approach the biblical text for intellectual pursuits or with a belief that God is known through the reason. Instead someone reads the Bible, as Warren says, to "become best friends with God."[82]

Becoming best friends with God also allows sentimental evangelicals to emphasize the connection between God and the individual as one of relationship, not religion. Religion is deprecated as something cold or lifeless, and the emotional connection to the divine is emphasized as being more authentic. The reason individuals need to be less concerned about doctrinal differences is that God cares not about religion but about relationships. In fact, sentimental ministers often pit religion against this relationship and suggest that religion will not lead to the relationship God desires. Jakes, for example, stresses that religion keeps human beings from God: "I'm not calling you to me, because I'm not better than you. I'm not calling you to a church, because the church is no Savior. I'm not calling you to a denomination, because I'm sick of all of them. I'm not calling you to religion, because I'm tired of religion, too. But I am calling you into a relationship with the Savior."[83] In fact, says Jakes, "there is a difference between trying church and trying Jesus."[84]

Lucado often echoes Jakes's antipathy to organized religion. In *No Wonder They Call Him the Savior*, for example, Lucado uses the Gospel account of Roman soldiers casting lots for Jesus' clothing at his crucifixion to criticize contemporary Christianity. "Here are common soldiers witnessing the world's most uncommon event and they don't even know it."[85] This scene reminds Lucado of modern-day Christians:

> It makes me think of us. The religious. Those who claim heritage at the cross. I'm thinking of all of us. Every believer in the land. The stuffy. The loose. The strict. The simple. Upper church. Lower church. "Spirit-filled." Millenialists [sic]. Evangelical. Political. Mystical. Literal. Cynical. Robes. Collars. Three-piece suits. Born-againers. Ameners. I'm thinking of us. I'm thinking we aren't so unlike those soldiers. (I'm sorry to say.)[86]

Such Christians, writes Lucado, are "so close to the cross but so far from the Christ."[87] He doles out judgment on Christianity for its doctrinal pettiness and divisions, but he believes that Christian unity is not an impossible dream. The solution is simple for Lucado—a dismantling of organized religion: "*One* church....Not Baptist, not Methodist, not Adventist. Just Christians. No denominations. No hierarchies. No traditions. Just Christ."[88] Even the dismantling of the denominational structure of Christianity receives Lucado's sentimentality: "Too idealistic? Impossible to achieve? I don't think so. Harder things have been done, you know. For example, once upon a tree, a Creator gave his life for his creation. Maybe all we need are a few hearts that are willing to follow suit."[89]

Whether it is asserting that one should be God's best friend or should try Jesus instead of the church, many evangelicals are moving away from the doctrinal aspects of Christianity. The encouraging of an antidoctrinal approach also provides a backdoor justification for anti-intellectualism under the guise of sentimentality. Because God loves all his children, doctrinal preferences— matters dealing with the intellectual investigation of scripture to determine the biblical view of whatever subject—are not as important as accepting the love of God in Jesus. Moreover, sentimentality obscures the subsumed and assumed commitments to certain evangelical doctrines. In addition, while ministers like Lucado or Jakes might rail against the abuses of organized religion, they are still situated in organized religion. Sentimental rhetoric obscures how firmly entrenched and financially dependent in organized religion they are. Abandoning doctrine and the intellect for feeling and an apparent anti-institutionalism, however, opens up the possibility for changes to occur.

A Tale of Two Hells: Max Lucado and Rob Bell

To say that those who rely on sentimentality in crafting their messages choose emotion over intellect does not mean that they avoid addressing Christian teaching altogether. Warren, for example, discusses doctrine in *The Purpose-Driven Life*, but frequently popular evangelical ministers frame those doctrines in emotional ways, not intending to explore these ideas intellectually. This sentimentalizing of Christian beliefs has the potential to lead to modification of traditional evangelical doctrines. A comparison of how two sentimental evangelicals—Max Lucado and Rob Bell—interpret a single belief reveals how sentimentality not only can participate in the construction of evangelical belief but also can lead to divergence among evangelicals. These two ministers both employ emotionality as the key authority for understanding God. Particularly insightful is paralleling the views of Lucado and Bell on a doctrine that would seem to be completely against evangelical sentimentality—hell.

As much as Lucado sentimentalizes Christianity and the believer's relationship to God, he still holds a belief in both the concrete reality and the eternality of hell. The existence of hell, like the sentimental tropes in the rest of his work, is related to the character of God. "If there is no hell," writes Lucado, "God is not just."[90] Because God reveals the existence of hell in scripture, Lucado continues, to refuse to believe in hell makes God a liar and the scripture untrue. Furthermore, the doctrine of a real hell is not inconsistent with the message of Jesus, according to Lucado, because "thirteen percent of the teachings of Christ are about judgment and hell. More than half of his parables related to God's eternal judgment of sinners."[91]

Not only do the scriptures describe the reality of hell, but they also insist on the eternality of hell. "There is no point which I'd more gladly be wrong than the eternal duration of hell. If God, on the last day, extinguishes the wicked, I'll celebrate my misreading of his words. Yet...God sobers his warnings with eternal language."[92] For Lucado, if heaven is eternal, hell is as well. "[Hell] may have a back door or graduation day, but I haven't found it."[93]

Despite his insistence on the real, eternal existence of hell, Lucado gives the topic of hell the sentimental treatment. While he believes that hell is a terrible place of torment, Lucado's God does everything he can to prevent people from going to hell. "He has wrapped caution tape on hell's porch and posted a million and one red flags outside the entrance. To descend its stairs, you'd have to cover your ears, blindfold your eyes, and, most of all, ignore the epic sacrifice of history: Christ, in God's hell on humanity's cross."[94] Individualism also comes into play in Lucado's doctrine hell. God so values the free choice of individuals that it is not God who sends people to hell, according to Lucado. Sinners and rebellious people freely choose to go to hell. "[God] simply honors their choice. Hell is the ultimate expression of God's high regard for the dignity of man. He has never forced us to choose him, even when that means we would choose hell."[95]

Because Lucado elevates individualism and relies on sentimentality so thoroughly, he fluctuates between fearful expressions of hell and a diminutive downplaying of its reality. The fear of hell is real for Lucado. Its suffering is eternal, and its power is destructive. Yet Lucado also encourages his readers to not be afraid of hell and uses language that is almost flippant to minimize the fear. Hell, for example, would be tolerable "if its citizens were lobotomized...Hell's misery is deep, but not as deep as God's love."[96] The doctrine of hell "teaches concepts that are tough to swallow, concepts such as 'conscious punishment' and 'permanent banishment.' But it also teaches a vital truth which is easily overlooked....the unimaginable love of God."[97] "How could a loving God send sinners to hell? He doesn't. They volunteer."[98]

Lucado's descriptions of hell are not those of eighteenth-century minister Jonathan Edwards's "Sinners in the Hands of an Angry God." For Edwards, the reality of hell was evidence of God's justice and the depravity of the nature of human beings. Edwards claimed, "The God that holds you over the pit of hell, much as one holds a spider, or some loathsome insect, over the fire, abhors you, and is dreadfully provoked; his wrath towards you burns like fire; he looks upon you as worthy of nothing else, but to be cast into the fire...you are ten thousand times so abominable in his eyes as the most hateful venomous serpent is in ours."[99] Instead Lucado uses the fatherly love of God to mask the terrors of the doctrine of hell, pushing them to the margins of his thought. He conceals this fearful language under the saccharine sentiment of God's love. Under the doctrinal-dismissive rhetoric, however, is a belief in a God doing (or at least willing to allow) terrible, wrathful things to those who do not accept Jesus as his son.[100]

Yet not everyone starts from a sentimental origin and reaches the conclusion that hell exists or that hell will exist eternally. In early 2011, Michigan pastor and author Rob Bell released his book *Love Wins: A Book About Heaven, Hell, and the Fate of Every Person Who Ever Lived*.[101] It set off a firestorm in the evangelical world that carried over into major media outlets. Critics denounced Bell for teaching universalism—that every person would be saved regardless of their faith in Jesus Christ. Warren took to Twitter to stress the reality of hell. Theologian John Piper tweeted, "Farewell, Rob Bell." Others joined the fray to challenge the book even before it had been released in stores. The controversy amounted to a large amount of publicity for Bell's book and HarperOne, the book's publisher. Although Bell claims he is "a pastor, not a theologian or a biblical scholar," here was a great "theological controversy" in evangelicalism.[102]

On the surface Bell presents us with a type of approach that is different from Max Lucado, Rick Warren, and Joel Osteen. Bell—like Warren—has a graduate degree from Fuller Seminary and bases part of his argument about heaven and hell in *Love Wins* on the Greek and Hebrew words of the original languages of the Christian Bible. While arguing that Jesus did not teach that hell would be eternal, he makes the claim that the Greek word in the New Testament "doesn't mean 'forever' as we think of forever."[103] Instead he claims that it "refers to a period of time with a beginning and an end."[104] Bell also cites Christian thinkers like Origen, Jerome, and Augustine.[105]

Bell also evidences postmodern sensibilities in his writing and thinking about evangelicalism. He refers to the first chapter of Genesis—God's creation of the world—as a "poem" about how life is "a pulsing, progressing, evolving, dynamic reality" instead of a literal account of creation as many evangelicals would see it.[106] Aesthetically the book has a lot of blank space, and many of Bell's points are put in the form of stanzas of a few words:

We live in several dimensions.
Up and down.
Left and right.
Forward and backward.
Three to be exact.[107]

Bell also frequently writes in a stream-of-consciousness format that bounces from point to point and raises questions and objections without clearly specifying his own views on the subject in a concise manner. By following his stream of thought, the reader is drawn to a conclusion instead of it being stated outright.

The clearest evidence of Bell's postmodern outlook is his willingness to allow polyvocality about hell in the history of Christian thought:

> People have answered these questions about who goes where, when, why and how in a number of ways. Or, to be more specific, serious, orthodox followers of Jesus have answered these questions in a number of different ways. Or, to say it another way, however you answer these questions, there's a good chance you can find a Christian or group of Christians somewhere who would answer in a similar way.[108]

Bell's postmodern proclivity toward polyvocality, however, also begins to evidence how much in common Bell has with Lucado and others. Polyvocality is another way to think about the downplaying of doctrinal differences. The route to arrive at this position might take a different direction, but it arrives at a very similar destination. In addition *Love Wins* appears in an epistolary format, addressing the reader as "you," making the book more like a conversation than like an investigation of theological truths. The tropes of sentimentality are also important for Bell, although they are less pronounced than in Lucado. Unlike the books of Lucado and others, there are no saccharine stories and platitudes. Bell, however, starts at the same position Lucado, Osteen, Warren, and others do—God is a father longing to be with his children, longing to let them experience his love.

While these ministers start at the same place—God's love—Bell and Lucado end up at a different place with respect to the issue of hell. Lucado asserts the reality and eternality of punishment in hell. As we have noted, Bell's position is different, drawing criticism from other evangelicals, because he diverges from traditional views about both heaven and hell. While he still believes in the reality of heaven, he suggests that the experience of heaven will be an experience of a recreated earth where "honest business, redemptive art, honorable law, sustainable living, medicine, education, making a home, [and] tending a garden" will continue.[109] So in some sense, for Bell, the experience of heaven begins with following Jesus in one's life now but also in the life to come.

His discussion of hell is similar to this in that Bell suggests that there is an experience and reality of hell in the present. He observes that there are not only those who experience hell in the present (e.g., victims of genocide, victims of child abuse, victims of rape) but also those who will experience hell in the future (e.g., those who reject God or oppress others or "reject the good and true and beautiful life that God has for us").[110] Bell suggests, however, that the Bible does not teach an eternal punishment in hell, claiming that the original languages of the Bible do not have that meaning: "So when we read 'eternal punishment,' it's important that we don't read categories and concepts into a phrase that aren't there. Jesus isn't talking about forever as we think of forever. Jesus may be talking about something else, which has all sorts of implications for our understandings of what happens after we die."[111]

What has been further troubling for evangelicals are the claims Bell makes in a chapter titled "Does God Get What God Wants?" Bell points to scriptures in the Bible that claim God desires the salvation of everyone and contrasts those scriptures with the beliefs of those who claim that God will eternally punish some individuals in hell. Hence, he asks the titular question: If God desires everyone to be saved, how could he allow some people to be unsaved? To suggest that some will go unsaved is to suggest that God will ultimately fail. The Bible offers a different picture, says Bell:

> The writers of scripture consistently affirm that we're all part of the same family. What we have in common—regardless of our tribe, language, customs, beliefs, or religion—outweighs our differences. This is why God wants "all people to be saved." History is about the kind of love a parent has for a child, the kind of love that pursues, searches, creates, connects, and bonds. The kind of love that moves toward, embraces, and always works to be reconciled with, regardless of the cost.[112]

Ultimately, Bell asserts that all people "will turn to God and find themselves in the joy and peace of God's presence. The love of God will melt every hard heart, and even the most 'depraved sinners' will eventually give up their resistance and turn to God."[113]

Lucado's God loves people so much that despite his warnings about hell he will ultimately let individuals make a decision that will eternally separate them from that love. Bell's God loves people so much that he will continue to give them chances to accept that love, no matter how long it takes and no matter what kind of pleasure or punishment is necessary. For Bell, God's love will not let anyone exist eternally in hell.

The influence of sentimentality halts the intellectual pursuits of both ministers. While Bell's investigation has the veneer of intellectuality—he references

Greek and Hebrew, he cites early Christian thinkers, he evidences the influence of modern approaches to biblical scholarship—both pastors hesitate to present their audiences with tougher intellectual questions. Both assume the overall veracity of the Bible and the authentic recordings of the statements of Jesus. Both accept the existence of God and the existence of evil without exploring the issue. Both assume some sort of punishment for evil and that bad things sometimes happen to good people.[114] Both ignore passages from scripture that challenge depictions of God as completely loving—ordering the death of women and children in 1 Samuel 15, for example. Instead both rely on God's love as the prime foundation for their depictions of hell.

Comparing Lucado and Bell demonstrates how sentimentality can provide the foundation for changing doctrine, but it also suggests that the individualism of evangelicalism that sentimentality has been so interwoven with might be in the process of transitioning. Bell's postmodern sentimentality is larger than the individual's relationship with God. While this individualism is still a central component of Bell's appeal, his concern with business ethics, redemptive popular culture, justice, and sustainable living is more than just about the individual and God but reflects a communal concern with an ethical society. It remains to be seen whether the vision of the sentimental moderns or the sentimental postmoderns will shape the next generation of evangelicals. What does seem clear, however, is that even postmodern evangelicals believe in the authority of the emotional, often at the expense of the intellectual.

Conclusion

In *Predestination: The American Career of a Contentious Doctrine*, religious studies scholar Peter Thuesen traces the history of the various ways Christians in the United States have understood the question of whether God specifically chooses which individuals will be saved and which will be damned.[115] In the epilogue Thuesen relates his interest in not only *The Purpose-Driven Life* but also Warren's Saddleback Church as examples of the complex development of predestination across American history. He notes that in his own visits at Saddleback and with some of the church's ministers and members he observed a "providence-without-predestination" mentality that empowers both Warren's book and the language at Saddleback.[116]

Thuesen's interests are historical and theological, leading him to wonder at how certain theological tenets moved from being fascinating and mysterious to being largely avoided, an issue he ventures some hypotheses about. What Thuesen overlooks, however, is the sentimental transition in evangelicalism that allows ministers like Warren to rely on fundamentalist beliefs but sidestep the theological questions that arise from those beliefs. When such individuals use language like "God has a plan for your life," it resonates with views of predestination, but the intent is sentimental. Parishioners are asked not to think about the validity of free will or predestination theology but to feel good that God cares so much about them that he set out what their life would be like.

Certainly, some individuals are both intellectuals and evangelicals. They represent a minority in the movement. In the past several decades contemporary evangelicalism has been an anti-intellectual movement, valuing expressing emotion over cultivating a life of the mind. The sentimental strand of evangelicalism is a particularly important part of that anti-intellectualism, moving even some evangelicals with advanced degrees to rely more heavily on emotion than intellect in appealing to the evangelical masses.

Sentimentality is a powerful tool; it is a product of anti-intellectualism and also exploits the absence of failed attempts of establishing evangelical intellectuality. The failure of Baconian Common Sense and of evangelicals to adapt to changes in science and biblical studies left evangelicals holding on to vestiges of a system that many did not find valid or viable. Sentimentality bypasses the intellectual challenges to evangelicalism by offering an emotional validity that trumps intellectual concerns. Why be concerned with whether or not an evangelical approach to the world is intellectually cohesive or logical if it feels emotionally true? Lucado and others use this feature of evangelical sentimentality quite effectively to create a simplistic message that softens concerns about most matters of doctrine.

Centering emotion as the core of people's religious identity lessens their need to be bound to specific doctrines like biblical inerrancy. In addition, it discourages the intellectual exploration of their faith to delineate what it is they believe, discouraging the presentation of their ideological commitments—whether religious or otherwise—in terms of a worldview shaped by logical consistency. If people's worldview is not well defined intellectually, it becomes difficult for them to converse with others who have different ideological commitments, perhaps providing an explanation for why nonevangelicals find certain positions of conservative evangelicals incomprehensible.

Furthermore, understanding evangelicalism only through the lenses of evangelical beliefs obfuscates the centrality of feelings in contemporary evangelicalism and the authority given to emotions by prominent evangelicals.

Biblical inerrancy and biblical literalism, which critics often examine and ridicule, become malleable in the writings of a sentimentalist. The historicity or veracity of the text is less important than the power of feeling that the sentimentally interpreted text may evoke. The fluidity of sentimentality works against concise definitional characteristics. Downplaying doctrinal distinctions and allegiances allows evangelical ministers to position themselves in the center of evangelicalism as a common person and a harbinger of Christian unity while obscuring—intentionally or not—the power relations that allow them to even make those claims to an audience. A reliance on sentimentality by these minsters and the acceptance of a sentimental approach by their audiences allow for this fusion that muddles the downplaying of intellect in favor of emotional response. Any investigation of evangelicalism, therefore, that ignores sentimentality or depends only on intellectual categories to examine the movement simplifies the complex reality that exists both in evangelical religious thought and evangelical practice.

3 "*NEW YORK TIMES* BEST-SELLING AUTHOR": CHRISTIAN MEDIA AND THE MARKETING OF SENTIMENT

A trip to a local Christian retailer can provide nearly all the necessary evidence of the prevalence of sentimentality in the American evangelical market. Christian bookstores carry not only many, if not all, of Max Lucado's inspirational titles but also versions of those works in book and DVD form directed at teenage and child audiences. Customers might purchase cards from Lucado's Hallmark line or calendars to provide inspirational messages from him throughout the year. They might find a Max Lucado gift book to sit on a bedside table next to a Max Lucado Bible and a Max Lucado wind chime to hang outside. They might buy a Max Lucado journal tied in to one of his books so that they could write down their thoughts while reading the book. A similar kind of product explosion is available for *The Prayer of Jabez*, *The Purpose-Driven Life*, *Your Best Life Now*, and a variety of other evangelical bestsellers. This extensive cross-media marketing and product tie-in proliferation demonstrates a push among evangelical book publishers to expand a book or its author into a product line that can garner more sales.

Because sentimentality is so much a part of evangelicalism, it appears not only in the therapeutic literature we have been examining but also in other evangelical material goods. Evangelical practice since the inception of the movement has frequently involved as much consumerism as it has consecration. Evangelicals' assimilation of a sentimental ethos in the nineteenth century introduced a predilection for consumption of emotional products into evangelicalism that has also increased the sheer volume of products directed toward both evangelical and nonevangelical consumers. The explosion of therapeutic materials geared toward the evangelical psyche has driven the evangelical publishing houses that produce these books to capitalize on emotions to sell products of every kind imaginable, promoting a way to connect to the divine through the emotions. An evangelical alliance with marketing techniques has allowed evangelicalism to spread but in turn has also created an atmosphere for an emotional religiosity to predominate.

Combining religious practice with emotionality also provides the opportunity to instantiate the authority of evangelicalism in the lives of practitioners. The success of marketing a brand to an audience opens a space for the acceptance of authority—whether of a specific minister or other media producer. The emotional appeal becomes a mode of authority to perpetuate evangelicalism to subsequent generations. The explicit saccharine message obscures this larger economic structure at work in evangelical emotionality.

Marketing and Media in the History of American Evangelicalism

Evangelicals have been relying on both the market and media products since the origins of evangelicalism. Max Lucado, Rick Warren, Bruce Wilkinson, and Joel Osteen are excellent examples of how evangelicals engage marketing principles to create a presence in the commercial sphere. Historically they stand at the apex of a long process of engagement between message and market. Evangelicals have often used the market to great success, but these ministers especially have achieved even greater success because of the tools and media available to them due to the technological developments of the twentieth and twenty-first centuries. Because of the business acumen of the marketing teams that work with them, they are able to achieve omnipresence in the market by emphasizing presence in the market over the purity of a distinct, concise, cohesive doctrinal position.[1]

Selling and finances have been a component of Christianity for a long time, and evangelicals have often relied on these aspects of culture to promote their message. From the eighteenth century onward, ministers and other religious people have taken advantage of economic, social, and political developments to broadcast their particular versions of Christianity.[2] Scholars usually look to George Whitefield as one of the earliest and most successful of these market innovators. Whitefield adapted newspapers and advertising to his benefit to market his revivals. By publishing his journals and advertising his upcoming meetings, Whitefield assured himself of large crowds and a widespread audience. Whitefield became "a pioneer in the commercialization of religion."[3] Others quickly followed.

Evangelicals who adopted the methods of the market struggled between trying to maintain the purity of their message and sustaining a presence in the secular arena. That presence was an important one for evangelicals since they saw competing messages in the market, including irreligious ones. An evangelical presence was also important in the market, especially as systems of distribution developed, because evangelicals could reach individuals they might never encounter face to face. The potential for proselytizing was great because they could send the message even if they could not send the missionaries. Methodists became especially resourceful in using market and print cultures in the colonial period and the early republic. Circuit riders were both ministers and merchandisers as they proclaimed the Methodist message and sold Methodist tracts or books. The impact of their teaching would be present while the circuit riders were gone.[4]

The presence of evangelicals in the market increased in the nineteenth century. Not only did technological changes in manufacturing and publishing allow for cheaper materials, but also disestablishment meant that evangelicals had to compete for an audience in new and different ways. Print culture in books and journals was one of the ways evangelicals coped with disestablishment. Many connected the rise of print culture and success in marketing with the onset of the Millennium. As human beings spread the gospel and thoughts about the gospel throughout the country, they believed they were working toward converting the nation and establishing the kingdom of God. This euphoria over the potential of human publishing and distribution was part of the general trust in the power of the institutions of the benevolent empire to enact God's will on Earth.[5]

Marketing, print culture, and material culture also combined in the realm of sentimentality. Sentimental literature was very popular in the middle of the nineteenth century, and authors like Harriet Beecher Stowe and Elizabeth Stuart Phelps wrote novels that became bestsellers. Because of the importance of the home and domestic values in sentimental thought, products for the home also became a big business. Religious art and architecture, along with other objects like family Bibles, fed into the consumerist lifestyle of sentimental Christians. Sentimentality itself became a commodity as these objects were connected to the feelings emphasized by the religious thought of the time.[6]

Marketing continued to be a vital part of evangelical millennial dreams and continued to shape evangelicalism even after many of those dreams faded. Not only did religious marketing continue in the realm of print culture, but it also impacted the oral presentation of the gospel. By the end of the nineteenth century ministers like Dwight Moody were expertly using different marketing techniques to attract large audiences. As they had been for George Whitefield, newspapers were especially useful for Moody to market his meetings. Moody, however, moved beyond just using newspapers to announce his meetings. He developed committees to prepare for events and used posters and other forms of advertising (like placards and handbills) to publicize his meetings and his message.[7]

Furthermore, Moody crafted his message into a product that could be received by mass audiences. He intentionally simplified his message to experience the widest acceptance possible. Avoiding doctrinal contentions and theological speculation, Moody focused on God's love for humanity. Concentrating on evangelism, Moody displayed "an irenic spirit concerned with holiness and saving souls" in the midst of the late-nineteenth-century challenges to evangelicalism.[8] Although the militancy of later fundamentalism shifts attention away from this strand in conservative evangelicalism, Moody's creation of a simplistic, good-natured product became a model for the success of later evangelicals.[9]

In the early twentieth century, Billy Sunday preached a practical gospel, and he used contemporary marketing methods to make sure people heard it. First as an assistant to revivalist J. Wilbur Chapman and then on his own, Billy Sunday knew the value of preparation, advertising, and general marketing for creating audiences who would then in turn contribute to numerical and financial success. As his popularity increased, Sunday looked for ways to increase the prestige and audience of his message. The incorporation of wooden tabernacles for large, sturdy, identifiable meeting space, the tailoring of his message to his audience by holding men- or women-only services during his revivals, and the introduction of music to the services to involve the audience in the revivals were responsible on one level for Sunday's success, but other facets of his ministry such as acquiring sponsors, strategically locating tabernacles, involving the religious and secular press, and creating an advance team to prepare and advertise his revivals also contributed—perhaps in greater ways.[10]

Sunday's popularity faded, and conservative evangelical Protestantism experienced marginalization from the mainstream American public sphere; thus, the importance of marketing to fundamentalism was greater than ever. The movement included many prominent businessmen of the day, who brought a marketing savvy that they applied to the religious message of fundamentalism. Many fundamentalists were outspoken about the dangers of modern American culture, but newspapers and radio provided opportunities to spread the message and to draw people to religious services.[11]

As the twentieth century continued on, fundamentalists looked for other opportunities to market their form of Christianity. Christian retailing especially exploded after World War II as more evangelicals saw the creation of religious products as a greater way to spread the evangelical message. A variety of religiously themed products from books to movies entered the marketplace. Hand in hand with the revival in the fifties, the religious marketplace expanded and offered consumers opportunities to envelop their lives in spirituality. Despite the challenges to established religious traditions that emerged in the sixties, the religious marketplace continued to blossom and also underwent great changes. When the "Jesus people"—individuals who embodied a hippie lifestyle as well as a strong commitment to Jesus—derided established religious institutions, this encouraged publishers to develop new tactics to create consumers. The rise of contemporary Christian music and other media that packaged religious themes in secular-like trappings led to entirely new forms for the fundamentalist gospel. T-shirts and bumper stickers also became a facet of Christian marketing, combining statements of belief with an evangelistic emphasis.[12]

Now many products are available in the evangelical marketplace. While books make up the largest part of evangelical merchandise, there are Christian toys, Christian music, Christian home decor, Christian products for children, Christian DVDs, and any other product that can be "Christianized."[13] Many of these products, however, reflect the core of the evangelical message: the sentimental connection between the human being and God. Marketers, publishers, ministers, and others in the production process have simplified the core emotional message to create some very popular Christian merchandise with well-known brand names.

Much of this merchandise is related to what we might broadly refer to as the *practice* of modern evangelical life. Although evangelicals, marketers, and publishers tend to emphasize the *message* of any particular object or media, these are messages presented in a format that requires some action on the part of the consumer. One *reads* a book, *listens* to a CD or MP3, or *looks* at a piece of artwork or other material piece with a devotional message. In offering these practices to their customers, evangelical authors, publishers, and producers are instantiating emotion into evangelicalism in more extensive ways than previously. In so doing, evangelicals consume products that construct religiosity as a practice of sentimentality instead of one of intellectual discovery, and publishing houses go to great lengths to encourage this practice.

Brand Knowledge, Brand Equity, and the Brands of Evangelicalism

In 2004, Thomas Nelson Inc. and W Publishing funded the Lucado Market Research Project in an attempt to gauge Lucado's readership so that they could "quantify Max Lucado's powerful national name recognition and broad readership base with empirical data."[14] In the wake of the findings, Thomas Nelson's executive vice president Jerry Park announced that the survey results would allow the publisher to "better present the Lucado story to retailers." Said Park, "We are now better equipped to explain Max's mission, history and success to our retail partners."[15] He went on to explain that "as a direct survey benefit to retailers, we are designing strategic in-store display systems for a variety of Lucado products."[16]

The surveyors found that 1 in 10 Americans had read one Lucado book. Consumers' awareness of Lucado was calculated (through random-digit phone surveys) at 21.8 percent. Lucado's awareness was second only to Billy Graham among Christian/Spirituality authors. In fact, when asked to name their favorite Christian/Spirituality author, Christian consumers listed Lucado more than any other author, although his percentage (16.8 percent) may be deceiving. Another statistic is telling as well. Lucado releases an adult inspirational title about every eight months or so. When asked about this release schedule, around 70 percent of Christian consumers thought this was a good schedule, with an additional 10 percent believing that an increased schedule would be welcome. Less than 10 percent thought that Lucado was "writing too many books."[17]

The project focused on retailers as well. Of retailers connected to the Christian Booksellers Association, 79 percent had read "several to most" of Lucado's books; 64 percent of "general market" retailers had done the same.[18] Retailers also noted that it was probably Lucado's message about God's grace that made him so successful. Both types of retailers also expressed that Lucado had "excellent brand equity."[19]

Brand equity refers to the value that a brand has that is "uniquely attributable to the brand."[20] In other words, equity can be conceptualized in terms of "certain outcomes result[ing] from the marketing of a product or service because of its brand name that would not occur if the same product or service did not have that name."[21] The concept of *branding* is a common one in American culture, one that often operates without conscious thought. Companies and marketers pay enormous amounts of money to create a brand that will sell. Not just the product but also the name attached to the product is important in the market. In extreme cases, the brand often becomes interchangeable with the product. For example, if I wanted to purchase an adhesive bandage to protect a cut, I might speak of buying a Band-Aid, even though the actual product is an adhesive bandage. Band-Aid is a registered trademark of the Johnson and Johnson Company, but the brand has become so ensconced in the American mind-set through branding that the brand name is interchangeable with the product. The same could be demonstrated in the interchange of Kleenex for facial tissue and Jell-O for gelatin. In such cases these companies have created brands that affect the way people think about their products. They have created an unconscious assimilation between a specific product, for example, facial tissue, and their brand of that product, Kleenex.

When a brand is created, it is linked to a variety of consumer experiences. For marketers, the hope is that consumers will become aware of the brand and remember it (brand awareness). Marketers also hope that what consumers remember about the brand will be positive (brand image). Brand awareness and brand image combine to form brand knowledge. Brand knowledge can be broken down into several key aspects: awareness, attributes, benefits, thoughts, feelings, attitudes, and experiences. In other words, brand knowledge consists of how a branded product addresses perceived needs, how it is characterized, what benefits it offers, how consumers respond to the brand cognitively and affectively, and how consumers purchase the brand.[22]

If Lucado's publishers are concerned about brand knowledge—which from the Lucado Market Research project it appears they are—then when W Publishing or Thomas Nelson puts out a Lucado book these are the elements that are connected to that enterprise. Lucado as a brand is managed so that his books meet the perceived needs of his consumers. The books are produced in such a way that consumers will attach value or meaning to them in hopes that they will purchase another Lucado book because they have had a positive experience with a previous one. The use of Lucado as a brand is controlled so that consumers will associate certain thoughts and feelings with "Max Lucado" and act on those thoughts and feelings and buy another adult inspirational book, children's book, DVD, journal, Bible, or whatever else is tagged with the Lucado brand. This is not just about selling an author's book; it is about selling both an author and an experience.

Lucado is not the only contemporary evangelical interested in marketing or the creation of a product line. As media studies scholar Mara Einstein showed in *Brands of Faith*, both Rick Warren and Joel Osteen are conscious about the importance of marketing to the success of their message.[23] Although Warren is rather deprecating toward equating his ministry with marketing, his approach to starting Saddleback Church involved market research. The *Purpose-Driven* brand includes not only the book *Purpose-Driven Life* but also *The Purpose-Driven Life Journal*, the *Purpose-Driven Life Scripture Keeper Plus*, a *Purpose-Driven Life* daily devotional, *Songs for a Purpose-Driven Life* CD, a two-year pocket planner, and a line of greeting cards featuring quotes from *Purpose-Driven Life*. Osteen's merchandise includes very similar products under his different brands based on his book—*Your Best Life Now Journal*, for example—and there is also a board game based on *Your Best Life Now*.[24]

Osteen and Warren, like Lucado, are also conscious of the presentation of their own personal image. They too want to be known by their first names and often eschew titles or other markers of ecclesiastical respect. Warren and Osteen also front images of themselves as everymen who are relatable and approachable. They have hired consultants to help develop and promote this image.[25] There is not necessarily anything insidious about using marketing, but it does demonstrate the commodification of sentimentality and why it is so prominent in contemporary evangelicalism.

One of the aspects of religious marketing that Einstein pointed out is the need for a message that is "simple and easily digestible in a short period of time."[26] What successful evangelical marketers have done is taken the core of evangelicalism—sentimental emotion—and turned it into big business.[27] In so doing, they have increased the authority of ministers like these. While these ministers were authorities already because they pastored local churches, the marketing of their books has expanded their authority. Every time someone turns to the books of Max Lucado, Rick Warren, or Joel Osteen for help with some personal problem, they have demonstrated that they have internalized the authority of that particular minister. In the practice of reading, consumers give authority to emotionality and the authors who rely on feeling to create their distinctive messages.

Yet this combination of market is message is not limited only to texts and authors. Evangelical music and children's products are two other examples of how prevalent sentimentality is in the practice of evangelicalism and how evangelicals attempt to introduce emotional habits to the consumers of such materials. Through media that encourage practice—through listening, watching, or reading—evangelicals perpetuate the sentimental core of the movement. These media practices allow evangelicals to instantiate sentimentality, perpetuate feeling rather than belief, and internalize authority.

Music and Emotional Evangelicalism

Although evangelicals have often relied on texts to carry their messages, another type of media where sentimentality is prominent is Christian music. Music has been an important aspect of Christian practice since it emerged out of the Jewish synagogues in the first century CE. Songs praising God have been created for millennia. Music itself is a powerful vessel for emotion, and it is no surprise that we would find emotional expressions in the music of modern evangelicalism. Music has the power to make us laugh or cry. It can move us to anger or can pacify us to calmness. It can also express sentimental notions of relationships between individual and deity, as it does in modern evangelicalism. Sentimental evangelical music evokes both familial and erotic love as it attempts to shape the attitudes of believers into conceptualizing the relationship between the believer and God in sentimental ways.

The sentimentalizing of evangelical hymnody occurred around the same time as the sentimentalizing of evangelical thought: the nineteenth century. As scholar June Hadden Hobbs noted, the gospel hymn—a specific type of church music Hobbs dates to the nineteenth century—provided the means to pass on truths about Christianity without engaging the challenge of science and modernism.[28] Positioning hymns in the first person and connecting them to an emotional experience encountered in the hymnist's personal life allowed worshipers to abstract the hymn from its historical setting, to adopt the affect of the hymn as the singers' own, and to bypass intellectual or theological questions that troubled many in the nineteenth century. Singers relied on the lyricist's authority as a conveyer of religious truth.[29]

The use of emotional music as a collective expression of worship legitimized sentimentality as an acceptable—perhaps even preferred—mode of communicating with the deity. The romantic currents in mid-nineteenth-century America became opportunities for new modes of declaration of one's commitment to the Christian God and also brought metaphors of domesticity into contemporary hymnody. Because many hymn writers in the mid- to late nineteenth century were women, it also gave women more of a public voice, especially among groups where women did not have access to positions of authority. By crafting hymns that were used in worship, these women were able to put their words and expressions of sentiment on the lips and in the minds of both men and women, sometimes for several generations.[30]

A multitude of hymn examples could demonstrate this transition to sentimental, domestic music in worship. It could be the plaintive strains of Sarah Adams's "Nearer, My God, to Thee" (1841) or the pleading of Elizabeth

Prentiss's "More Love to Thee, O Christ" (1869). Even "What a Friend We Have in Jesus" (c. 1855) by Joseph Scriven shows the influence of the sentimental mood, especially when the worshipers tell each other that "In His arms He'll take and shield thee/Thou wilt find a solace there."[31] Fanny J. Crosby's songs, however, clearly show how much sentimental imagery had permeated evangelical hymnody.

Crosby was perhaps the most prolific of hymn writers. She claimed to have written 8,000 hymns during her lifetime. Quite often she had to write these works under pseudonyms because publishing companies did not want it known that Crosby was producing such a large amount of the hymns in evangelical hymnals, work for which she was grossly underpaid. A common feature in many of her hymns is their sentimental or domestic imagery.[32]

In the hymn "Tell Me the Story of Jesus," for example, Crosby asks to hear about the story "most precious" about Jesus' life on earth, his birth, his temptations, his ministry, his crucifixion, and his resurrection.[33] This is the story about which Crosby asks, "Write on my heart ev'ry word."[34] She tells an imagined respondent, "Love in that story so tender/Clearer than ever I see/Stay, let me weep while you whisper/Love paid the ransom for me."[35] The hymn presents the story of Jesus' life as one that should create an affective response—"let me weep while you whisper" the story.[36] This "sweetest [story] that ever was heard" is not about believing facts about Jesus' identity and his resurrection; it is about how the story moves the emotions.[37] It asks not for intellectual consent but for weeping for what Jesus has done for the singer.[38]

The intertwining of sentimental imagery and domestic motifs is evident in Crosby's hymn "Jesus Is Tenderly Calling." In this hymn the worshiper is told that "Jesus is tenderly calling thee home."[39] Yet the worshiper continues to move away from "the sunshine of love...farther and farther away."[40] Jesus, however, continues to call to the worshiper. In successive verses he is "tenderly calling"; he is "calling"; he is "waiting"; he is "pleading."[41] The place where Jesus is, however, is "home." Through the singers, he calls sinners with their "burdens" to "Come with thy sins/At His feet lowly bow."[42]

The imagery behind this hymn—and many other Victorian hymns—is Jesus' parable of the Prodigal Son from Luke 15, one of his more emotionally moving stories. In the parable a father has two sons. The younger son asks for his inheritance and then leaves. He spends his money on immoral living and is soon broke. He gets a job working on a farm. One day he realizes that his father's servants have a much better life than the one he is living. He resolves to return to his father and become a servant. Seeing his son returning, the father runs to meet him. The father will not entertain any thoughts of the son becoming a servant and calls for a celebration for the son who has returned home. Crosby invokes this story in "Jesus Is Tenderly Calling." The song calls any sinner to come home to Jesus who will "tenderly" welcome that sinner home.[43]

A romantic tone marks some of Crosby's other hymns, like "I Am Thine, O Lord." In this hymn the worshiper confesses to hearing God's voice, which has told the worshiper of God's love. In response to this love, the worshiper professes that "I am Thine, O Lord" and asks to "be closer drawn to Thee."[44] The rest of the hymn talks of the singer's will being lost in God's will, of "the pure delight of a single hour" in God's presence, and of the "depths of love that I cannot know" and of the "heights of joy that I may not reach" until reaching heaven and being with God.[45] The chorus pleads with God for closeness: "Draw me nearer, nearer blessed Lord/To the cross where Thou has died./Draw me nearer, nearer, nearer blessed Lord/To Thy precious, bleeding side."[46]

Such hymns emphasize that believers should have an erotic desire for God. Worshipers sing to the deity that they want to be drawn to his side, to experience intimate closeness. Such intimacy, it is believed, will bring about delight, love, and joy. It has not happened for worshipers, but they express that "I long to rise in the arms of faith/And be closer drawn to Thee."[47] Connected to this erotic longing is an expression of submission ("my will be lost in Thine") evoking surrender to the deity that may also be read as romantic.[48]

Sentimental music became so popular in the last half of the nineteenth century that revivalists like Dwight Moody used it strategically in their meetings. Moody and his choirmaster, Ira Sankey, incorporated music into their productions to stimulate their audiences' emotions and perhaps to garner a larger response. The music Sankey chose was often sentimental in tone and emphasized the importance of the domestic sphere. He also chose songs that recalled the prodigal son parable and others like it. Historian Charles Lippy argued that the music Moody and Sankey used called audiences to capture or encounter supernatural power while emphasizing the importance of the individual believer. One of the key tropes used in such hymns was the *possession* of Jesus. As Lippy noted:

> The sense of personal possession of Jesus in these hymns brings the supernatural presence into everyday life and endows the heavenly sphere with greater meaning and power than empirical reality....One might feel lost amid the seeming chaos of factory and city, but those who tapped into the reservoir of supernatural power knew that they

were in actuality "lost in his love" [a line from Fanny Crosby's "Blessed Assurance"] and hence not lost at all in the ultimate sense but, rather, at "the gate of life eternal" [a line from Crosby's "Closer to Thee"].[49]

Sankey was more a composer and hymn compiler than lyricist, and women, including Crosby, wrote many of the hymns for which he composed the music. As Moody's music leader, however, the hymns he chose emphasized the closeness of Jesus and not Jesus' divinity. These hymns focused on "the intimate love of Jesus rather than the awesome power of his Father."[50] The Moody–Sankey evangelistic team chose to emphasize the relational aspects of Christianity instead of other intellectual aspects, to great numerical success. "In the Sankey hymns, Jesus was a human being who could be known and loved and imitated."[51]

Revivalists were not always strong public supporters of sentimentality. Hobbs noted that Billy Sunday was strongly against types of Christianity that "would domesticate and feminize Christian men."[52] Even before Sunday's time, however, many of these so-called feminized, sentimental hymns were a part of the collective consciousness of evangelicals and a staple of their worship. Audiences would ask Sunday's music leader Homer Rodeheaver for songs like "Blessed Assurance," despite Sunday's preference for songs like "Onward Christian Soldiers" and "The Battle Hymn of the Republic." Sunday may have railed against "sissified" Christianity, but this was counteracted when Rodeheaver led an audience to sing, "Filled with His goodness/ Lost in His love."[53]

Sentimentality had become a part of evangelical practice even if rhetorically ministers and theologians deprecated it. Sentimentality buoyed the militancy of fundamentalism, and evangelicals incorporated it into the youth culture that they attempted to develop in the middle of the twentieth century. The Youth for Christ movement affected both evangelical organizations and music. Evangelicals, especially ministers holding crusades, tried to reach large audiences of young people by creating new styles of music that they believed would attract and keep those large audiences. Even though they faced resistance, Youth for Christ organizers created new music that they believed was entertaining and upbeat, some of which used revivalistic lyrics. It was "repackaging Fundamentalist spirituality as both fun and fulfilling."[54] It was also a transition between the music of the late nineteenth century and the late twentieth century. Music focused on evangelizing youth in the postwar period served as a foundation for Jesus rock—the music style of hippies who attempted to Christianize the bohemian lifestyle of the sixties—and its later mainstream form, contemporary Christian music (CCM). Part of that transition was bringing to the forefront the impact of sentimentality and the language of romance in evangelicalism.[55]

Historian David Stowe noted that evangelicals became aware of the need to create new styles of music to reach a new style of youth: "To save hippies inspiring music was needed."[56] Jesus rock incorporated evangelical teachings with music that tapped into the emotion-laden culture of the sixties and seventies that influenced not only hippies but evangelical churches as well. Praise music or worship choruses became a staple of a new style of churches and megachurches throughout the last part of the twentieth century. These praise songs simplified Christian theology and focused on emotional language. According to Stowe, this transition to a simplified, emotional music style "has been a key factor in the expansion of evangelical Christianity since the seventies."[57]

Like much within modern evangelical popular culture, CCM has expanded in the past four decades. Although there had been recordings of gospel music prior to the late twentieth century, from the 1960s on evangelicals have made religious music a big business.[58] Coming out of the Jesus Movement and Jesus rock, CCM evidences an attempt to connect to both evangelicals and nonevangelicals in an effort to distance religious music from its institutional stereotypes. Much like the people of the Jesus Movement criticized *Churchianity*—the institutionalized religion of the sixties—the musicians of early Jesus rock thought that older forms of music were too reminiscent of church services and wanted to mimic the styles of nonreligious music, particularly rock and roll. The oft-repeated phrase—by Jesus rock artists and in scholarly pieces afterward—"Why should the devil have all the good tunes?" reflected the mind-set of this new style of music.[59]

Although they were new styles of music for evangelicalism, Jesus rock and CCM reflect the themes of earlier sentimental evangelical music, perhaps even more explicitly. Artists relied on the tropes of sentimentality—especially the fatherhood of God and nostalgia for home—but they also tended to couch their expressions of piety in the language of romance. Media scholar Heather Hendershot noted that the ambiguous romantic language of some CCM songs appears to be an attempt to reach an audience wider than evangelicals. For example, instead of singing "Jesus loves me," a CCM singer might sing, "He loves me." Instead of singing, "I love God," a band might say, "I love him." The intent is to be inoffensive to a non-Christian audience, believing that a Christian audience, which is in the know, so to speak, would understand the true meaning of the lyrics.[60] Whether or not this is what occurs,

CCM artists evidently believe that it is often appropriate to sing to the deity through love songs and sentimental music.

The band dc Talk's song "Consume Me" is a perfect example of this combination of romantic sentimentality and religious devotion.[61] Michael Tait, one of the band's members, starts the song by singing of how God moves him and he seeks no escape from God's presence. He affirms that he is incomplete without God and "It's hopeless."[62] The rest of the band joins in to sing that God consumes them and that he runs through their veins like fire. The second verse, mainly sung by Toby McKeehan, is more explicit. McKeehan (who also goes by tobyMac) asserts that he is immersed in God, asking God to baptize him in God's love. As the band again joins in, they sing that they are God's no matter what they might lose. The same type of language continues in the bridge; each of the individuals in the band is in God's hands, under God's command, "Like a puppet on a string."[63]

The group recognizes, even embraces, the "passionate" language of "Consume Me."[64] On the now-separated band's official website, the lyrics to "Consume Me" are called "smoldering."[65] McKeehan states that the intimacy of the song is intentional because of the band's view that the relationship between believers and deity is personal. He goes on to say, "Some people might get upset because the relationship in 'Consume Me' is so passionate and real, rather than ritualistic. We wrote this as a spiritual song because to us, faith is a passionate, personal, committed love relationship with Jesus Christ."[66] Their message, therefore, is not about the intellectual validity of Christianity or the theological nature of Jesus Christ but about the romantic relationship they should have with Jesus. Like lovers, they want Jesus to "consume" them, to "run through their veins."[67] In some sense this is a working out of the Christian belief of the indwelling of Christ, but it is couched in language that appeals to the emotions, not the intellect. It takes the language of romantic love and projects it onto a relationship between the divine and human. The rituals and feelings of adolescent love become the language that people should speak to God and the expectations that they should anticipate from a relationship with God. Note McKeehan's statement about critics: those who do not have the type of relationship with Jesus reflected in "Consume Me" have a ritualistic approach to God, not a real one.[68]

The use of romantic language is also present in "Love Song," written by Mac Powell of the group Third Day.[69] In the song, the relationship between believer and deity is compared to that between lovers. Singing from the viewpoint of Jesus, Powell notes that a man might overcome a variety of challenges—like climbing a mountain—to be with his lover. But human love is replete with promises that lovers have broken. Jesus has not climbed a mountain, but he went up Calvary to be crucified to be with human beings. In fact, "There's no price I would not pay."[70] The second verse starts by discussing the possibility of a man swimming the ocean to be with his beloved. Such human claims are "empty emotion" that will not be fulfilled.[71] Jesus did not swim the ocean, but he walked on the "raging sea."[72] Again Powell sings that to be with "you" Jesus was willing to do anything including, giving his "life away."[73] Jesus' love is the subject of the bridge as well, where Powell sings that, although human beings do not fully understand that Jesus' death on the cross was for their sins, he would do it again if needed. The song closes with Powell repeating that Jesus gave his life away just to be with the individual human being: "you."[74]

"Love Song" intertwines human romance with the deity–believer relationship. The message appears to be that human romance is filled with failure and empty promises but that the romance between a believer and God is filled with success and sure promises. The Jesus of "Love Song" is so in love with human beings that he died for their sins. The atonement, a subject of great debate throughout Christian history, is reduced to a declaration of affection. The point is not about limited or unlimited atonement or whether the death of Jesus is substitution, expiation, or propitiation. All that one needs to know about the atonement is that Jesus loves the individual, and he loves the individual more than any human being can.

Jason Gray's "More like Falling in Love" is much more explicit that a relationship with the deity is more authentic than following a religion.[75] From the very beginning Gray states that he would not be able to follow a system of rules and laws, something he would break. Instead of a "truth to believe," he needs a truth "to sweep me off my feet."[76] For Gray, Christianity is not about the intellect. Instead it should be "more like falling in love."[77] In the bridge he explicitly states that it was "falling in love with Jesus," not beliefs or creeds, that changed his life.[78]

The sentimentalizing of the individual is the motif of "Sea of Faces" by the group Kutless.[79] Lead singer Jon Micah Sumrall starts the song with a melancholic examination of the massive number of people around him. In a city of millions of people, for example, it is unlikely that anyone would care about anyone else's problems. But someone does care. In God's eyes, the singer is not overlooked in a "sea of faces."[79] Jesus traded his life for the singer's life. How could the singer be unimportant? The second verse echoes the first. Although people's lives might feel insignificant, God still finds time for and loves them. The chorus repeats the sentiment that he is important and not just one other person. The bridge further emphasizes the importance of one person in God's eyes. Sumrall rhapsodizes that, if he were the only person that Jesus would have redeemed through his sacrifice, Jesus "would have still been a man/With a reason/To willingly offer your life."[80] Although Kutless may fit into the categories of Christian rock or Christian alternative music, its singers still rely on sentiment to express to their audience what they think God feels about them.

In the previous examples from contemporary Christian music, like those from Warren, Osteen, and Lucado, the reliance on sentimentality and its tropes are obvious. While sentimentality is not blatant in every song, CCM artists rely on emotionality to encourage their listeners to believe that God loves them as individuals and cares deeply about having a relationship with them. Intentionally or not, they draw on a long tradition of evangelical music constructing how believers should understand God and the world around them. It is this sentimental product that is marketed through Christian magazines and Christian radio. These artists are asking people to engage in a religious practice of listening to their music, perhaps singing along with it, and accepting their views of God and how God sees the listeners. The listener is so important to Jesus, these artists sing, that he would—as Kutless says in "Sea of Faces"—still have died if it had saved only the listener and no one else.[81] The repetition of the songs on Christian radio or frequent listening of the song off an album provide multiple occasions for listeners to hear this message and make it part of how they see the world.

Listening to CCM is not the only way emotion-laden music reaches evangelicals. The use of sentimentality in modern worship hymns also demonstrates how important it is to the practice of evangelicalism. Many hymnals are available in the evangelical market, although they often contain the same songs. One example of the genre is *The Worship Hymnal*.[82] LifeWay Christian Resources produces *The Worship Hymnal* as one of the hymnals offered through LifeWay Christian Stores, a popular outlet for evangelical Christian material. LifeWay is a part of the Southern Baptist denomination and claims to be "one of the world's largest providers of Christian resources."[83] *The Worship Hymnal* is indicative of evangelical music, even though it may not be used extensively by evangelicals. As an attempt to get their product into the pews of evangelical churches, LifeWay would certainly attempt to collect songs for *The Worship Hymnal* that they believe evangelicals would use or would be interested in using.[84]

In the song "Draw Me Close," worshipers sing to God or to Jesus, asking the deity to pull the worshipers in and never let them go. The worshipers then tell the deity that they are willing to surrender everything to hear God assert that he is their friend. The second verse, however, takes on a more sensual tone: "You are my desire," the worshiper sings, and "no one else will do," telling the deity of the longing for his "embrace."[85] In romantic language, the chorus swells with proclamations of the deity being all the worshiper wants and needs, begging, "Help me know You are near."[86]

A similar aesthetic appears in the song "Breathe."[87] Although the song evokes a centuries-old doctrine of the presence of God among believers, the desire for God is couched in romantic language. God's "daily presence" is "the air I breathe," according to the song.[88] The chorus is much more explicitly amorous. The believers tell the deity that they are desperate for God and lost without him. The lyrics read almost as a love letter. The attitude encouraged in the song is a passionate one. One approaches the deity through desire as opposed to the intellect. Desperate for God's presence, the believer cries out for the deity to come and be the vital essence of life ("the air I breathe").[89] Both male and female CCM artists have recorded the song, and males and females would both be singing in a worship service, signifying that the attitude of the song is one all believers (regardless of gender) should aspire to.

The verses of "Beautiful One" do not necessarily betray a romantic connection between the singer and God.[90] The verses speak of wonder, power, might, and mercy. There is some mention of beauty, but it is a minor part of the declarations that mostly focus on how, for example, God's "glory fills the skies."[91] By the chorus, however, emotions for the deity overtake the worshipers, and they declare that God is the "beautiful one" whom they love and adore, who causes their soul to sing. The romance is even clearer in the bridge, when believers sing about opening their eyes to God's wonder and how "You captured my heart with this love."[92] The bridge concludes with the observation that "nothing on earth is as beautiful as You."[93]

Sentimentality is present not only in CCM, which may be listened to sporadically, but also how in how evangelicals worship when they gather together. The continual performance of sentimentality reinforces the belief that one should understand God through this aesthetic. Although evangelicals would certainly give lip service to theological descriptions of God that emphasize ideas like transcendence, sovereignty, inscrutability, and distance, the rituals of evangelicalism encourages its practitioners to accept that the way God most often relates to human beings is through a certain type of affect. God may be a great, terrible, and mighty judge of humanity, but he is primarily a loving God to be desired.

Yet the God of love is still an authoritative God. Instead of crafting God's authority in terms of fear as evangelicals of previous generations might, evangelical musicians have appealed to their audiences to desire God's authority because God is love. In language that evokes adolescent romance, evangelical worshipers plead for God to be present, to sweep them off their feet, as Jason Gray sings. In much of evangelical music, evangelicals proffer to God the submission of their ego if God will just show his favor.

The Rise of the Evangelical Child

In the eyes of sentimentality, all human beings are called God's children. Since the nineteenth century, however, children have played an important role in evangelicalism. Evangelical creators of culture in the nineteenth century, as historian Colleen McDannell noted, saw the home as "a vehicle for the promotion of values."[94] They stood at a pinnacle of a Christian tradition that had moved from the house churches of the earliest centuries of Christianity to a domestic religion found in American Puritanism to the elevation of domestic piety in the Victorian United States. The Enlightenment and the rise of republicanism led to changes in family piety that made the home the center of religious life for Victorians. Nostalgia became an important facet of domestic piety as individuals and families looked to an imagined colonial period as the height of familial commitment to religiosity. Changes in architecture and the market led to reconceptualizations of home and family that bifurcated the public and private spheres in the minds of many. Whatever the reality, Americans idealized the Victorian home and what it should represent. They thought of the home as a stronghold of safety against the deteriorating forces of the market and the secular world. Attendant with this idealization of domestic space came a rise in domestic products that could both fill and sacralize that space. According to McDannell, "By linking morality and religion with the purchase and maintenance of a Christian home, the Victorians legitimized acquisition and display of domestic goods."[95] Theologians like Horace Bushnell provided an ideological foundation for accepting the home and family as the center of a Protestant faith that emphasized the religious duty of fostering a Christian home.[96]

In addition to changes in conceptualizing domestic space and domestic piety, children especially came to serve an important role. Conceptions of children underwent changes theologically and educationally. The traditional view of children as bearers of original sin—and thus born sinful—gave way to a romantic view of children as inherently innocent from birth. Based on philosopher John Locke's view of the mind and the senses, families and ministers viewed children as blank slates who were malleable and ready to be molded. In the Early Republic, individuals followed the thinking of people like Joseph Addison, Frances Hutcheson, and Jean-Jacques Rousseau along with the Scottish Common Sense philosophers and emphasized the importance of instilling republican virtues and good citizenship in children. Evangelicals began to focus on parent–child relationships as the key to living daily life in the United States. Mothers frequently took on this responsibility to make children good citizens, and they did this through the inculcation of religious values.[97]

By the middle of the nineteenth century, conceptions of children experienced another evolution. With Bushnell's thoughts on Christian nurture and the writings of the sisters Catherine and Harriet Beecher, children moved from being vessels whom parents should fill with republican virtue and pieces of clay that parents and educators need to mold to spiritual guides adults should follow.[98] Perhaps the most famous spiritually guiding child of the mid-nineteenth century was Harriet Beecher Stowe's literary figure, Little Eva, a character in *Uncle Tom's Cabin*. Eva served as an example of tolerance and spirituality not only for her father, Augustine St. Clare, but also for Stowe's readers. Despite Eva's explicit paternalism, Stowe's narrative made her a guide for both black and white characters around her.[99]

Quite accurately, historians usually connect Bushnell and the Beechers with a liberal strand of American evangelicalism. Yet the sentimental approach to children appears even within conservative thought. Dwight Moody, for example, used the image of a child as a spiritual guide in several of his sermons. In his sermon "The Child Angel," Moody related a narrative of a child very similar to Little Eva, who, although dead, still led her father to a conversion. A little girl is able to move Abraham Lincoln to have compassion on her brother in "The Child and President Lincoln." Another little child's faith that God would provide a house because she had prayed for one in faith reproves a mother's disbelief in "Faith." These three sermons are representative of the importance Moody placed on children as models of a good Christian. Although a liberal theology might connect Bushnell to liberal Protestantism, children were also a part of conservative theology.[100] As historian George Marsden noted, "The emphasis on motherhood and domesticity in Moody's preaching was part of the widespread evangelical conviction that stability in the home was the key to the resolution of other social problems."[101] Individual conversion was the focus of Moody's preaching, but the family—especially children—played an important role in the relationship between believer and society.[102]

The family was also important to fundamentalists even as they retreated from society. Since fundamentalists began to feel shut off from shaping American culture and politics, the family became the important sphere in which to protect Christianity. Furthermore, the status of the home reflected as well as impacted the moral stability of the nation. "As the home goes, so society will go," said minister Charles Fuller in one of his radio broadcasts.[103] Fundamentalists continued to conceive of the home and family as a fortress to protect individuals from the perils of the world. Victorian notions of domesticity continued to empower fundamentalist conceptions of the home and family as divinely sanctioned and ordered. The home was particularly important because in the home children learned and expressed the piety that would shape their entire lives. Victorian views on gender also motivated the fundamentalist home, especially concerning the relationship between parents and children. Fundamentalist mothers provided the instruction that would safeguard children from the dangerous ideologies in the world, particularly evolution. Fundamentalist fathers provided discipline that would theoretically prevent children from straying from fundamentalist teachings.[104]

The contemporary rise in evangelical products brought with it those focused on children. For example, in 1992 Max Lucado released his first children's title, *Just in Case You Ever Wonder*.[105] Since then he has released over 30 children's and teens' books and DVDs. Some of those works are child or adolescent versions of his adult inspirational titles. Others draw on themes found in his adult books but are completely new works. Lucado has some books and DVDs that are part of a series, including Hermie & Friends and Wemmicks. Others are stand-alone stories. Sentimentality is the ruling motif; individualism and the individual's relationship to God are the key points.

In *Just in Case You Ever Wonder*, for example, Lucado shapes his narrative around a one-sided conversation between a parent and a child. Throughout the story the parent emphasizes to the child that God made the child both as a special child and as a unique child: "God made you like no one else."[106] The parent further tells the child that because of her or his special, unique nature God specifically picked a home: "God wanted to put you in just the right home...where you would be warm when it's cold, where you'd be safe when you're afraid, where you'd have fun and learn about heaven. So, after lots of looking for just the right family, God sent you to me. And I'm so glad he did."[107] The parent also wants the child to know about God: "He loves you. He protects you. He and His angels are always watching over you."[108] Furthermore, it is the parent's responsibility to tell the child about heaven: "It's a wonderful place. There are no tears there. No monsters. No mean people.

You never have to say 'good-bye,' or 'good night,' or 'I'm hungry.' You never get cold or sick or afraid."[109] Finally, the narrator connects the parental role to the role of God: "In heaven you are so close to God that He will hug you, just like I hug you."[110]

These themes appear in other examples of Lucado's material for children, especially in his Wemmicks series. The first of the Wemmicks books is a work titled *You Are Special*.[111] The book opens by describing a group of wooden people called Wemmicks who had been created by a woodcarver named Eli. The Wemmicks spent quite an amount of time giving each other stickers. If they approved of another Wemmick, they gave that Wemmick a gold star. If they disapproved of another Wemmick, they gave that Wemmick a gray dot. There was a Wemmick named Punchinello who always received dots because the other Wemmicks did not like him. One day Punchinello met a Wemmick named Lucia who did not have any stickers. Neither the gold stars nor the gray dots would stick to her. She told Punchinello that the stickers did not adhere to her because she went to see the Wemmicks' maker, Eli. Punchinello visits Eli, who tells him that Punchinello should not care what the other Wemmicks think of him. Instead he should rest assured that Eli, his maker, thought he was special. Eli continues by telling Punchinello that Lucia does not have stickers because she does not care about what the Wemmicks think of her: "The stickers only stick if they matter to you. The more you trust my love, the less you care about their stickers."[112] As Punchinello leaves Eli's house, he begins to understand what Eli tells him, and the gray dots start falling off.[113]

You Are Special is an allegory in which the child reading or hearing the story is put into the role of Punchinello. Eli represents God or perhaps Jesus. The stickers represent the praise (i.e., the gold stars) or disapproval (i.e., the gray dots) of the people around the reader. What is important, according to Lucado, is not what other people think about a person but what God thinks about a person. The individual is inherently special in the eyes of God because God created each individual. Furthermore, every individual is a child of God and is special in that way as well.

Lucado's children's books, however, may not live up to the expectations of the author, the publishers, or even parents who buy them for their children. Professor Ann Trousdale studied children's responses to *You Are Special* by having them read the book and discuss it with her. In her findings Trousdale noted that the children did not make a connection between the character Eli and God until Trousdale specifically asked if Eli reminded them of God. The children had previously related Eli to family members that they knew, but only when Trousdale made the connection for them they did see some similarities. After de-allegorizing the character of Eli, the children believed that the lesson of *You Are Special* had to do with personal autonomy and self-esteem. Having understood Eli as God, most of the children did agree that what was most important from the book was what God thought about that individual.[114]

While children may not always understand the nuances of evangelical children's literature, books and other products directed toward children perform important functions for the adults of the evangelical community. Children's materials offer the hope of a stable community—one that will continue after the death of contemporary adults. The materials are a way for parents and other adults to convince themselves that they are passing on their faith to the next generation. Related to this feature, children's literature also provides socialization to the evangelical community. It introduces evangelical virtues and standards to children. It tells children—through cartoon characters or easy-to-read narratives—what matters to the community and how one should act in the community. Lucado's children's books evidence the same practical piety found in his adult titles. Self-concept, sharing, telling the truth, love, and following the rules are just a few lessons found in Lucado's children's books. They provide children with figures whose qualities they should emulate. Colorful cartoon characters or adults reading to children transmit values that are important to the community. These works do not present doctrinal or philosophical arguments, but neither do Lucado's adult titles. The overall message of God's love for human beings permeates his media, making it easy to associate the Lucado brand with an easy-to-identify idea: a Max Lucado children's book will tell a child about God's love.

The themes present in Lucado's works make their way into forms of evangelical children's material like the video series VeggieTales. Using computer animation, its creators have invented a cast of characters that are anthropomorphized vegetables who provide lessons on various issues of morality. Bob the Tomato and Larry the Cucumber are the leaders of a cast that teaches children reconceptualized versions of biblical stories or various character traits like honesty, bravery, loyalty, and sharing. The creators also incorporate references to popular culture and frequently include a "silly song," an often ridiculous song that may or may not have a point or a moral but serves a non-sequitur break in the overarching narrative of the video's given lesson. The videos are often available not just in Christian bookstores but also in general market retailers.

That the creators also rely on evangelical sentimentality is obvious in the VeggieTales video *Rack, Shack, and Benny*.[115] The writers get their inspiration for this episode from the biblical story of Daniel and his friends Shadrach, Meshach, and Abednego in Daniel 1-3. In the biblical narrative the Babylonians have taken many Jews into captivity. The text of the book of Daniel specifically mentions these four Jewish lads who serve in the court of King Nebuchadnezzar. Daniel and his friends uphold Jewish food laws and refuse to eat the food of the Babylonians, which they believe would ritually defile them. The court officials are concerned that this will cause these Jews to appear less healthy than the king's other attendants, but they allow it anyway. After a certain period it becomes obvious that Daniel, Shadrach, Meshach, and Abednego are much healthier than the other young men. Not only are they healthier, but they also are wiser and more discerning than even the king's advisors.

Two chapters later the king's officials call into question Shadrach, Meshach, and Abednego's service to Nebuchadnezzar. The king had decreed that everyone in his kingdom must bow down and worship an image that he had created. The Jews refuse to do so because of their allegiance to the God of Israel. The penalty for not worshipping the image is death, and after providing them another opportunity to do so, Nebuchadnezzar sentences the three men to death in a furnace. When the Jews are put in the furnace, however, God protects them from harm. Nebuchadnezzar orders their release, blesses their God, and promotes them in his court.

The VeggieTales writers conflate the refusal of food and the refusal of worship into one story and remove reference to Daniel altogether. Shadrach, Meshach, and Abednego become Rack (Bob the Tomato), Shack (Junior Asparagus), and Benny (Larry the Cucumber). They work—with other "boys and girls"—in Mr. Nebby K. Nezzar's chocolate bunny factory.[116] Mr. Nezzar is a chief executive officer who is a bit "big for his britches" although he is "not a bad man; he just gets confused sometimes."[117] The narrative presents the children as essentially a conscripted labor force given some sort of compensation that they plan to send to their families who live in some undisclosed location. When the company ships its two millionth chocolate bunny, Nezzar allows everyone to have all the chocolate bunnies they can eat in 30 minutes.

Although Rack, Shack, and Benny begin eating with everyone else, Shack tells his friends that they should probably stop eating or they will get sick. "Don't you remember what our parents taught us?" he asks. "We shouldn't eat very much candy because it's not good for us."[118] Rack responds that their parents are not present and everyone else was eating the bunnies. Shack then tells Rack and Benny of a song his mother used to sing to him. In the song Shack's mother sings to him about the importance of obedience to parents and that when children listen to their parents' teaching it is like the parents being present even if they are far away. Rack and Benny listen to Shack's story and respond—with tears in their eyes—that they will not eat any more bunnies. Rack even tells him, "I'm doing it for my mom!" "Me, too," Benny says.[119] Since they refrain from eating more bunnies, the three boys are the only workers not sick when Mr. Nezzar arrives to inspect the factory. Nezzar makes Rack, Shack, and Benny junior executives because they appear to be more industrious than the other workers.

When Rack, Shack, and Benny arrive at the factory the next day, Nezzar tells them of his plan to construct a 90-foot bunny statue so that everyone will "love the bunny" like he does.[120] He expects that when his workers see the statue that they will bow down and sing the bunny song. "The bunny song," says Nezzar, " is how all my employees will show just how much they love the bunny, how nothing is more important than the bunny, [and] how they would do anything for the bunny."[121] Anyone not singing the bunny song would be thrown into the furnace for bunnies that have some sort of manufacturing defect. Someone not singing the song is essentially a "bad bunny."[122] At the unveiling of the large bunny, Rack, Shack, and Benny refuse to bow and sing because their parents told them to "stand up for what [you] believe in" and that God wants them to "do what's right."[123] Since there was "a lot of stuff in that song that's not right," they cannot sing it.[124]

Nezzar orders his other workers to take Rack, Shack, and Benny to the furnace. When the three fall into the furnace, darkness covers the factory, and a strange ethereal light shoots out of the openings of the furnace. One of the other workers notices that Rack, Shack, and Benny are not burning up. Nezzar calls for their release, noting that God had saved them from the furnace. He also admits that he was wrong to "try and make [them] do things [they] weren't supposed to do."[125] Nezzar asks for forgiveness from Rack, Shack, and Benny, which they are happy to give.

Hendershot observed that part of the reason for the success of VeggieTales is shrewd practices on the part of the creators of the series. They present, argued Hendershot, an amorphous religious message instead of one that is explicitly evangelical. Although the episodes in the series clearly reference God, there are very few references to Jesus or conversion, a concession that Hendershot sees as partly materialistic. The videos sell better in a general retail market if they do not include the express views of a specific religious subgroup. Unlike other video series that maintain an explicitly evangelical message, VeggieTales succeeds commercially because it is "more secular."[126]

There is much to commend Hendershot's conclusions about the video series, especially if we understand evangelicalism in terms of doctrine, beliefs, and even politics. If we understand evangelicalism in terms of emotional practices and aesthetics, however, it becomes evident that VeggieTales is promulgating an explicitly evangelical worldview. As we saw in *Rack, Shack, and Benny*, the appeal to moral behavior is an emotional one. When Shack encourages Rack and Benny to stop eating chocolate bunnies, he does so by reminding his friends that their loving parents want them to do what is right. The response Rack and Benny give—that they will stop eating bunnies—comes with tears in their eyes. Shack's memories of his mother and her instruction causes Rack and Benny to be saddened—probably through a nostalgic response of remembering their own parents' teachings—and to vow that they will follow what Shack has presented as the right course of moral action. When the boys have to make a decision about whether they will bow down to the bunny and sing the bunny song, they determine the right course of action again through this emotional, nostalgic appeal. The song of Shack's mother is reprised to set the stage for what their parents, and God, would want them to do—refuse to worship Nezzar's bunny.

The evangelicalism of VeggieTales is further evident in the other ways sentimentality pervades the series. Not only do the series creators rely on familial pressure for moral decisions—as seen in *Rack, Shack, and Benny*—but they also assure their viewers that they have individual value to God. The importance of the individual melds with the promotion of the need for an emotional connection to the deity in the closing line of nearly every VeggieTales episode. After teaching their viewers a moral lesson about some character trait, Bob the Tomato and Larry the Cucumber encourage their audience to "remember God made you special, and he loves you very much."[127]

But the sentimentality of children's media conceals as much as it reveals. Sentimentality often obscures the issues of power that are continually being negotiated in relationships of parents and children. "God made you special and he loves you very much," but he also expects you to act in certain ways. The simplified message of sentimental creators of popular culture rests on the concealed evangelical framework of the reliability of biblical texts. Although the creators of VeggieTales are willing to take a lot of license with the biblical text to present a humorous and entertaining product, they close with a Bible verse that connects to the presented character trait or to the message of the episode. The Bible becomes a guide to day-to-day living, a reliable sourcebook for what both parents and God expects. Sentimentality, therefore, instanti-ates systems of authority and power and is a conservative force.

It is also the path to a type of self-surveillance. As Junior Asparagus notes in *Rack, Shack, and Benny*, "Don't you remember what our parents taught us?" The sentimental and the nostalgic are intended to trigger emotional responses to enact appropriate behavior. They become a conduit for both internalizing and invoking ethical behavior. God loves me, thinks I'm special, wants the best for me. The Bible—literally accepted—tells me what is best for me. Authority is internalized—I want to do what God wants me to do and what's best for me. Then, when I stray from that norm, emotional appeals can evoke that internalized emotional authority. "Don't you remember what our parents taught us?"

The commodification of sentimentality also participates in this prolifera-tion of authority, often extending the authority of the author or creator of a piece of popular culture. The works of Max Lucado and VeggieTales are just two of the never-ending number of brands—albeit two very popular ones—marketed to evangelicals. The sentimental and religious nature of the message hides that at the end of the day Max Lucado books and VeggieTales videos are produced by companies with a bottom line. They produce media not only to spread Christianity—although in the modern market many Christian publishers are owned by secular parent companies—but also to sell product. The purpose of creating a brand—an author or product line—is to produce repeat customer business because of the emotional connections consumers have with the brand.[128]

Sentimentality and branding combine to instantiate the authority of the author or other producer of popular culture. A child may relate to the Hermie brand and want the latest Hermie DVD or a kids' meal with a Hermie toy, like what has been offered by Christian-based fast food restau-rant Chick-fil-A. When children watch a Hermie DVD, Lucado introduces them to a variety of evangelical values. These values are practical ones. The Hermie videos feature evangelical ideas about God and Jesus, but their main focus—emblazoned on the front of each DVD—is on encouraging children to tell the truth, be unique, get along, behave, be friendly, and share as well as engage in certain religious practices, such as believing God or praying. The parent or adult might feel comfortable buying a Hermie DVD because it is *Max Lucado's Hermie & Friends*, and they have come to trust Max Lucado. If such is the case, the branding has worked effectively. Lucado and his publish-ers and marketers, then, have successfully identified "Max Lucado" as a brand that people can rely on and trust to present godly, positive, life-affirming material meant to draw audiences into a closer relationship with God. Children are spiritually safe with Max Lucado products, and Max Lucado will help parents prepare their children to be godly. Lucado becomes an authority to be trusted.

Conclusion

"The exchange of Christian goods and the construction of religious environments is not something that has appeared recently in American culture and it is not something that will disappear," wrote McDannell in *Material Christianity*.[129] The choices evangelicals have available to materially construct those environments, however, has increased in recent years. There is a plethora of religious options even just within evangelicalism that they can appropriate and inject into the worlds they inhabit. The religious goods of Max Lucado and others and the ideas that they embody provide individuals an opportunity to see the world with sentimental eyes. If people adopt the worldview these evangelicals offer, they can make sense of the world and the people around them in the context of a sentimental God who interacts with human beings in sentimental ways. A calendar that offers a daily quote from Joel Osteen, a Lucado DVD for the children to watch, a *Purpose-Drive Life* journal to record one's thoughts, a Lucado Bible to read devotionally, and an inspirational title to motivate can theoretically work together to create a dependence on the part of the consumer. They turn to such ministers to understand the Bible, God, and the world: reality itself and their place in it. Omnipresence in the market offers the opportunity to bathe one's life in sentimental sacredness—for a price.[130]

That price is not just financial. The economics and marketing of modern evangelical sentimentality has led to the emphasis of presence in the market instead of purity of theological stance. Evangelical popular culture becomes a means to seek stability—stability found in emotional boundaries not doctrinal ones. Such products offer a vision for what Christianity should be about. Publishers market that vision in the hopes of saturating the market with branded products that will help their bottom line. They play on the trust consumers have for the name Max Lucado, for example, encouraging them to accept that Max has the answers to life's questions and can give them practical advice.

This chapter began by briefly tracing some contours of evangelical marketing. It was obviously incomplete and selective, but it is a standard narrative of the ways evangelicals have used marketing to promote their message. The narrative has been one of religious innovation. Whitefield, Moody, and others often appear as astute observers of market forces who manipulate the market for their own purposes. What Lucado and others reveal about the history of marketing and evangelicalism, however, is how they appear much more dependent on marketing than before. Even Whitefield, Moody, and Sunday did not have the kind of team that these contemporary evangelicals have. This reliance on marketing for presence puts modern evangelicals in a quandary because, if Lucado is any indication, it appears that quite often evangelicals must downplay purity to be present.[131] Minimizing doctrinal purity hides larger issues in evangelicalism including the reliance on fundamentalist theology and Scottish Common Sense in modern evangelicalism, the importance of the bottom line to evangelical marketers and publishers, and the constructedness of evangelical authors.

The trajectory of evangelicalism and marketing from Whitefield to Lucado, therefore, is not simply one of religious innovators manipulating the market to spread evangelicalism. There were certainly instances of that, but it is also about evangelical celebrities becoming more and more dependent on the market for success. Market research, publishers, and economics all factor into the production of evangelical popular culture. Whether or not Dwight Moody, for example, would have incorporated high-tech market research, modern evangelical ministers must take it into consideration. Publishers must consider profitability and not just the religious values and teaching that a work presents. The success of these evangelicals shows not only sentimentality's profitability but also how important sentimentality is to understanding modern evangelicalism.

Through an examination of marketing, practical piety, and children's media we see how much evangelicals, especially evangelical publishers and authors, have come to depend on the commercialization of sentiment and religiosity for survival. They seek to find stability in evangelicalism through the production of religious materials to shape a constituency that will continue to buy their religious materials. Evangelical publishing finds itself in much the same position that promoters of tourism in Branson, Missouri, do. As American studies scholar Aaron Ketchell noted in *Holy Hills of the Ozarks*, Branson tourism relies on a simplified Christianity that allows for the appearance of *family values*, but it is a capitalistic venture that has crafted a religiosity of broad appeal, not doctrinal positions.[132] It is an "amorphous Christian outlook" presented "in a buoyant and consumable manner."[133] Because of the capitalist bottom line that marketers, whether of religious tourism or religious books, must consider, scholars cannot simply accept that religious marketing is about the message. It is not. It is about what will sell, and diminishing doctrine in favor of emotional rhetoric will.

Although sentimentality is a commodity, it is also important to see it as a vital part of evangelical culture and the practice of evangelicalism. From the middle of the nineteenth century, sentimentality became a core part of evangelical practice. As evangelicals read sentimental works, heard sentimental sermons, and sang sentimental songs, nostalgia, familial love for God, and the importance of the domestic sphere became an important rhetorical part of how evangelicals understood God and the world around them. Although fundamentalists and those who espoused a *muscular Christianity* (often not mutually exclusive) employed rhetoric that was antagonistic to the sentiment Christianity of the nineteenth century, they used sentimental songs in their services placing "Blessed Assurance" alongside "Onward, Christian Soldiers." Unintentionally, militaristic evangelicals further incorporated the very sentimentality they deplored into the evangelical consciousness.

Among contemporary evangelicals, the singing of sentimental music, whether from the nineteenth century or from more modern periods, continues to reproduce a culture of emotion that evokes a rhetoric of familial and erotic love for the deity. Listening to contemporary Christian music also furthers this development. Reading popular inspirational ministers like Max Lucado, Rick Warren, and Joel Osteen legitimizes sentimentality not only as the way God deals with humans but also how humans are to interact with God. It also authenticates such language as the appropriate way to converse with and about God. In other words, the authority evangelicals give to musicians, authors, and ministers who use sentimental rhetoric cyclically proves that such languages is the "true" way to understand and approach God. The very activities of singing, listening, and reading in a devotional manner often works to hide how these activities instantiate sentimentality even more deeply into evangelicalism. As ritual theorist Catherine Bell noted, "Ritual practices are produced with an intent to order, rectify, or transform a particular situation."[134] Sentimentality in practice—as part of *religious* practice—replicates itself to become a fundamental characteristic of modern evangelicalism.

Sentimentality is not just about positive feelings of God's love. It is also a means to perpetuate the evangelical community and instantiate religious authority. Cute cartoon character or saccharine writing elides the deeper structural work that this type of evangelical emotionality does. It perpetuates a specific religious worldview, not through the intellectual assent to beliefs but through the internalization of emotional habits of seeing that world through sentimental eyes. Contemporary evangelical sentimentality is a conservative force to perpetuate authority. It is not just about telling people that God loves them.

4 AMERICA LOOKS UP: SENTIMENTALITY, POLITICS, AND AMERICAN EVANGELICALISM

Sometimes evangelical sentimentality appears in a place where one would not expect to find it. Multiple examples could be produced of evangelicals using emotional language tinged with fear or hatred, but occasionally beneath such expressions is the foundation of the very emotionality we have been examining. Consider the following tract titled "Somebody Loves You."[1]

The tract contains very few words and little spoken dialogue. It opens with an image of the exterior of a cabin in a torrential rainstorm. Inside the cabin a father sends his child out into the storm to beg for money. The father is a drunk, as evidenced by liquor bottles scattered across the floor of the cabin and the word *hic* in a thought balloon. The androgynous, large-eyed child exits into the rain with a large cup to collect money. Most of the people that the child encounters pass by; the child receives a penny from only one individual. Upon returning, the child, shivering and wet, presents the money to the father. The father, seeing only a penny, is furious, and in a drunken rage he beats the child. After the beating, the father tosses the child out of the house into the storm. The child crawls away from the house and eventually into an alley, falling asleep in a box by a garbage can. While the child sleeps the scene shifts. The rain has stopped and a new breeze is blowing. It is particularly blowing a card with the words SOMEBODY LOVES YOU written on it. The wind blows the card to the child who picks it up and reads it. The child does not understand the message, as evidenced by the large question mark over the child's head while reading it. Noticing a woman passing by, the child holds the card out to her wondering what it means. "JESUS LOVES YOU!" the woman tells the child.[2] In some of the tract's only spoken dialogue, the woman tells the child that she will go to get help. The child is overjoyed with the news and thinks, "JESUS LOVES ME!"[3] The child lies down clutching the card, as hearts connected by dotted lines radiate off the child's body. Help for the child, however, does not come, and the child dies. In the last panels of the comic an angel bends into the box holding the child and grabs the child's body, taking it to heaven. The angel then presents the child to someone off screen. The child's face beams as it reaches out for whatever it sees. The author tells the reader, "AND THE LORD JESUS LOVES YOU TOO!"[4] The tract is titled "Somebody Loves Me" and is a product of Chick Publications.

Although usually demonstrative of evangelical hatred and appeals to fear, Chick tracts represent one example of evangelical visions of transforming society through the transformation of individuals. In the past four decades especially, evangelicals have been prominent in the public arena, desiring to see both a more moral American society and a return to a time when Christianity was more prominent in shaping the agenda of the United States. Sentimentality participates in defining the concerns of evangelical politics as well as providing the nostalgic authority for evangelical involvement in politics. Yet sentimentality fails to provide the ability to recognize the structural issues at work in a variety of moral and political situations.

Creating a Contemporary Culturally Active Evangelicalism

Nineteenth-century evangelicals were politically active with respect to a variety of social and political issues. As liberals and conservative evangelicals split from each other in the latter nineteenth century, conservative evangelicals—and later fundamentalists—still believed that they needed to provide the moral agenda for the United States. The experience of the Scopes Trial, however, caused evangelicals to concede that not all Americans were willing to follow their lead. Although fundamentalists still involved themselves in politics in some cases, they also developed a separatist mentality that led to the construction of a variety of fundamentalist institutions.[5]

In the 1940s several conservative Christians became dissatisfied with the separatism of fundamentalism. Individuals like Harold Ockenga, Carl Henry, Harold Lindsell, Charles Fuller, and Billy Graham looked for ways to move conservative Christianity into more contact with American culture. Several factors motivated these individuals to reconceptualize fundamentalism. They believed that Christians had to be involved in culture to evangelize effectively. They also were frustrated with the anti-intellectual position of many fundamentalists. Finally, they sought social and political engagement with the world through activism. They assumed they could not maintain the disengagement of fundamentalism and accomplish these goals.[6]

One of the ways they began to distinguish themselves from other fundamentalists was through the formation of the National Association of Evangelicals (NAE) in 1942. Organizers like Ockenga pictured the NAE as a response to the liberalism of the Federal Council of Churches and the divisiveness of the American Council of Churches, a fundamentalist group. At its origin the NAE worked against separatism by being more inclusive with regard to the groups that it admitted. Groups like Pentecostals, Methodists, and Mennonites—excluded from the American Council of Churches— joined the NAE. This inclusivity angered fundamentalists, but it was a sign of the changes to come.[7]

Another major milestone in the developing fundamentalist cleavage was the creation of Fuller Seminary in California. Minister and radio personality Fuller and minister Ockenga started Fuller Seminary in 1947 as an attempt to give intellectual legitimacy to the movement. Like the NAE, the founders of Fuller conceived of the school as a conservative school that moderated between the fundamentalist hard line found in schools like Dallas Theological Seminary and the liberalism of places like Princeton. Especially Ockenga believed that a rigorous intellectual life was the key to the success of the neo-evangelical movement—a term not commonly used until the 1950s—as well as the way evangelicalism would make an impact on the larger American culture. As historian George Marsden noted, Ockenga believed that a "true scholarly center" would create outstanding scholarship and "all the world would have to notice."[8] Whether or not the world noticed, Fuller Seminary educated many in the subsequent generations of evangelical ministers and theologians including Rick Warren and Rob Bell.[9]

While Ockenga and Fuller were recreating evangelicalism on the West Coast, others were making an impact on the East Coast. In the East the focus was not on scholarship but youth. Ministers like Percy Crawford and Jack Wyrtzen produced radio programs geared at preaching a fundamentalist-evangelical gospel to a young audience. Based on their success on the radio, Crawford (in Philadelphia) and Wyrtzen (in New York) held rallies of young people in large venues—like Madison Square Garden— drawing tens of thousands of people. Other ministers used a similar format and began holding Youth for Christ rallies. Gradually these rallies were institutionalized into a Youth for Christ organization, which opened offices in Chicago. In 1944 the Youth for Christ movement started a series of Saturday night rallies. The inaugural speaker, who later became officially associated with the movement, was a 25-year-old Wheaton College graduate named William "Billy" Graham.[10]

By 1948 Graham had left Youth for Christ to start holding citywide revival campaigns. He preached across the country and even took several preaching tours of Great Britain, much like Dwight Moody had done at the end of the nineteenth century. His success at these campaigns was modest compared with the audience he had reached in the Youth for Christ rallies. In 1949 Graham agreed to be the featured evangelist in a crusade in Los Angeles. The result this time was much different. After several weeks, several noteworthy conversions, and the publicity of a press motivated by Graham's success as well as his anti-communist message, attendance at the crusade exploded. He followed this success with success in Boston and then elsewhere. Billy Graham and neo-evangelicalism was catching the attention of American culture.[11]

A few years after Graham's Los Angeles crusade, a candy-salesman-turned-failing-Fuller-Seminary student named Bill Bright claimed to have received a vision from God to start a ministry to college students. Bright's goal in 1951 was "to recruit one hundred seminary and Bible-college graduates to be 'dispatched in teams of five' across the country to hold evangelistic meetings and meet student leaders."[12] Things did not work out as planned. Bright's initial forays into creating Campus Crusade for Christ were modest but highly publicized conversions by notable college athletes, smart use of the media, and persistence allowed Bright to grow Campus Crusade in fits and starts.[13]

The separation between fundamentalism and neo-evangelicalism solidified in the 1950s. Much of the break was due to the work of Graham and those who supported him. Graham began accepting support from nonevangelicals and nonfundamentalists in publicizing his crusades. His ecumenical attitude angered many fundamentalists, and they denounced his work. The publication of *Christianity Today*, an evangelical magazine supported by Graham and other neo-evangelicals, also precipitated the break. The editors and writers of *Christianity Today* intentionally distanced the magazine and the movement from fundamentalism and evidenced a more tolerant attitude toward modernism, the decades-old enemy of fundamentalists. The creation of neo-evangelicalism also brought together Graham, Fuller Seminary, and Campus Crusade for Christ as part of the institutionalization of neo-evangelicalism. Graham endorsed Fuller Seminary. Fuller Seminary and its faculty threw their weight behind Graham, and Campus Crusade eventually broke ties with fundamentalist Bob Jones University to find acceptance and patronage with Billy Graham and his coterie.[14]

The 1960s brought both challenges and adaptations for evangelicalism. Billy Graham tried to be racially inclusive while standing at a distance from the Civil Rights movement. Campus Crusade met protests on college campuses. Fuller Seminary experienced a division among the faculty regarding whether or not they should continue pushing the idea of biblical inerrancy, the idea that the Bible was literally true word-for-word and contained no errors, or should adopt the idea of biblical infallibility, a position that claimed the message of the Bible was true and effective but that the text might contain errors. The majority of the faculty of Fuller chose infallibility, and conservative faculty members like Harold Lindsell left. Yet Graham also became politically prominent during this time. He continued to succeed in his crusades but also began a shift into becoming an advisor to presidents by aligning himself with Richard Nixon.[15] Campus Crusade changed tactics. Bill Bright simplified the message of the group to the Four Spiritual Laws, making the presentation of the message much easier on staff members. The first of these laws was "God loves you and has a wonderful plan for your life."[16] Not only did Campus Crusade simplify its message, but it also adopted some of the activities and interests of the New Left and the counterculture to present this message. Grassroots organizing and collective protesting became a part of evangelicalism. At Fuller Seminary faculty, including the dean Daniel Fuller, son of Charles Fuller, turned to the thinking of theologian Karl Barth and his notions of biblical infallibility to mediate a commitment to scripture as God's word while recognizing the possibility that scripture contained errors. These individuals could no longer accept the doctrine of biblical inerrancy, but they wanted to cling to scripture as a revelation from the divine. While they could not accept all of Barth's neo-orthodoxy, his position on scripture was a welcome substitute for the problems of inerrancy.[17]

If evangelicals had made somewhat successful attempts to reassert themselves in American culture from the 1940s through the 1960s, the decade of the seventies brought evangelicalism much more prominently back into the public sphere in a sustained way. Yet the move from generally separated from culture to fully integrated into culture did not leave evangelicalism unchanged. Many scholars have focused on the political shifts of the time period: the rise of the Moral Majority, protests over abortion, and the election of Jimmy Carter. These events changed the political face of evangelicalism.[18]

Newsweek magazine called 1976 the Year of the Evangelical due to Jimmy Carter's candidacy for president, among other things. Jerry Falwell created the Moral Majority as an organization to create political change. In the 1980 presidential election all three candidates identified themselves as evangelicals, and Ronald Reagan successfully appealed to evangelicals for their support. Dissatisfied that neither Carter nor Reagan lived up to his expectations of evangelical presidents, Marion "Pat" Robertson, a televangelist, ran for the Republican nomination in 1988. Although he was unsuccessful in acquiring the nomination, Robertson continued to shape the Republican Party's agenda by starting the Christian Coalition, a grassroots evangelical movement that intended to reshape American politics at all levels of government to look more like the imagined Christian America of the past.

Robertson's candidacy also demonstrates other ways evangelicals were prominent in American culture toward the end of the twentieth century. Televangelists, like Robertson, Oral Roberts, Jimmy Swaggart, and Jim and Tammy Bakker, used the airwaves to reach millions of viewers and acquire millions of dollars. While televangelists had been using television since its inception, the eighties marked both a proliferation of ministries and a proliferation of scandal. Swaggart and Bakker were separately involved in high-profile sexual scandals, and Bakker was also indicted on issues related to the mishandling of money from viewers. Despite the scandals, televangelists continued to use media to garner viewership and financial support.[19]

Evangelicals also made their presence known in other media areas in the late twentieth century to greater levels than they had before. The proliferation of contemporary Christian music occurred not only on Christian radio and in Christian bookstores but also in mainstream markets. Crossover artists like Amy Grant, Michael W. Smith, Jars of Clay, and Sixpence None the Richer brought an evangelical message to secular radio stations and music stores. Other forms of Christian media like Christian movies, videos, and books also became prominent. Whether or not Ockenga, Henry, and Fuller intended this kind of presence in American culture when they formed the National Association of Evangelicals, by the end of the century American evangelicals had thrown off the separatism of fundamentalism to make their presence known.

In creating that presence, evangelicals have relied on sentimental tropes to understand who they are and how they should be involved in the world. These tropes have provided not only the foundation for evangelical political engagement but also the justification for evangelicals to be involved in politics. With this sentimental base they have made their political presence known as they relied on emotional language, particularly about domesticity, to motivate people for political causes as well as to try to explain their beliefs to others, quite often using the sentimental discourse of God's love and the sanctity of the domestic sphere as the foundation for an evangelical political agenda. Sentimentality has also provided evangelicals an apparatus to over-look the consequences of that political activity, providing them the authority they needed for political engagement.

The Politics of Evangelical Sentimentality

Many scholars have addressed the rise of evangelicalism to renewed politi-cal power and focused on how evangelical leaders have motivated individuals to politically support conservative and primarily Republican causes since the last third of the twentieth century. Often the focus of these scholars has been outspoken figures like Robertson, Jerry Falwell, and James Dobson and orga-nizations like the Moral Majority, the Christian Coalition, and Focus on the Family.[20] While these vociferous individuals and groups and others garner the attention of journalists, scholars, and the American public, there is another side to evangelical politics that provides us with a slightly different type of evangelicalism and political involvement. Max Lucado, Rick Warren, Joel Osteen, and others have made the claim that they are pastors, not politicians. Sociologist Christian Smith also found that a sizable group of evangelicals is hesitant to be involved with politics or thought they should not be political activists: "The vast majority of ordinary evangelicals, even those animated by Christian Right issues, clearly disavowed such aspirations to domination."[21] Instead of legislating morality, those Smith and his team surveyed believed that converting others should not occur through coercion but through "living a life of good example."[22] How do we reconcile such apparently discordant approaches to politics that we see in evangelicalism?

Sentimentality provides the foundation for this dichotomous approach to politics in evangelicalism. In *Christian America?* Smith pointed to his infor-mants' claims that they believed in the importance of aligning oneself with the Christian message and then transforming society through the spread of one's loving influence that will produce voluntary converts.[23] Yet according to soci-ologist D. Michael Lindsay, George W. Bush received large majorities of the evangelical vote in his two presidential runs—72 percent in 2000 and 87 per-cent in 2004.[24] By stressing the power of the individual to transform society and the ability of the sentimental message about God to convert individuals in society, evangelicals can be political while denouncing being overtly political. Sentimentality also provides the means for resolving the cognitive dissonance of acting in political ways while rhetorically eschewing political domination. The views of common evangelicals might not align with outspoken talking heads like Robertson, but the political outcomes align in the election of evangelical—or conservative Republican—candidates or the electoral support of political measures, like the question of same-sex marriage.[25]

In many respects modern evangelical sentimentality taps into the same cultural milieu that scholars of eighteenth- and nineteenth-century sentimentality have pointed out. Evangelical sentimentality is not solely about conceptions of God or humanity or about feeling happiness and joy. There are important political components to the presentation of the sentimental, nostalgic images that sentimental evangelicals offer their audiences. The political aspects of sentimentality are ironic in some ways because of how much such evangelicals attempt to rhetorically shun politics and a politicized faith.

In 2005, for example, Lucado was chosen to be the spokesperson for the National Day of Prayer. Not surprisingly, he wrote a book about it. The book, *Turn*, is a call to the people of America to be involved in prayer.[26] As his text, Lucado chose 2 Chronicles 7:14: "If my people, who are called by my name, will humble themselves and pray and seek my face and turn from their wicked ways, then will I hear from heaven and will forgive their sin and will heal their land" (NIV). Although the book is subtitled *Remembering Our Foundations*, it is not an explicit appeal to return to the supposed religion of the founding fathers, nor is it civil religion. America is God's nation only insofar as every nation is God's nation, writes Lucado. On the other hand, Lucado is concerned that prayer is limited in schools, the Bible is not allowed to be studied in schools, what he sees as God's idea of family is being overturned, and the phrase *under God* is in danger of being removed from the Pledge of Allegiance.[27]

Rhetorically he attempts to characterize the message of *Turn* as simply theological. Christians and others should be concerned about the "removal" of God from the public sphere not because America is God's nation but because America exists by God's power. "God determines every detail of every country. He defines all boundaries. He places every milestone. While we applaud Mayflower pilgrims and Lewis and Clark expeditions, they did nothing apart from God's power."[28] Lucado argues that such is the case of all nations. God sets up authorities and governments, and Christians are expected to submit to those governments: "Such words test our trust. We think of Nero, Stalin, Hitler, and Saddam Hussein. We may wonder why God permits despots and dictators their day. But we can be sure of this: no one rules without his permission."[29] Lucado does issue a dire warning, however. Because America exists by the power of God, God is ultimately in control of whether America continues to exist or is destroyed. We ignore God "only at a terrible risk."[30]

Despite an apparent rejection of Christian nationalism, Lucado does suggest that something is lacking in American culture. In rejecting God, the United States has lost some of its prominence. To return to greatness, changes are needed. Part of the answer lies in a return to prayer and the Bible. For Lucado these are the two most neglected things in American culture. Citing James 5:16 from the New Contemporary Version of the Bible, "When a believing person prays, great things happen," Lucado urges his readers, "Lay our great nation at His feet."[31] Such a national repentance does not begin with an enforced political morality. It begins with, yes, recognizing that "America needs to change" but following that up with "the change begins with me."[32]

Lucado cites the parable of the Pharisee and the publican told by Jesus in Luke 18. He presents the two characters as ways Americans as individuals can look on American society:

> We begin feeling like the man at the prayer session. During the time of private prayer, he stood alone and prayed, "God, I thank You that America has people like me. The man on the corner needs welfare—I don't. The prostitute on the street has AIDS—I don't. The bum at the bar needs alcohol—I don't. The gay caucus needs morality—I don't. I thank You that America has people like me." In the same meeting, a man of humble heart, too contrite to even look to the skies, prayed, "God, have mercy on me—a sinner. Like my brother on welfare—I'm dependent on Your grace. Like my sister with AIDS—I'm infected with mistakes. Like my friend who drinks—I need something to ease my pain. And like those You love who are gay—I need direction, too. Have mercy on me a sinner."[33]

When Americans humble themselves like this, writes Lucado, God "will heal our land."[34]

Lucado, much like the informants in Smith's study, emphasizes the importance of—in Smith's words—"civility, tolerance, and voluntary persuasion" while recognizing that God is ultimately in control of the destiny of all nations.[35] Smith pointed out that his informants reiterated eight different attitudes toward nonevangelicals that Lucado's approach in *Turn* reflects. Christians, they believed, should "practice what they preach," act toward others in loving ways, be respectful and tolerant of others, listen to the opinions of others, avoid forcing their beliefs on others, refrain from hostility, recognize the power of one's personal example, and rely on persuasion for conversion.[36]

Lucado's approach to the issue of same-sex marriage, however, deviates from this pattern. In 2004 Lucado posted "What God Says about Gay Marriage" to his website.[37] It has since been removed from the list of articles. The article opens with Lucado's characteristic syrupy language. Breaking his argument into three sections, Lucado addresses the issue of the biblical messages about marriage in the first section. Since "God created marriage," claims Lucado, "marriage is a divine match" and "God's plan."[38] Indeed, wives are "a godlike presence" for men. The creation of human beings in monogamous, heterosexual relationships is the standard for Lucado to judge other types of pair bondings. "Homosexuality, by its very nature, resists" the truth about God ordaining monogamous, heterosexual pair bondings.[39] In the second section, Lucado becomes more explicit and less sentimental about same-sex marriage. Although "nothing can separate us from the love God…[including] homosexuality," Lucado's God sees homosexual activity as an "abomination" and makes this position plain throughout the Bible.[40] This less sentimental Lucado continues into the third section, in which he repeats common evangelical arguments against same-sex unions. According to Lucado, they will "erode the traditional family," they will lead to legitimation of "polygamy and other deviations," and they are against God's plan.[41] In stating that individuals should oppose same-sex marriage because "God does," Lucado returns to his sentimental motif.[42] God opposes same-sex marriage "because He loves us" and "Jesus had your best interest at heart" when he supported monogamous, heterosexual marriage as the standard relationship.[43] Marriage, argues Lucado, restores the Edenic state of humanity. Also in this third section Lucado is his most political. He encourages his readers to contact their senators to support passage of the Federal Marriage Amendment, which would have limited marriage to heterosexual partners. "We cannot budge," writes Lucado. "Too much is at stake."[44]

The controversy surrounding same-sex marriage also provides an opportunity to see this cognitive dissonance between the apolitical rhetoric and political activity in the life of Rick Warren as well. In 2008 Proposition 8 was on the ballot in the state of California. Proposition 8 was an attempt to define marriage as only being between one man and one woman. In the weeks prior to the election, Warren sent a video to members of his Saddleback Church in support of Proposition 8. When president-elect Barack Obama invited Warren to offer a prayer at his inauguration, there was controversy because of Warren's support of Proposition 8. In response to the controversy, Warren participated in an interview with the website *beliefnet* regarding his position on gay marriage. In the context of that interview, Warren made comments that appeared to parallel same-sex unions with incestuous or pedophiliac ones. He quickly attempted damage control, releasing statements and giving interviews—including one with CNN talk-show host Larry King—that claimed he did not see homosexual activity in the same light as incest or pedophilia.[45]

While doing his damage control, Warren appealed to sentimental tropes. Like Lucado, Warren believes God created marriage. Because God created marriage as a union between one man and one woman, any other grouping "causes broken hearts, broken families, emotional hurt and shame, painful memories, and many other destructive consequences."[46] In further clarifications to his *beliefnet* interview, Warren asserted that the rejection of Proposition 8 would have led to children being "taught to approve what most parents disapprove of."[47] In these comments Warren invoked the divine sanctity of the home as well as the need to protect the innocence and spiritual purity of children, two important devices as we have seen. In attempting to salvage his image, Warren also made repeated claims that he was a pastor not a politician or activist. Although he did admit to providing a video in support of Proposition 8 to his church—clearly a political activity—Warren claimed to Larry King as well in a press release sent to Christian publications that he was not involved in organized activity related to Proposition 8, which provided his rationalization to claim that he is not involved in politics.[48]

Despite Lucado's and Warren's statements evidencing their commitment to the issues of conservative politics, they appear to work hard to intentionally present themselves as apolitical and nonpartisan. Such evangelicals can reach a broader audience because they do not publicly identify with Republicans or Democrats, liberals or conservatives. Their stated concern is about religious matters and not political ones. The answers to the individual's problems are spiritual not governmental. Furthermore, such a position distinguishes them from other evangelicals like Robertson and Dobson or others who have a blatantly political faith. The sentimental rhetoric that presents an apolitical image, however, is perplexing. Modern evangelical sentimentality, in fact, does political work and is ensconced in politics. It allows individuals to claim an apolitical stance by emphasizing the sanctity of the individual and the power of influence but justifies acting politically when the tropes of the sentimental worldview—marriage, family, innocent children—are threatened in the political arena.

These sentimental appeals also disguise the authority wielded by ministers like Lucado and Warren. While they assert they are pastors, not politicians, they encourage their congregants and their larger audiences to engage in political activity in certain causes. Another important aspect is that by being *pastors* and not politicians, they can set themselves up as being above politics while offering political opinions through the use of sentimentality.

The observations of scholars Julia Sterns, Jane Tompkins and Ann Douglas provide a framework to see how the sentimentality of modern evangelicalism is different from the sentimentalism of the eighteenth and nineteenth centuries, but the types of sentimentality have resonances. By placing them parallel to each other, especially in light of the political work sentimentality does, we can see important differences. As Sterns and others have observed, the use of sentimentality often reveals important details about culture and historical moments.[49]

In *Sensational Designs,* Jane Tompkins elucidated a feature of the cultural and political work that sentimental rhetoric does. In attempting to rescue the literature of nineteenth-century sentimental authors, Tompkins noted the cultural authority that they wielded because sentimentality provided them avenues to create a public presence that society had previously denied them. The elevation of the domestic sphere and feminine piety became a foundation for some women to enter the public sphere. These authors, many of whom were women, attempted to "reorganize culture from the woman's point of view."[50] They created and participated in a mythos of domesticity as an ideal for society and offered that to a large audience. Because these women drew on the social, religious, and political categories of the day, they were able to create successful literary works that relied on the mores of contemporary America while also critiquing aspects of them. Sometimes the works of these authors had great political consequences. Tompkins made the case that Harriet Beecher Stowe's *Uncle Tom's Cabin* provided the groundwork for the American Civil War through its creation of a moral judgment on slavery based on feeling, not on an intellectual or scriptural argument against the practice. The audience's participation in this shared sentimentality bestowed cultural power on these authors.[51]

Sentimentality also provides cultural authority to modern evangelicals. As already noted, deploying sentimental rhetoric is an attempt to create a bond between minister and audience, a bond where the audience accepts the minister's view of reality and the minister's authority. The minister invites the audience to accept a view of God, humanity, and the world around them. When they do, they give the ministers power to shape their thinking about religion. It appears that they use most of their authority in creating more authority by retaining and procuring new customers. While Lucado and Warren in recent years have been more vocal about social issues like poverty and AIDS, their rhetorical evasion of the political often works to legitimate society in some form. While they may decry the lack of morality in society, the locus for social change appears to be the sentimental reconstruction of the individual and not a collective political expression of solidarity and change. The transformation of society will occur, in their view, through personal influence.

Ann Douglas argued that the evangelical reliance on the power of personal influence to effect social change is a product of nineteenth-century sentimentality. Ministers and sentimental authors had no tangible power due to disestablishment and the abstraction of the means of production from the home. Instead, they sought authority through influence. Through influence these individuals believed they could actually exert more authority because influence would be something "discreetly omnipresent and omnipotent."[52] They could be "unobtrusive and everywhere at the same time."[53] Ultimately, for Douglas, influence was essentially conservative and worked to instantiate culture not radically change it.

Furthermore, influence was nostalgic in many respects. Although many clergy eventually embraced disestablishment in the nineteenth century (at least rhetorically), the use of influence as a symbol to assert power served as a reminder that they were separated from the traditional power to which clergy were accustomed. According to Douglas, disestablishment left clergy "to substitute political rhetoric for genuine political leadership, to imitate rather than assert political authority."[54] Such a generalization is surely an overstatement, but for most clergy they could look only back to a time when clergy wielded widespread political authority. As historians like Jon Butler have argued, however, the creation of a Christian America was a product of the late eighteenth century and the early Republic.[55] While Christians eventually wielded great political authority in religiously shaping the policies of the United States, it had not always been so across the colonies. In the minds of clergy and many Christians, however, they were attempting to recover what they believed had been lost, but they were actually creating something new and different. Sentimentality was an important part of this recreation.[56]

Nostalgia still marks this desire to see a political return to an imagined Christian America. It can be a part of how evangelicals envision a political return to this imagined past. Language of *restoration* and *return* are almost ubiquitous throughout conservative rhetoric about Christian America. The family and politics about the family—including the politics of sex—are often the key for this conservative reconstruction. The post–World War II period is also important for this nostalgic reimagining of Christian America, especially the imagined family of the 1950s.[57]

Even the apolitical rhetoric of Lucado and others participates in this politics of nostalgia. When Max Lucado or Rick Warren or Joel Osteen says, "I'm a pastor not a politician," they demonstrate the culmination of the historical trend of disestablishment. In this mind-set pastor and politician are two distinct, and importantly distinct, offices in this rhetoric. Moreover, being a pastor is rhetorically more important than being a politician in a culture that is suspicious of politicians and politicized faith. This apparently apolitical stance participates in the grief of a certain segment of culture that feels disenchanted with politics, politicians, and clergy masquerading as politicians. The rhetoric obscures the political roots of an apolitical agenda. The politics of the apolitical participates in the same grief and nostalgia over a lost Christian America. Although Lucado shuns political expressions about a political return to America, for example, the rhetoric he uses in books like *Turn* of *return* and *America bless God* evidences his involvement in an evangelical mind-set that postulates pristine Christian origins for the nation and that grieves that America has left those origins. Lucado may be rhetorically satisfied to adopt a pastor persona distinct from politics, but by doing so he demonstrates that he shares in a politics of grief and nostalgia that mourns the loss of Christian influence in the shaping of the United States.[58]

Here, too, sentimentality works in concealing ways that allow evangelicals to make claims that do not stand up to close scrutiny. We have seen throughout the book the importance of the image of the everyman for the ministers featured in this study. Lucado is Max, Warren is Rick, and Osteen is Joel. People can relate to them; they consider their audience as friends. There is an assumed authenticity presented in those images. Max, Rick, and Joel are people that one can trust. They care about their congregants. Included in that image is the apolitical nature of Max, Rick, and Joel. They are pastors, not politicians. They are concerned about greater matters; they are concerned about one's soul and spiritual destiny. While they are outside the halls of power, their calling is greater than what occurs in the halls of power. Their mission is an eternal, divine one that transcends politics.

The image of Lucado, Warren, and Osteen as everyman pastors begins to crumble in light of the fact that they have all had access not only to channels of politics but also to political figures. President Obama did not pick an everyman to word the prayer at the inauguration. He chose a best-selling author, a pastor of a large megachurch, and a friend of the president of Rwanda. Lucado has also been to the White House at the invitation of President George W. Bush. While these men might claim that they do not have constant access to or influence on the president of the United States, they certainly have more access than an everyman would.[59]

In many respects their apolitical political vision is closely related to the ritualistic character of their works. By creating a particular way of viewing the world through the consistent presentation of biblical narratives in certain ways, these evangelicals encourage their audiences to accept that individuals have behavioral power based on their individual connection to God. They entice their readers to believe that by performing specific acts or behaving according to a specific manner—usually an emotional one—they can affect the course of the world around them. These behaviors are deeply embedded in the emotions and the repetitive schema that they have developed to cultivate those emotions. Constructing God and humanity in his characteristic ways through a repetitive formulation of how to read scripture is the foundation for healing that results in a type of behavior for being in the world.

Sentimentality is an important part of how these evangelicals create an authoritative relationship with their readers. This emotional worldview also gives these ministers the authority to speak out about political issues from a position where they can denounce political involvement. Because they have sentimentalized the role of the pastor, they can cognitively distance themselves from the political process while being firmly entrenched in it. In so doing, they distance themselves from a process that usually involves a different emotional tenor. The political realm is usually the realm not of sentiment but of fear.

The Politics of Fear and the Power of Sentiment

In his book *Religion of Fear,* religious studies scholar Jason Bivins traced the interconnections between the use of fear tactics and the political aspirations of American evangelicalism.[60] He mapped out how intricately conservative evangelicals have tied themselves to a culture and worldview that attempts to use fear both as a motivator for conversion and as a political outlook meant to motivate the faithful to rally around specific political causes. Although he noted that not all evangelicals tap into this religion of fear, Bivins observed that within politically engaged, conservative evangelicalism there is an intense fascination with describing evil and lewdness in the utmost detail and a horror that such things will spring up in the minds of the faithful. For these evangelicals, popular culture is awash in symbols that will taint the soul and must be avoided. And they will explicitly describe what those evils are to frighten believer and nonbeliever alike.[61]

One example Bivins used to demonstrate the combination of evangelicalism and fear is Chick tracts. These small, comic strip-style mini-brochures combine often heavily stylized artwork with text meant to be evangelistic. The artwork is usually lurid and demonstrates an elevated fascination with violence or morbidity. Jack T. Chick, the recluse inventor of Chick tracts, started publishing his gospel in 1961, with his first tract appearing in 1964. Since then, many individuals and churches have purchased and distributed the tracts in telephone booths, at nightclubs, on cars, and after parades. The website boasts the sale of over 700 million tracts in English.[62]

With titles like "The Sissy?," "The Death Cookie," and "Who Murdered Clarice?" it is not surprising that scholars have focused on the violence and religious intolerance of Jack Chick and his gospel tracts. The stories quite often read as evangelical noir, while the illustrations are often graphic, especially in terms of violence. In "Somebody Loves Me," for example, the beating of the child is horrendously graphic, even though it is seen from behind and little actual detail of the abused child is seen. The father uses a large piece of wood and beats the child several times. In the next panel, the father stands over the child's body, and some sort of liquid, most likely blood, is dripping off of the wood he used. The next panel shows the child's bruised and broken body.[63]

Religious intolerance is another staple of the Chick tracts catalog. Chick often rails against nonevangelical religions through his medium, intending to prove that they are false and evangelical Christianity is true. Catholicism is one of Chick's favorite targets, although he has written tracks against Mormonism, Islam, Hinduism, and Buddhism. In his attacks on Catholicism, for example, Chick questions whether they are Christians, blames them for the Holocaust, condemns Christians who fellowship with Catholics, and makes light of Catholic doctrines like transubstantiation, the belief that the elements of the Eucharist become the body and blood of Christ. Yet religious intolerance and graphic depictions of violence are not all there is to a Chick tract. Underlying Chick's religion of fear is evangelical sentimentality.[64]

The Chick tract "The Present" combines Chick's penchant for violence and fear with evangelical sentiment.[65] It opens with a story about a king who lived in the sky. This king had one son whom he loved very much and wanted everyone else to love the son as well. One day the king tells his son to invite everyone he can find to come live in the castle with them. When the son goes to the people, they are suspicious. Although the son tells the people that the king has "a *wonderful* present" for them, the people believe he is lying and they kill the son.[66] When the king hears what has happened, he is greatly angered.

The townspeople had rejected his gift and killed his son. So the king attacks the town and kills everyone in it. The tract transitions from this parable to a different section by asserting the veracity of the second part of the tract and asking the reader to continue reading to learn about "a wonderful present" available for the reader.[67]

The second part of the tract is the story of Jesus. The parable at the beginning is simply an allegory for the story of how Jesus became human to die for humanity's sins. In one panel an amorphous light—representing God the Father—tells Jesus that those accept Jesus will "live with us in heaven FOREVER!"[68] This is God's "present" for human beings.[69] The people who Jesus goes to—who are never explicitly identified as Jews—reject him and crucify him. Among the last panels of the tract, the reader learns that those who do not follow Jesus and reject "His wonderful present" will be sentenced to eternal hellfire.[70] On the other hand, "those who receive God's present" will live forever in heaven with God and Jesus.[71] The tract concludes with telling readers how to get God's present by saying a specific prayer and noting that "the most wonderful present in the universe" is available for the reader immediately if the reader will simply accept it.[72]

Jack Chick relies on fear, violence, stereotypes, and prejudices to convey his message. Yet at the core, parts of that message come from sentimental evangelical thought. Calling salvation God's present or using a comic tract to tell readers that someone loves them demonstrates that even in the most deplorable presentations of evangelicalism there is a sentimental heart. Chick may or may not explicitly detest sentimentality—and a majority of his tracts suggest this might be the case—but he relies on it consciously or unconsciously because of how much it has infiltrated how evangelicals understand God and the world around them.

Another example of the politics of religious fear for Bivins is the *Left Behind* series of novels. The *Left Behind* series is an example of contemporary approaches to a literal interpretation of the Bible and dispensational premillennialism, a belief that history was divided into distinct periods and that the world was soon coming to an end. Over the course of 16 novels, Tim LaHaye and Jerry Jenkins create a narrative of their view of what it might be like on Earth in the last days. Believing that biblical books like Ezekiel, Daniel, and Revelation provide a plan and timeline for the arrival of the end times, LaHaye and Jenkins tell a story of the Rapture of all the faithful Christians from the earth, the onset of a period of trouble known as the Great Tribulation, the rise of a world leader called the Antichrist, and the final battle between good and evil, Armageddon, which culminates in the return of Jesus.

Though similar tales have been and continue to be told by others, LaHaye and Jenkins achieved great success with the *Left Behind* series, selling several million copies of each book in the series as well as making the bestseller lists of many newspapers and magazines. Whatever else can be said about *Left Behind*, a large audience has read these books.

When scholars have looked at *Left Behind*, though, they have tended to focus on the reception of the books, the concessions made in transforming the books to movies, and the political framework that the authors use to map out the apocalypse. It becomes apparent in their studies that readers of the series approach the books through social networks and cultures that shape their thinking about apocalyptic literature in general. It is also evident that evangelicals often make challenging decisions about how overtly proselytizing they should be in creating media for consumption by evangelicals and non-evangelicals alike. Finally, scholars have shown that the authors can strongly critique American culture while encouraging and legitimizing violence, as long as it is violence that takes places somewhere in the future.[73]

While these analyses provide great insight into what motivates evangelicals to create and read apocalyptic fiction, sentimentality is downplayed. In her discussion of *Left Behind* Amy Johnson Frykohlm examined the complicated ideologies about gender that are at work in the series and connected Rapture fiction and Victorian culture, ideologies that are connected to the themes of evangelical sentimentality we have been examining. She noted that the use of images of female piety are the stock themes in trade for Rapture fiction—the raptured church as the *bride of Christ*; the raptured wife versus the left behind husband; the home as the realm of the feminine. She spent little time exploring these tropes in *Left Behind*, however, preferring instead to look at how gender relations in dispensational fundamentalism inform both the characters of the novels and the readers who interpret them. Bivins also picked up on Frykohlm's analysis and interwove the use of gender in the novels with other ideas of gender that LaHaye has conveyed in other writings.[74]

Yet the depictions of gender in *Left Behind* reveal the ways sentimentality informs the evangelical worldview, even in militaristic, violent constructions of religiosity. As Bivins pointed out, the trope of the pious woman and worldly husband appears in the relationship of airplane pilot and main character Rayford Steele and his wife, Irene. Rayford is a nominal Christian contemplating an affair when the Rapture occurs. After hearing about the disappearance of large numbers of people, Rayford realizes what has probably happened and knows that Irene is among those who have disappeared. Irene is presented as a virtuous woman who was the spiritual leader of her household.

She tries to convince her family (including the two children, college-aged Chloe and preteen Ray Jr.) of the truth of her faith, but she makes an impact only on Ray Jr. The virtuous wife is taken to heaven; the adulterous husband is left behind.[75]

Gender depictions are not the only ways sentimentality affects the thought of *Left Behind*. Some women are pictured as particularly pious, but so are children. Like other authors we have seen, LaHaye and Jenkins encourage childlike faith. After Rayford prayed along with a videotaped message and achieves salvation, he wanted to continue praying: "He knew he was forgiven, but in a childlike way, he wanted God to know that he knew what kind of a person he had been."[76] The childlike faith of Ray Jr. is also emphasized—he also was raptured. The clearest sign that the authors believe in the spiritual superiority of children is what happens to young children and infants during the Rapture:

"Mr. Williams," she sobbed, "you know we lost several old people, but not all of them. And we lost several middle-aged people, but not all of them. And we lost several people your age and my age, but not all of them. We even lost some teenagers." He stared at her. What was she driving at? "Sir, we lost every child and baby on this plane." "How many were there?" "More than a dozen. But all of them! Not one was left."[77]

This scene, which takes place on an aircraft, is repeated in several chapters and in several regions of post-Rapture Earth. Several times in the novel, characters remark that children are taken in the Rapture. In addition, even unborn children are taken. Women who were pregnant before the Rapture are not pregnant after it. In one scene Rayford watches a CNN broadcast of a pregnancy home video: "CNN reran the footage in superslow motion, showing the woman going from very pregnant to nearly flat stomached, as if she had instantaneously delivered."[78] The reason for the disappearance is made clear in an "in-case-of-Rapture" video that Rayford watches. The pastor on the video—who has been raptured as well—tells his audience, "Up to a certain age, which is probably different for each individual, we believe God will not hold a child accountable for a decision that must be made with heart and mind, fully cognizant of the ramifications."[79] The pastor goes on to note that unborn children will probably disappear as well, stating, "I can only imagine the pain and heartache of a world without precious children."[80] In another place children are referred to as innocents. Children, being unable to sin, are raptured with the Christians.[81]

Chapter 3 discussed how sentimental conceptions of children became a part of evangelicalism in the nineteenth century. Even though the rapture of children is a minor detail of the overall plotline of the *Left Behind* series, it is evidence of how evangelicals have internalized sentimental conceptions that have retained potency even through fundamentalism and dispensational premillennialism. Although the political aspects are most apparent because they are foregrounded, sentimentality is foundational to certain parts of the evangelical worldview.

The endorsement of childlike and feminine spirituality further demonstrates the importance of the domestic sphere to LaHaye and Jenkins. Much like views of nineteenth-century evangelicals, the world of LaHaye and Jenkins is bifurcated into two spheres. Irene and Ray Jr.—who Rayford had thought of as a "mama's boy" and as "too compassionate, too sensitive, too caring"— inhabit the private or domestic sphere.[82] This sphere is where the mother exerts spiritual influence, primarily over the not quite "effeminate" son.[83] The inhabitants of this sphere are the spiritual giants of the family, the ones who disappear in the Rapture. Rayford and Chloe—who takes after Rayford more than Irene—primarily live in the public sphere and retreat from the domestic sphere as much as possible. Because they spend most of their time in the public sphere, they are open to worldly influences. Rayford ponders having an affair while his wife and son are being raptured. He also has issues with alcohol. After the Rapture he reminisces about getting drunk at a holiday party. Chloe too has gotten drunk before and attends a non-Christian university, Stanford. The "masculine" characters of Rayford and Chloe are left behind when the "feminine" characters Irene and Ray Jr. are taken to heaven.[84]

The destruction of the domestic sphere in the Rapture awakens Rayford to his condition before God. The loss of his wife and son causes him to realize the truth of their religious worldview. The items he finds at his home that confirm their disappearance are intricately attached to the domestic sphere. He finds pajamas and a nightgown, a locket with his picture in it, and Irene's wedding ring; these items reinforce that the Rapture had indeed occurred. The damage done to his family causes Rayford to realize his sinful state: "Losing his wife and child made him realize what a vapid relationship he had been pursuing with a twenty-seven-year-old woman....He felt guilty for having considered it."[85] The loss of his family also motivates Rayford to study the Bible—he wants to be able to share heaven with them. It is true that his daughter is left behind as well, but that further evidences the destruction of the domestic sphere. Because Rayford and Chloe are similar in attitude and temperament, they had withdrawn from the domestic sphere, and now that it is gone Rayford wants both of them to try to reestablish it. Through reconnecting with his daughter and convincing her about the truth of evangelical Christianity, Rayford hopes to recover a semblance of what was lost.[86]

To reestablish the domestic sphere, Rayford turns to Irene's evangelical faith. Since the Rapture had occurred, Irene must have been right, especially since she had been raptured as well. Rayford decides that he wants to find what she had found. In these depictions of salvation, aspects of evangelical sentimentality feature prominently. LaHaye and Jenkins attempt to divert questions about the tension between God's goodness and the doctrine of the Rapture to affirm that God is loving and kind and wants a relationship with human beings. When Rayford confronts his daughter with his theory that people disappeared in the Rapture, Chloe is upset: "Daddy, what does this make God? Some sick, sadistic dictator?"[87] Rayford asks Chloe to consider the possibility that he is right. She responds, "Then God is spiteful, hateful, mean. Who wants to go to heaven with a God like that?"[88] Rayford asserts that he does, if that is where his wife and son are. Chloe retorts:

> I want to be with them, too, Daddy! But tell me how this fits with a loving, merciful God. When I went to church, I got tired of hearing how loving God is. He never answered *my* prayers and I never felt like he knew me or cared about me. Now you're saying I was right. He didn't. I didn't qualify, so I got left behind? You'd better hope you're not right.[89]

Rayford has no answer at the time, but he is convinced of the truth of the Rapture.

Chloe's assertion that the Rapture would suggest a sadistic God is a perceived objection that LaHaye and Jenkins are trying to head off. Their response is that God is a loving and forgiving God. He loves human beings and wants to have a relationship with them. In fact, for LaHaye and Jenkins, the Rapture is not an expression of God's sadism but of God's love:

> Strange as this may sound to you, this is God's final effort to get the attention of every person who has ignored or rejected him. He is allowing now a vast period of trial and tribulation to come to you who remain. He has removed his church from a corrupt world that seeks its own way, its own pleasures, its own ends. I believe God's purpose in this is to allow those who remain to take stock of themselves and leave

their frantic search for pleasure and self-fulfillment, and turn to the Bible for truth and to Christ for salvation.[90]

Because fear and violence are the primary motifs of the *Left Behind* series, it is easy to overlook the sentimental aspects of the evangelicalism presented here. It is also not as pronounced as in the writings of the ministers we have been examining, but it is present as something that forms the foundation for the ideology of *Left Behind*. The fear and the violence serve as a warning of what LaHaye and Jenkins believe is coming for non-Christians, but the threat of fearful, violent times is meant to motivate people to seriously consider becoming a child of God because they believe the primary way God interacts with human beings is through loving ways. The fear and violence of *Left Behind* is intricately connected to an evangelical core of sentiment.

In pointing to the presence of sentimentality in Chick tracts and *Left Behind*, we should not discount the presence or appeal of what Bivins calls the religion of fear. It is evident, however, that its presence does not negate a *religion of sentiment* or vice versa. As revealed by Chick tracts and *Left Behind*, evangelicals who participate in religion of fear tactics see what they are doing partly as expressions of God's love. They believe that if individuals will not respond to direct exclamations of God's love, then fear is a good motivator to drive people to God's love. LaHaye and Jenkins, for example, think that the Rapture and the Tribulation are expressions of God's love. Fear and violence are a wake-up call to non-Christians that God loves them so much that he will use any means necessary to get their attention and their love. A sentimental view of the world in the case of the Chick tracts and *Left Behind* provides justification for a politics of fear. The authority for using fear is the belief that it will drive people to accept God's love. Despite the obvious paradox, the violence and hatred are conceptualized as intricately connected to sentimentality. Sentimentality provides the authority to engage in fearful rhetoric and practices because the fear serves higher purposes.

The Sentimentalizing of Evangelical Social Action

Many of the sentimentally constructed issues that are important to evangelicals are deeply connected to understandings of what constitutes a Christian domestic sphere. Evangelicals interpret abortion, same-sex marriage, and school choice—a voucher program to fund private or religious schooling with taxpayer funds—through their understandings about the power and sanctity of the domestic sphere and what they believe the home represents to society. So evangelicals create *attack on the family* rhetoric and use sentimentality and fear as forces to construct boundaries between the home and the so-called world. Victorian culture and sentiment have influenced evangelicals theologically and ecclessiologically, but they have also impacted the means and motivation for being involved in the world around them.[91]

There are two main ideologies behind the evangelical opposition to abortion: the sanctity of human life and the holiness of children. In his 1988 encounter with Robertson's burgeoning presidential campaign, historian Randall Balmer mused that conservative evangelicals rallied around antiabortion politics because of their symbolic identification with the "alienation and vulnerability" of a human fetus.[92] In other words, evangelicals felt alienated and vulnerable in American culture and attached themselves to an image that resonated with their feelings of displacement—an unborn fetus under attack by "pro-abortionists." While this is an insightful examination of symbolic identification, Balmer overlooked the important conceptual role children have had in evangelicalism. He noted appropriately the power of Victorian notions of domesticity and feminine piety in modern evangelicalism but ignored the Victorian spiritual ideal of the child that was just as important. Antiabortion evangelicals are adamant to point out that the unborn fetus is a child, that is, a human life. As discussed previously, the angelic image of the child as spiritual guide and the desire to preserve or protect this image have been important parts of evangelicalism since the middle of the nineteenth century. This mind-set, that children are innocents, still forms the foundation for how evangelicals conceive of children, even unborn ones.[93]

Opposition to same-sex marriages comes from a similar sentimental ideology. Victorian domesticity and imagined godly family life of the past help construct a vision of marriage that evangelicals are trying to defend. *Sanctity of marriage* or *destruction of marriage* rhetoric that evangelicals use to protest same sex-marriage relies on a belief in the role that the domestic sphere—the *home*—should play in society. In this way of thinking, the home is the backbone of civilization. It is believed that as the home goes, so goes society. If the home (marriage) is destroyed, as these evangelicals believe that the acceptance of same-sex marriage will do, the destruction of society will not be far behind. Furthermore, those who are against same-sex marriage rely on the bifurcated role archetype from the nineteenth century. They believe that it is necessary for the home to have both a mother and a father because mothers and fathers have different roles in creating a stable domestic sphere. While the roles and spheres of mothers and fathers have changed since the nineteenth century, the idea that each gender must fulfill its roles to maintain the home and society is still a part of evangelical domestic ideology. Closely aligned with this is a fear about what will happen to children in same-sex households. Selectively using social scientific research, evangelicals like Dobson appeal to studies (questioned by scholars) that claim that children need both fathers and mothers in their lives to succeed. Evangelicals who listen to and respect Dobson and his organization thus cite these studies: mothers and fathers prepare children for adult life differently, and both are need to raise healthy, happy children to provide stability for subsequent generations.[94]

The same type of reasoning that leads evangelicals to protest abortion or vote against same-sex marriages forms the foundation for their support of school choice legislation, despite the question of whether it breaches the wall of separation between church and state by funding schools that are religious in nature. The theological or ideological question for why school choice is necessary, however, is a sentimental one, or at least rests on sentimental foundations. Just like abortion and same-sex marriage, those who support school choice are concerned about what their children might encounter in public school curricula, particularly issues evangelicals are opposed to like homosexuality or evolution. The rhetoric supporting school choice is two-pronged. First, there are the financial considerations. Advocates argue that funds to provide scholarships to private schools are not a governmental support of religion, nor do they take away from public school funding. Second, those who push for school choice contend that such options would give parents more control and force parents to be more involved in educating their children. Again, the rhetoric of the defense of domesticity is vital to the appeal for school choice. Advocates urge parents to "protect the hearts and minds" of their children. Homosexuals and evolutionary scientists become the enemy in this rhetoric. They present a danger to innocents who will abandon their parents' values because of the indoctrination the children will receive if there is no opportunity for parents to school their children according to their own values.[95]

The ways evangelicals engage in social and political action demonstrate the importance of sentimentality—especially nostalgia and domesticity—in understanding evangelicalism. Evangelicals rely on certain sentimental tropes to conceptualize the world and their participation in it. This understanding of the home and the domestic sphere both motivate and validate certain political and social activities. Abstracting sentimentality and focusing only on evangelical belief or evangelical political rhetoric gives just part of the picture of evangelicalism and ignores how sentimentality flows through all aspects of evangelicalism and continues to be reproduced and instantiated within the movement.[96]

An excellent example of how emotionality and social conceptions work together in the context of evangelicalism is the August 1, 2012, Chick-fil-A Day. This quick-service restaurant predominantly sells chicken sandwiches, chicken biscuits, and chicken nuggets. It also claims to use biblically based principles for business and to "glorify God by being a faithful steward of all that is entrusted to us and to have a positive influence on all who come into contact with Chick-fil-A."[97] This commitment to biblically based principles drew public attention in July 2012 when chief operating officer Dan Cathy, son of Chick-fil-A founder Truett Cathy, gave an interview to the *Biblical Recorder,* a Christian newspaper. The piece is predominantly focused on how Chick-fil-A incorporates biblical principles into its corporate policy, including being closed on Sunday, but it also covers Chick-fil-A's financial support of college football conferences like the Atlantic Coast Conference and the Southeastern Conference through sponsoring scholarships, football games, and universities. At the end of the article, however, is the comment that ignited a media firestorm. When asked whether Chick-fil-A as a company supports the "traditional" family, Cathy responded, "Well, guilty as charged."[98]

In the aftermath of Cathy's comments, there was an outcry from a variety of arenas including several politicians against Chick-fil-A's apparent antigay sentiments. Other individuals were vocal about their support for Chick-fil-A and Cathy's position on traditional marriage. When mayors of several cities noted that they did not want Chick-fil-A stores in their cities and claimed that they would work against their presence, former governor, Fox News commentator, and Southern Baptist minister Mike Huckabee organized a Support Chick-fil-A day. He encouraged individuals who supported Dan Cathy's position to show up to Chick-fil-A on August 1, 2012. Huckabee's grassroots initiative was successful. Although the Chick-fil-A corporation did not take an official position on Chick-fil-A day, they certainly benefited from it, boasting long lines and record sales.[99]

Many who showed up to patronize Chick-fil-A or who offered vocal support for Cathy's position claimed that they were concerned about the first amendment issues involved in Cathy's comments and the backlash from them. It was about freedom of expression and religion against those who would try to silence such voices. While these issues might have been used to encourage individuals to come out and buy chicken, it was specifically the freedom of expressing certain views about the domestic sphere that motivated such a response. Although it might be foolish to speculate on counterfactual history, in our context one cannot help but wonder what other issues would have garnered such an extraordinary response. It does not appear that evangelicals are mobilized to such an extent either to support or protest a cause when it is not related to the sentimental tropes we have been examining. While evangelicals can be very active in social causes, what appears to motivate them to be active is sentimentality or efforts connected to evangelical sentimentality.

The combination of sentiment and conservative politics has important consequences for gender rhetoric and gender roles. In the selection of abortion, same-sex marriage, and school choice as indicative political identifiers, evangelicals rely on the combination of sentiment and fear to police gender roles. In this worldview, the use of fear creates a boundary between the sentimental domestic sphere and the world and attempts to trap women within that boundary. A virtuous woman, in this conception, is to maintain the home and remain in it, teaching the innocent children she has brought to full term. The sentimentalizing of children, feminine piety, and the home provides justification for homeschooling—with the mother expected to train the children in the sacred home. Sentimentality and fear align to create a social world ordered by evangelical principles that is also extremely fragile because of the cultural forces of chaos that wait outside the boundaries. Without fear this boundary would not exist; without sentimentality there would be no need for this type of boundary.[100]

Many evangelicals are engaged members of society and are active in their communities. Not all of the causes that galvanize evangelicals are necessarily sentimental in nature, but in the past several decades the issues that have motivated widespread action from evangelicals across the United States have been cast in sentimental tones or have drawn on sentimental tropes. This appeal seems to be the most effective in garnering evangelical support.

Sentimentality and Speaking Truth to Power

We have considered thus far the power that sentimentality evokes in political issues and how evangelicals are often active on hot button issues connected to sentimental themes. Yet while sentimentality might provide justification for some sorts of political or social action, it also participates in the confusion of the unjust structures at work in other aspects of political life. Lucado, Warren, and Osteen have recently been more vocal about a variety of global issues that humans across the planet are facing, including poverty, the AIDS crisis in Africa, environmental issues, and the genocide in Darfur. However, their approach to answering these problems has relied on sentimental tropes that do not speak truth to power but instead offer platitudes about the changes individuals can make in shaping the world for God, or, as Lucado put it in a recent book, these are opportunities for individuals to "outlive your life."

Releasing the book *Outlive Your Life* marked Lucado's twenty-fifth year of publishing.[101] In many respects the purpose of this book was quite different from some of his other books. Using the biblical book of Acts, Lucado attempts to bring the issues of poverty, hunger, and exploitation to the attention of his audience. Throughout the pages of the book, he introduces his readers to individuals who have lost jobs, who live on very little funds, and who have experienced homelessness and to those who have devoted their lives to serving such people. It is a call to action, a call for his readers to demonstrate the same kind of devotion of serving those who are disadvantaged.

That call relies on the sentimental foundations that all of Lucado's books provide. Lucado and his readers are just "simple folks," but they too can make a difference in the lives of those who are disadvantaged.[102] The "missing ingredient for changing the world is teamwork," which he conceptualizes as the collective result of individual actions.[103] Lucado holds up ordinary individuals as the locus for great changes in the world in ridding the globe of poverty, hunger, and unequal wealth distribution. Common concern for helping others will override doctrinal differences. The key to activating such great changes is the compassion that a relationship with God and Jesus will inspire.[104]

Evangelicals with a sentimental outlook certainly do good deeds. Lucado and Warren especially appear to give sizable parts of their income either to their ministries or to charities. Lucado even donated 100 percent of his royalties of *Outlive Your Life* to "faith-based compassion ministries."[105] They speak for and support other organizations intent on relieving poverty, addressing the AIDS crisis in Africa, or distributing clean water and food to those who need it. Nor do they appear to be acting out of nefarious motives in these charitable endeavors. It seems that Lucado, Warren, and others are deeply concerned about these issues and not interested in just selling more books. Yet sentimentality has provided the way to discuss issues of inequality without challenging the structures that cause such inequality.

This lack of "speaking truth to power" is perhaps clearest in a chapter of *Outlive Your Life* titled "Blast a Few Walls." Lucado opens the chapter with a story about a high school football game between a Christian school and maximum-security correctional education facility. The athletes from Gainesville—the prison school—"wear seven-year-old shoulder pads and last decade's helmets and show up at each game wearing handcuffs."[106] The coach for the Christian school encouraged the team's fans to root for the Gainesville team and provide them support during the game. As a result, according to Lucado, "a squad of bigotry-demolition experts" blasted "bias into dust."[107] They broke down "barricades that separate God's children from each other."[108] Lucado goes on to give other examples of how Christians have "blasted" walls that separate people.[109]

While it is admirable that football fans were willing to root for the opposing team because the opposing team had no fans, Lucado certainly misses the opportunity to dig further into the issues surrounding the Gainesville State School. He does not mention that 44 percent of people incarcerated with the Texas Youth Commission—which includes Gainesville—are Hispanic, 34 percent are African American, and 93 percent are male. In addition, "72 percent had high or moderate need for alcohol or other drug treatment."[110] Over half of these individuals came from low-income homes. Here are issues of poverty, drugs, gender, race, and violence that go unaddressed. The structures that support such inequalities and the proliferation of violence and oppression are ignored in favor of valorizing a few fans who cheered at a football game and provided burgers afterward.[111]

Like Lucado, Warren in recent years has been active in bringing global issues to the attention of Americans, especially evangelicals. Warren's main focus has been on using what he calls the P.E.A.C.E. plan—an acronym for plant churches, equip leaders, assist the poor, care for the sick, and educate subsequent generations—to mobilize Christians across the world to address five global, "giant problems": "spiritual emptiness, self-centered leadership, poverty, disease, and illiteracy."[112] The main concern for Warren is how these giants have kept people around the world "from knowing the saving grace of a loving God who sent his son, Jesus Christ, to die for their sins allowing them eternal hope and security."[113] Warren also claims that human organizations are unable to rid the globe of these evils. The "only successful solution is the global Church of Jesus Christ."[114]

The P.E.A.C.E. plan represents the transition that evangelical social action is undergoing. The issues Warren is concerned about are not just abortion and same-sex marriage—the stereotypical concerns of evangelicals. Through the plan he and those working with him hope to also address issues like human trafficking. Such an outlook demonstrates the beginnings of a transition in evangelical social concern. Warren and others are starting to realize that there might be structural issues related to the problems they hope to address. One of Warren's evil giants, for example, is corrupt leadership. The P.E.A.C.E. plan's website also has several resources that suggest structural reasons for generational poverty: "cultures oppress women and families, intentionally keeping them from educational opportunities that illuminate a way out of poverty."[115]

Even as there is recognition of more than just individual choice at the heart of problems like poverty and illiteracy, there is still a reliance on sentimentality at the heart of motivation for evangelical social action, which limits the vision for transforming global society. The key for the success of the P.E.A.C.E. plan is not political activity. It is not national or global pressure for governments and nations to change their oppressive ways. Instead it is the sacralized power of the ordinary individual that sits at the core of the appeal to be a part of the P.E.A.C.E. plan. On the homepage, the visitor is told, "What if there was a way for ordinary people—people like you and me— to make an extraordinary connection and a lasting difference in the world? If you've ever imagined joining a movement of people dedicated to serving, but weren't sure who to contact or how to begin, start here. Welcome to the PEACE Plan—your portal to a world of difference. Enter, and discover just how powerful you can be."[116] On another page, the visitor learns that "God made you to fulfill a purpose. He has given you a calling and the capacity to answer it; He wants you to put your gifts into service. You CAN make a difference in someone else's life, community, and in the world."[117]

Sentimentality still provides the means for dismissing the power of those structures in the face of individual activity. For example, Warren sees "equipping servant leaders" as the answer to corrupt leadership.[118] Although it is certainly an important transition to see evangelicals active in global social issues, what we continue to see is both how prevalent sentimentality is in the evangelical political ethos and how sentimentality shapes the appropriate responses to those issues. The emphasis on individualism and the relational aspects of Christianity actively work against attacking the structural inequality present in systems of power, making the sentimental approach ineffective to creating real social change. Sentimentality provides the authority to be involved in politics, what constitutes appropriate issues to be political about, and the authority to ignore structural problems at work in inequitable situations.[119]

Furthermore, many evangelicals are still convinced that the interior experience—especially the individual's relationship with God—is more important than exterior conditions. Joyce Meyer in *Beauty for Ashes*, for example, asserts that "the Lord's main concern is our *inner* life, because that is where we enjoy His presence.... Our inner life with God is much more important than our outer life."[120] As long as evangelicals are consumed with this narcissistic focus on the individual and the individual's conversion as the primary—or sole—means to transform society, it is unlikely that they will be largely successful in transforming corrupt world governments into the kingdom of God.

Conclusion

For the past three decades scholars and others have been interested in the political impact evangelicalism could and should make on American culture. Whether those interests have been supportive of or concerned about evangelical political engagement, most of the attention has focused on the intellectual justification for political activity or specific political positions or the intellectual ways evangelicals have intellectually united themselves to the Republican party. Moving beyond the intellect, however, provides a different perspective. The emotional, especially the sentimental, is a vital component of evangelical politics.

Jason Bivins and others have focused on the importance of fear in evangelical politics, but the sentimental is just as (if not more than) important in understanding the aesthetics of evangelicalism and the political implications of those aesthetics. The sentimental provides the foundation for delineating not only what issues evangelicals should be concerned about but also the appropriate responses to those issues. Certainly for particular individuals or organizations we could imaginatively plot a continuum of emotionality where different "ratios" of fear and sentimentality are mixed where some groups would be more apt to emphasize fear while others would be ready to emphasize love, family, or nostalgia. In any case, at the core of evangelicalism are those tropes that provide meaning and perspective for evangelicals to encounter the world even in the context of politics.

To ignore the emotional and focus solely on the intellectual, however, does not provide us with a complete picture of evangelical political success. As Christian Smith and others have shown, many evangelicals (perhaps even most) and many evangelical leaders present themselves as disinterested in reshaping American life into a theocratic utopia. Yet evangelicals in recent years have been responsible for the success of the election of political candidates and the passage of certain pieces of legislation. This incongruity cannot be explained through an appeal to evangelical beliefs but can be understood through an examination of evangelical emotional appeal. Because of their reliance on sentimentality, Max Lucado, Rick Warren, Joel Osteen and others can say they are pastors and not politicians and then preach or write against what they see are the problems in global and American society and conceptualize them as problems with spiritual, or more accurately emotional, solutions.

Certainly throughout their history, even recently, evangelicals have been mobilized in great numbers to effect change in American society. Sentimentality has often been the mode of appeal that has been successful in this organizing in the recent past. Yet evangelicalism's reliance on narcissistic appeals seems unlikely to be a long-term strategy to mobilize evangelicals for extensive social change. Sentimentality is not at issue here but instead how it has been intertwined with a therapeutic culture of narcissism that works against collective action. Sentimentality, on the other hand, works to conceal the structures of power at work in social issues and thus provides evangelicals with the assumption that issues like poverty, racism, slavery, and oppression have simplistic solutions. Because evangelicals have so widely adopted this melding of sentimentality and narcissism, they face difficult challenges in shaping this world into the kingdom of God.

CONCLUSION

CURE FOR THE COMMON HISTORIOGRAPHY: THE FUTURE OF EVANGELICALISM AND EVANGELICAL STUDIES

In May 2008 a group of evangelicals released "An Evangelical Manifesto: A Declaration of Evangelical Identity and Public Commitment."[1] They claimed that it was an attempt to redefine what it means to be "Evangelical"—with intentional capitalization—and to decry the politicization of evangelicalism in recent years. Arguing that they should be defined by their theology and not in cultural or social ways, Evangelicals offered seven beliefs that marked them as distinctive from other Christians, among them the dual nature of Christ as divine and human, the importance of the crucifixion for salvation, the transformation and new birth that comes from the Holy Spirit, the veracity and authority of the Christian Bible, and the hope of the Second Coming. In addition to these five beliefs, the manifesto noted that Evangelicals believe that they should be involved in both social and ecclesiastical spheres, particularly with the socially disadvantaged, and should be environmentally conscious. Evangelicals should also "know and love Christ through worship, love Christ's family through fellowship, grow like Christ through discipleship, serve Christ by ministering to the needs of others in his name, and share Christ with those who do not yet know him."[2]

The authors aimed the document at several different audiences. Although they wrote that they were speaking only for themselves, they wanted others to agree to their description of who evangelicals are and how evangelicals should be involved in the political arena. Fellow Americans were asked to read the document and be active in "restoring liberty and civility in public life."[3] Additionally, the writers addressed those who belonged to other religions, claiming that these Evangelicals would work for their liberty and rights in the United States and asking that the peoples of other faiths work for the liberty and rights of evangelicals in other countries. They called on those in power to recognize that they had given their allegiance to God first, which meant that they were answerable to God and God's standards before the standards of any particular country. Any who were concerned about the oppressed were encouraged to work with them in common cause. They appealed to spiritual seekers to consider the evangelical gospel. Finally, they pled with "scholars, journalists, and public policy makers" to "abandon stereotypes and adopt definitions and categories in describing us and other believers in terms that are both accurate and fair, and with a tone that you in turn would like to be applied to yourselves."[4] The document was written by the nine-person Evangelical Manifesto Steering Committee, which included businessmen, theologians, the editor-in-chief of the *Christianity Today* Media Group, and author Os Guinness. The manifesto was signed by a group of charter signatories, among them clergy, the president of Dollar General, theologians, academics, the publisher of *Forbes* magazine, a filmmaker, and Max Lucado.[5]

In juxtaposing "An Evangelical Manifesto" with what we have investigated, it becomes obvious that some evangelicals are concerned about the direction of contemporary evangelicalism. They appear to nostalgically long for the revival of a rational, broadly engaged religion like nineteenth-century evangelicalism. Modern evangelicalism in their view has capitulated to American culture and thus has committed a variety of "sins." Ironically, several of these sins are the very aspects of evangelicalism we have explored. Therapeutic evangelicalism—and the marketing of it—along with anti-intellectualism and a politicized faith are the target of the Evangelicals behind the manifesto.

Max Lucado, Joel Osteen, Rick Warren, and others are at the pinnacle of a centuries-long development of the confluence of several trends in evangelicalism. They represent developments that predate the nineteenth-century evangelicalism some so highly prize. For example, since the eighteenth century evangelicals have embraced the market as an avenue for their message. Some evangelicals have been very astute in how they have exploited the market and its tools; others have been hesitant to involve themselves in commercializing evangelicalism. Evangelicalism has changed and shifted with these cultural and commercial forces since its beginning. In fact, Christians have always modified their thought and the presentation of that thought in response to audiences and the intellectual currents of their day from the time of Paul. Evangelicals are no different.

In the nineteenth century, it was sentimentality that appealed to many evangelical ministers and authors—though certainly not all. Sisters Catherine and Harriet Beecher and Horace Bushnell may be among the most famous of sentimental authors and ministers of the middle of the nineteenth century; however, they were not the only ones, nor did the influence of sentimentality in evangelicalism end there. The appeal to sentiment became a part of evangelical rhetoric and practice.

The sentimentality that contemporary evangelicals draw on became an important part of conservative evangelical thought with the rise of biblical criticism and Darwinism. These challenges to both scripture and evangelicalism led evangelicals to two approaches. On one hand, there were theologians and ministers who returned the challenge of biblical criticism with a position of scriptural inerrancy and literalism. They denounced higher criticism as un-Christian and deceptive. They held to traditional ideas about the composition and authorship of the biblical books. They developed a fortress mentality when it came to Christianity that eventually led to a retreat from American public life, which they viewed as harmful to Christians. The other type of thought embraced sentimentality, which became a way to avoid the challenges of biblical criticism and Charles Darwin. Revivalists like Dwight Moody appealed to individuals through sentiment, not intellect. Through narratives meant to produce certain types of emotion, Moody became a very successful minister and set a pattern for others to follow. Ministers and authors today who appeal to sentiment and experience also sidestep the intellectual challenges that evangelicalism still faces. Where the Evangelicals of the manifesto see sins, we have seen a very important strand of evangelicalism that provides meaning for a large group—perhaps even a majority—of ordinary evangelicals.

Therapeutic Culture

The historical and cultural changes of the twentieth century increased the presence of sentimentality and combined it with a therapeutic concern about individual psychological well-being. The mixture of Scottish Common Sense, sentimental romanticism, and therapeutic culture nurtured an evangelicalism heavily marked by narcissism and the cult of personality. Charismatic leaders with an individual gospel centralized the message of Christianity in God's desperate desire for a relationship with each particular human being. In these messages, God's overwhelming concern appears to be the happiness of individuals, despite a countermessage that "it's not about you." Some of these charismatic leaders have joined their sentimental message with market acumen to create dominance in Christian and general retail bookstores and to craft media empires built on definable brand qualities.

This therapeutic evangelicalism draws the ire of the Evangelicals of the manifesto because they believe it adulterates the evangelical message. In a section titled "We Must Reform Our Own Behavior," the authors write:

> All too often we have trumpeted the gospel of Jesus, but we have replaced biblical truths with therapeutic techniques, worship with entertainment, discipleship with growth in human potential, church growth with business entrepreneurialism, concern for the church and for the local congregation with expressions of the faith that are church-less and little better than a vapid spirituality, meeting real needs with pandering to felt needs, and mission principles with marketing precepts. In the process we have become known for commercial, diluted, and feel-good gospels of health, wealth, human potential, and religious happy talk, each of which is indistinguishable from the passing fashions of the surrounding world.[6]

The polarities they set out in this confession of evangelical sins are intertwined in evangelicalism, some for a very long time. While the separation of biblical truths from therapeutic techniques and mission principles from marketing precepts may seem like an attainable goal for these Evangelicals, the conjoining of these approaches is part of the reason evangelicalism has been so successful in the United States. It is unlikely that this situation will change.

It is also doubtful that most evangelicals would like to see such changes. Since its inception, the evangelical movement has been a diverse one. It has found success across ethnic, racial, and national barriers. It has encompassed people of a variety of political positions. It has bypassed denominational barriers. It has even held in tension a rational strand and an emotional one. Although evangelicals have often lauded one of these strands while deprecating or ignoring the other, both have played important roles in the development of this movement. In the twentieth and twenty-first centuries, however, many evangelicals have demonstrated an overwhelming preference for the emotional strand with relatively few preferring the rational one.

The irony is that Scottish Common Sense philosophy provided the ideological foundation for the development of both strands. Providing a method for approaching the natural world and the Bible, it emphasized the importance not only of facts and a methodological approach to discovering truth that evangelicals adopted but also of the emotions to encourage individuals to engage in moral behaviors and to develop moral habits. As we have seen, this focus on the motivational powers of emotion integrated a romantic worldview and fostered sentimentality as the primary means of emotional appeal.

While the Evangelicals of the manifesto might deprecate the therapeutic strand in their movement, it is a source of comfort and vitality to many other evangelicals. People turn to ministers like Lucado, Warren, or Osteen because they are struggling with a variety of problems. Therapeutic evangelicals offer them healing that they do not find in the outside world. Instead of seeing such literature as "indistinguishable from the passing fashions of the surrounding world," many probably turn to therapeutic evangelicalism because they want religious answers to their psychological, emotional, physical, and spiritual problems. They see it not as "religious happy talk" but as a reminder that God cares for and wants to help them. We can certainly see how therapeutic evangelicalism can be conceptualized as a comprehensive approach to life: if God is a loving God and cares about human beings, would he not want them to have positive, fulfilled, psychologically stable lives?

The therapeutic turn of evangelicalism does not necessarily mean that evangelicals are more interested in therapeutic concerns or that they are more narcissistic than other citizens of the United States. Instead, it demonstrates how American culture has shaped contemporary evangelicalism. Therapeutic evangelicalism is the culmination of the fusion of sentimentality and the self-help culture of the United States. This has led evangelicalism down a path evangelicals did not intend but has climaxed in a popular but narcissistic approach that focuses on the individual's concerns as God's primary interest.

Anti-Intellectualism

The therapeutic concern with psychological well-being serves for the Evangelicals as a symptom of larger anti-intellectual impulse within evangelicalism. God called these Evangelicals to love him with their minds as well as their hearts and souls, but too often many had relied on "an unbecoming anti-intellectualism" that the authors saw as sinful.[7] Such rhetoric displays that these Evangelicals believe other evangelicals have made the movement appear moronic or unsophisticated in the public sphere. They do not specify a particular group of individuals, but they are particularly disgusted with how some evangelicals have approached science: "some among us have betrayed the strong Christian tradition of a high view of science, epitomized in the very matrix of ideas that gave birth to modern science, and made themselves vulnerable to caricatures of the false hostility between science and faith."[8]

Yet in their critique of anti-intellectualism, the authors are essentially pitting the two strands of evangelicalism—emotionality and rationality—against each other, with their obvious preference for the latter. Because of this preference for rational evangelicalism in the manifesto, Lucado is an ironic promoter for its agenda. As we have seen throughout, the ministry and works of Lucado and others like him manifest a primary component of popular contemporary evangelicalism. As best-selling ministers, they represent both the therapeutic evangelicalism and the anti-intellectualism that the Evangelicals rail against. They want belief and doctrine, instead of feelings, at the core of evangelicalism. In their minds, definite beliefs comprise evangelicalism, and subscribing to these beliefs is the sine qua non of what it means to be evangelical.

Yet belief is a very fluid category in the works of inspirational ministers like Lucado. While they promote some concrete beliefs—Jesus as God's son, the reality of hell—they downplay the importance of doctrine in favor of emotional expressions and relationships. Lucado's evangelicalism is less about intellectual construction of doctrine than it is the management of sentiment. Because evangelicals have been unable to convince nonevangelicals that their view of the world is valid, they have turned to the emotions and experience for legitimacy.

Both rational evangelicals and sentimental evangelicals employ their particular approaches to bring about unity, especially Christian unity, but each has staked a claim on what such Christianity should represent. For rational evangelicals it is unity based on a shared set of doctrines. Sentimental evangelicals—especially those we have been examining—depend on the audience not intellectually investigating their claims and views. Because they promote an affective evangelicalism and attempt to create an ecumenism based on sentiment, their vision of evangelicalism essentially operates counter to the cerebral evangelicalism the Evangelical Manifesto Steering Committee endorses. Christian unity for sentimentalists is found in common emotional experience. Even where sentimentalists like Lucado might support a rationalistic, belief-centered religion, this aspect of their ideology is subsumed to the emotionality. Although they might agree with doctrines about the nature of Christ, the truthfulness of the Bible, and the necessity of the new birth, these beliefs are either assumed or deployed for therapeutic, emotional ends. Doctrine is secondary to experience. In the end, the rationalists are correct about one aspect of sentimentality; it does foster—and count on—the anti-intellectualism of evangelicalism.

Yet the charge of anti-intellectualism that the Manifesto Committee chooses to level against others is problematic. As we observed in Chapter 2, anti-intellectualism has been a part of evangelicalism since the late nineteenth century. The Evangelicals of "An Evangelical Manifesto" appear to want a reunion between Christianity and science because the separation has "unwittingly given comfort to the unbridled scientism and naturalism that are so rampant in our culture."[9] Such language makes me wonder what kind of reunion they desire. Do these Evangelicals accept evolution—which some do? Are they taking a position similar to liberal Protestants in the nineteenth century that saw evolution as God's mechanism for creation? Or do they want to recast modern science into resurgent Baconianism in an attempt to give scientific validity to creationism or intelligent design? The appeal to "the very matrix of ideas that gave birth to modern science" seems to be a veiled reference to Bacon's approach to nature and scripture.[10] It is apparent, then, that the attempt to disparage those who "have betrayed the strong Christian tradition of a high view of science" is really to affirm that evangelicals are intellectuals when it comes to science without parsing out what the authors mean by science or anti-intellectualism.[11]

Historian Richard Hofstadter wrote in 1964 about the anti-intellectualism present in American culture, partially laying the blame for its predominance at the feet of evangelicalism.[12] Evangelicals are probably no more anti-intellectual than other Americans. However, because of the intellectual challenges that the worldview of evangelicalism (and Christianity in general) faces in modern life, most are still following their hearts, although some are trying to incorporate more of a "life of the mind" into the movement. It is probably also worth noting that should any of the ministers investigated here decide to address the "tougher" intellectual questions that Christians face, they would probably lose their bestseller status.[13]

Politics

Not only are the authors of the manifesto discouraged by the therapeutic and anti-intellectual nature of their religion; they are also deeply concerned about the evangelical engagement in politics. Implicitly denouncing the Religious Right, the authors claim that as Evangelicals they should be involved in the public sphere but not in such a way that they could be "completely equated with a party, partisan ideology, economic system, or nationality."[14] They announce that "the Evangelical soul is not for sale," and they encourage fellow Christians not only to be concerned with the political issues of abortion or marriage but also to be active in "engaging the global giants of conflict, racism, corruption, poverty, pandemic diseases, illiteracy, ignorance, and spiritual emptiness."[15] Noting that Evangelicals have contributed to social movements of abolition, suffrage, "the voluntary association," as well as "the understanding of key notions as civil society and social capital," the authors plead for the creation of a "civil public square," by which they mean "a vision of public life in which citizens of all faiths are free to enter and engage the public square on the basis of their faith, but within a framework of what is agreed to be just and free for other faiths too."[16] Troubled about both a completely secular public discourse and a religiously monopolized public discourse, these authors call for a "liberal" approach to the public square, wherein they would support giving any Christian rights to those with no religion or who practice other religions, including Islam, Mormonism, and Scientology.[17]

Here again, the manifesto is both revealing and problematic for the study of evangelicalism. It is revealing in that it evidences dissatisfaction with the *religion of fear* and the political activities of the Religious Right in recent years. The manifesto authors apparently believe that certain politically active conservatives have made Christians "useful idiots" for political gain.[18] On the other hand, they contend that "the politicization of faith is never a sign of strength but of weakness."[19] That other evangelicals feel the same way is apparent in the comments section on the Evangelical Manifesto website. Many—although obviously not all—of those who commented on the document offered their wholehearted support and expressed gratitude for the presence of this stance.[20]

This denouncing of a politicized faith represents another problematic area of the manifesto. The steering committee wants to call evangelicals away from "single-issue" politics to broader concerns for human life in general.[21] They claim that the document relates a theological repositioning of evangelicalism that is above politics and is committed to ending oppression and bringing justice. The fact that "An Evangelical Manifesto" is essentially a political document, however, escapes the notice of the steering committee members. Perhaps they are just concerned about the politicization of evangelicalism in certain ways—ways that have led to ridicule and marginalization. They note that "a politicized faith is faithless, foolish, and disastrous for the church," but what they are arguing for is a politicized faith—one that is different from the Religious Right's total support of the Republican Party.[22] Any faith wanting to be actively involved in public life, especially in dealing with social issues, cannot avoid politicization. Becoming actively involved in working for social justice *is* a political position. Furthermore, how does such a position work out in actual practice? Would these Evangelicals support a candidate who was working toward alleviating poverty, illiteracy, racism, corruption, and abortion if that candidate supported same-sex marriage?[23]

Concern about politics and faith is shared across the different strands of evangelicalism. In spite of even the solipsism of therapeutic narcissistic evangelicalism, evangelicals as a group still seem to be concerned about transforming society. Ultimately it appears that they still share the Reformed Protestant notion that something is broken in the world and needs to be set right. Yet the sentimentality that is so important to contemporary evangelicalism seems like it will be an ineffective conduit for this societal transformation.

Perhaps evangelicals have been useful idiots for certain candidates, politicians, and politicized ministers. If so, the evangelical culture of feeling that developed in the nineteenth and twentieth century contributed to evangelicals becoming a manipulated constituency. When some evangelicals chose to accept sentimental tropes as the core of their religion and other evangelicals followed them, they positioned themselves as a community swayed not by rational discourse but by strong feeling. Because evangelical practice and culture have been so shaped by sentimental and domestic concerns, evangelicals are often easy prey to political currents and politicians that play on fears or anxieties related to preserving the sanctity of the domestic and sentimental sphere. Moreover, most evangelicals are unaware that the very ideological commitments that they made in their religiosity have made them pawns in the realm of politics.

The Transforming and Obfuscating Nature of Sentimentality

As we have observed throughout the book, sentimentality obscures structures and forces that operate in the emotionality of evangelicalism. It has great power to move people to action and to bring about personal change, but it can also conceal other factors at work. Sentimentality's obscurantist nature is particularly unfortunate because of the consequences of the sentimental worldview. It appears that some evangelicals are concerned about the anti-intellectual, commercial, therapeutic, and political nature of their religion, but most would not pinpoint emotional rhetoric and practices as the problem.

While millions of people draw strength and create meaning from the sentimentality present in evangelical sermons, inspirational books, romance novels, domestic products, music, calendars, birthday cards, and numerous other formats, there is another side to evangelical sentimentality. The hypocognized nature of sentimentality implicitly discourages evangelicals from exploring not only the reason sentimentality should be used in evangelicalism but also the structures of power and authority that are covered by a syrupy, sweet veneer. Even many of the evangelicals who deploy sentimentality prolifically are probably unaware of how they are legitimating their own authority and also instantiating other authorities including those in the political realm. If sentimentality were not so hypocognized in evangelicalism, perhaps evangelicals would realize that they are ultimately undercutting their own efforts at societal transformation.

The commercialization and commodification of sentimentality participates in the hypocognized character of evangelical emotionality. Yet this development is an old one that shows no indication of slowing. The evangelical publishing machine continues to expand, and sentimentality remains a large part of the success of evangelical publishing. As long as evangelicals remain convinced that they should understand and approach God based on emotionality, marketers will continue to provide them products that will ostensibly offer emotional avenues to encounter God while at the same time further establish the connection between sentimentality, the divine, and evangelicals.

Obfuscation in evangelicalism—whether from sentimentality or not—is probably another consequence of Scottish Common Sense. The Scottish philosophers suggested that certain truths—particularly moral truth—were intuitive and a part of the "common sense" of human nature. Morality especially was essentially intuitive. Combined with the belief that reality could be understood as it was through the senses, evangelicals approached the world with a commonsense, straightforward mind-set, often accepting the "obvious" nature of reality. Although evangelicals in the nineteenth century accepted Scottish Common Sense in various amounts, it has continued to linger on. When joined with anti-intellectualism, it would make sense that most evangelicals would not be inclined to inquisitively investigate sentimentality and its consequences, preferring instead to accept that sentimentality was a transparent, emotional connection with the divine.[24]

Even the Evangelicals of the manifesto evidence an interest in straightforwardness, especially in religion. The authors want scholars to accept what Evangelicals say at face value. They reserve the right to define who they are and what their motives are: "We are who we say we are, and we resist all attempts to explain us in terms of our 'true' motives and our 'real' agenda."[25] Obviously humanistic religious studies scholars cannot entirely accept such a position. It is important that scholars pay attention to their informants and note closely what they say, what they do, and how they live their lives. Yet religion is not an isolated aspect of human lives. It is deeply entwined with the results of other forces like history, culture, economics, and politics. These very forces undergo elision so that religious people often do not see the impact because of the nature of these forces and the often intentionally forgetful memory of groups. Because of the vantage point of the scholar, these forces are more visible because they are the kind of data we are hunting. We seek explanations beyond simply accepting what our informants tell us.

Moreover, even evangelical scholars studying evangelicalism do not simply rely on what their informants tell them, especially if these scholars are doing historical work. In his book *America's God*, for example, historian Mark Noll, one of the signers of the "Evangelical Manifesto," takes great pains to dissect the historical and cultural changes that theology experienced in the early Republic.[26] Noll points to broad trends in Western intellectual thought as being responsible for these theological shifts, concluding that in the United States evangelicals combined their Protestantism, "a republican political ideology," and Scottish Common Sense to create an American theology.[27] To the best of my knowledge, Noll had no sources declaring that this is what they were doing in describing who God was or what evangelicalism should look like in the United States. The far-reaching view of the scholar allowed Noll to outline the importance of Scottish Common Sense to antebellum evangelical thought. Essentially he was going beyond what his evangelical subjects claimed that they were.[28]

This is the murky legacy of evangelicalism and sentimentality. Evangelicals relying on sentimentality have shaped a religious movement that looks quite different from its nineteenth-century antecedents. In so doing they have helped many people make meaning and find healing in their lives. The sentimental rhetoric of therapeutic evangelicalism has had real and positive effects in the lives of those touched by it.[29]

But sentimentality has had real consequences as well. Reliance on sentimentality is beginning to transform the doctrinal positions that undergird evangelicalism. We can see developing in conservative evangelicalism many of the ideological positions that historian William Hutchison pointed to as marking the development of liberal Protestantism in the late nineteenth and early twentieth centuries.[30] Liberals tended to emphasize that God was immanent, that universal religious sentiment and experience that was more important than creeds or institutions, that individuals should value good works, and that Christians should focus on the importance of the Incarnation. These components contributed to the theological change that moved liberals away from their conservative counterparts.[31] Yet in the latter part of the twentieth century, conservative evangelicals were emphasizing these very things as well. Although many of the individuals we have examined here would be theologically and politically conservative, the evangelicalism they are espousing does not need to remain that way. Chapter 2 outlined how sentimentality provided Rob Bell with the foundation to question the validity and eternality of hell. Recent surveys have also indicated that young evangelicals are diverging from older evangelicals on a variety of moral issues.[32] Most of this work has been done by sociologists defining evangelicals through their connections to specific denominations, through their self-identification as evangelical, or through their holding of certain theological doctrines. Education, gender, income, race, and other variables are also explored to determine whether these factors provide insight into why younger evangelicals appear more progressive than their religious ancestors.[33]

One issue that has gotten particular attention is the divergence over the moral acceptability of same-sex marriage. Younger evangelicals are more open to being supportive of same-sex marriage for various reasons, including their increased use of the Internet, the liberalization of higher education, and the increased presence of positive gay characters in popular culture. Yet many of these explorations have largely focused on doctrinal and theological questions instead of connecting the doctrinal divergence to emotional trends in evangelicalism.[34]

If scholars were to inquire more deeply into the emotional concerns of evangelicals—young and old—a clearer picture of this trend might develop. A younger generation who was raised in an evangelicalism that centralized sentimentality and the message of God's love for all human beings could certainly transition to a position that is more favorable toward same-sex marriage. If God desperately loves all human beings as his children, then God would certainly love gays. The steps between God loving gays and God approving of a loving relationship between people of the same sex are not very far conceptually. Although older evangelicals have been very vocal about their condemnation of same-sex marriage, they also have been very vocal about a loving, fatherly God and not as vocal about the importance of maintaining doctrine. Such an emphasis on emotionality would certainly participate in changes among younger evangelicals who—like their peers—are more likely to emphasize the importance of one's conscience instead of moral absolutes in making moral decisions.[35]

At this stage it is unclear whether sentimentality is motivating younger evangelicals to move away from older evangelicals on moral issues. More empirical research needs to be done, certainly. Whether or not sentimentality is participating in this change, it is contributing to changes in evangelicalism. Evangelicals may be traveling light because they have abandoned the burdens of theology and the life of the mind, but in so doing they have acquired additional baggage—a politicized faith manipulated by those who shape the evangelical market and those who want to shape the political course of the United States.

Defining and Redefining Evangelicalism

On the margins of this exploration of sentimentality is a question about the definition of evangelicalism. The term *evangelical* has become problematic in modern scholarly usage, primarily due to the inexact nature of definition. Who is an evangelical? Should we use it in a broad sense to describe Protestants in general? Should the terms evangelical and *fundamentalist* be interchangeable? In *Mine Eyes Have Seen the Glory,* Randall Balmer somewhat facetiously noted that one way people—even scholars—think about evangelicalism is to apply former Supreme Court Justice Potter Stewart's explanation of pornography: "I can't define it, but I know it when I see it."[36]

The problem of defining evangelicalism is evident in the work of a variety of scholars. It often appears as if every study in evangelical historiography contains a section where the author delineates how they are defining evangelical for their particular study. These definitions tend to follow a few scholars who have laid out more comprehensive definitions of evangelicalism. Many scholars have tended to follow historian George Marsden's definition of evangelicalism: a unified whole based on a small selection of beliefs, particularly "the Reformation doctrine of the final authority of Scripture..., the real historical character of God's saving work recorded in Scripture..., eternal salvation only through personal trust in Christ..., the importance of evangelism and missions..., [and] the importance of a spiritually transformed life."[37] These categories are very broad for two reasons. First, there is a lot of variety between evangelicals. While evangelicals are unified on some aspects of Christianity, they often disagree on other doctrines, beliefs, and practices. Second, to be any more specific would cause someone interested in evangelicalism to overlook the overarching evangelical umbrella for the specificity that would isolate movements from each other.

Other scholars have preferred to look to different aspects to define evangelicalism. Historian David Bebbington's identifies evangelicalism as being focused on four centers: conversionism; activism; Biblicism; and crucicentrism.[38] Upon further examination, this seems to be a partial rearrangement and reformulation of Marsden's categories.[39] In addition, the way Bebbington describes these centers also demonstrates the importance of *belief* to defining evangelicalism. Conversionism is not just the practice or experience of conversion; it is a practice "bound up with major theological convictions."[40] Activism is not about being involved in social causes or just some sort of change in one's attitude toward others; it is the *belief* that one should be involved in converting others. Bebbington claims that one of the principal modes for this activism was *preaching*. Biblicism is not the use of the Bible, but instead it is evangelical "devotion to the Bible," which is "the result of their belief that all spiritual truth is to be found in its pages."[41] Furthermore, the way Bebbington describes this biblicism resonates with Marsden's description of Reformation beliefs about the final authority of scripture. Finally, curcicentrism is not about the use of crosses in religious practices or religious architecture. It is not even a notion that a believer must share in the experience of Christ and "take up one's cross." Instead it is "the doctrine of the cross."[42] Specifically it is the doctrine that "Christ died as a substitute for sinful mankind."[43] While Bebbington uses different words, he essentially mirrors Marsden's emphasis on belief.

The general trend of defining evangelicalism, exemplified in these important scholars, is to delineate the boundaries of evangelicalism through the lens of distinctive doctrine. A group or individual can be identified as evangelical on the basis of holding certain beliefs. More recently, however, scholars have begun contesting some aspects of belief-centered definitions. In her study of *Left Behind* readers, Amy Johnson Frykohlm argued that scholars *must* pay attention to the notion of belief in evangelicalism. As she investigated the impact of apocalyptic fiction, she noted that there are complex relationships at work in the assimilation of texts and the production of belief statements and understandings. Many of her informants read *Left Behind*, which developed or reinforced in them dispensational premillennialist views that then were exhibited in social living. Yet she demonstrated that the entire experience is culturally constructed. The apocalyptic tenets of *Left Behind* are a combination of not only traditional fundamentalist dispensational premillennialism but also depictions of apocalypticism in popular culture. Readers who accept the *Left Behind* view of eschatology do so based on culturally constructed understandings of evangelical fiction. They engage social living based on a view encouraged by the publishers—specifically the claim that *Left Behind* can be a good witnessing tool for unsaved friends and family. Frykohlm demonstrated that while evangelicals emphasize the importance of belief to their identity it is constructed in culture through relationships and symbols.[44]

Ultimately, we must explore definitions of evangelicalism that move beyond a singular focus on belief. As Lynn Neal noted, essentializing evangelicalism through the category of belief "neglects evangelical practices, elevates the church over the home, and as a result obscures women's lives and the audibility of their voices."[45] Codifying evangelicalism in a series of beliefs also disregards the dynamic and diverse nature of the movement. Are evangelicals only what they believe or best understood only by what they believe? Is something or someone evangelical because of the thing or person's connection to a series of belief statements? Neal wanted to move away from evangelicalism described through beliefs to make audible the voices of women. This is, of course, an excellent scholarly task, but she never defined what evangelicalism is or how she determined how her romance novels and their readers are *evangelical*. Is it because the authors and the reader self-identify as evangelicals? Is it because such novels can be found in evangelical bookstores or are published by evangelical publishing houses, or is there some other determinant?

Using belief as the sole lens to understand evangelicalism not only elides the voices of women but also obscures certain larger tensions within evangelicalism in general. In a historiographical article in *Church History*, historian Douglas Sweeney pointed out that many of the prominent historians within the field of evangelical history approach evangelicalism from a background he labeled the *Reformed model*.[46] The Reformed model included historians like Marsden and Noll, who came from traditions which privileged the importance of belief and the intellect as an expression of religiosity. In opposition to the Reformed model is the *Holiness model*, which is meant to reflect evangelical scholars from Wesleyan traditions. Holiness historians, like Donald Dayton, Leonard Sweet, and Timothy Smith, argue instead for seeing the impact of forms of evangelicalism that would privilege experience over belief.[47] The tensions between these two schools have often marked a stalemate among evangelical scholars, with Dayton even suggesting that perhaps scholars should discontinue using evangelicalism as a useful term to describe a particular group of Christians.[48]

Defining evangelicalism in terms of belief, therefore, participates in a struggle within evangelicalism over self-identity, as revealed in "An Evangelical Manifesto." As scholars—evangelical and not—delineate what evangelicalism is, they make political choices while attempting to make historical ones. This process conceals as much as it reveals. It also becomes very frustrating in trying to elucidate who we are discussing when we cannot even decide whom we are seeking or how we know when we find them. It is tempting to accept some of the tongue-in-cheek expressions: "the difference between an evangelical and a fundamentalist is that a fundamentalist is an evangelical who is mad about something"; and "an evangelical is anyone who identified with Billy Graham."[49]

It is not a fruitless situation, however. Rethinking the focus of defining evangelicalism can yield benefits that will allow scholars to be more attentive to the vitality of the movement. Because sentimentality and sentimental expressions of piety are an important aspect of evangelicalism, especially in religious practice, any definition of evangelicalism that wants to take practice seriously as a vital component must include openness to the sentimental aesthetic. Appealing to sentimentality certainly does not explain everything in evangelicalism, nor can scholars reduce evangelicalism to sentimentality. There are other vital sociological, cultural, and political facets of evangelicalism that are not connected to sentimentality. Nostalgia, familial and romantic love, and particular conceptions of the domestic sphere, however, are part of the evangelical worldview that ministers, hymn writers, authors, and others have created for evangelicals. They appeal to sentimentality to motivate their audiences to live certain types of lives, to understand God in certain ways, to worship through certain tropes, and to be involved in the world in certain political and social activities. The success of sentimentalists, the presence of sentimentality even in the most unlikely of works, and the continued use of sentimental music implies that sentimentality has integrally changed evangelicalism from the nineteenth century to the present.[50]

For scholars of evangelicalism and American Christianity in general, this evolution means that our definitions and methods must adapt as well. Although in the past several decades we as scholars have begun to reconceptualize our approach to religion, moving from doctrine and belief to the realm of practice and daily life, Christianity, and especially evangelicalism, still seems generally to be understood as a set of beliefs requiring intellectual assent. As we continue to open up new horizons for investigation, we must begin to recognize that contemporary Christianity might be better understood through emotion and emotional practices. It is emotion that validates Christianity in the modern age and not rational propositions, at least for an apparent majority of Christians. Attention to emotion might better help scholars understand the vitality of the variety of options in American Protestantism. If we focus on the emotionologies of various groups and the general evacuation of doctrine in Christianity, we might better understand why people are drawn to evangelicalism in its diversity. Emotion might better help us theorize the appeal of conservative evangelicalism, the Word of Faith movement and other prosperity-driven groups, and Pentecostalism.

And so we return to the definition I advanced at the beginning of the book:

Evangelical refers to an aesthetical worldview fashioned by belief in the truthfulness of the Bible, by experience of new birth into the Christian community, by emotional relationship between individuals and God through Christ, by concern to share the message of Christ with others, and by interest in shaping human society into the kingdom of God.

We have been tracing broad contours of this aesthetic throughout the work. In so doing we have noted throughout the impact American culture has had on evangelicalism. Yet it is important to remember that as that influence has occurred evangelicals have attempted to Christianize certain elements of that culture. So, for example, although the therapeutic culture of the United States has affected evangelicalism, the therapeutic culture that evangelicals have developed is shaped by understandings of the Bible. It is distinctly *evangelical* therapeutic culture. The same can be said about other media in evangelicalism. Evangelicals have mapped their aesthetic onto media to proffer to consumers apparent alternatives. Understanding the term evangelical in terms of an aesthetic allows us to understand how being evangelical refers to a way of seeing and being in the world that encompasses the entirety of life and not just a set of propositions to which one adheres.

Aesthetic also allows us to better understand the fluidity between belief and practice that exists in evangelicalism. Evangelicals throughout their history have privileged belief or "the message" as the important component in their version of Christianity. Yet this message is intricately tied to the practice of evangelicalism and the message has often existed in material objects like books. The beliefs of evangelicals do not exist separately from the practice components and objects that transfer those beliefs between evangelicals. Whether through listening to a sermon or music or reading a book or even a greeting card, evangelical ideas exist and perpetuate through practice. As Frykohlm emphasized, the beliefs of evangelicalism are vitally important to what it means to be evangelical. To be evangelical is to be connected to certain ideas, even if they are not always complex ideas. But those ideas are entrenched through religious practice. The conflation of belief and practice through the integration of emotion becomes a habitual way of seeing the world that defines evangelicals and evangelicalism in the contemporary period. Evangelicalism has evolved from its origins to the present; our definitions of it must evolve as well.

Both evangelicals and evangelical studies are at a crossroads, as evidenced by "An Evangelical Manifesto." For evangelicals, there are surely some who will continue to seek political power or political solutions to the events of the twenty-first century. Many will continue to align themselves with the Republican Party and conservative politics. For other evangelicals the future presents different options. There are those dissatisfied with the politicization of their religion and the hijacking of the image of evangelicals by the Religious Right. They do not want to return to the separatism of fundamentalism, but they do not want to be removed from the public sphere. They want a voice, just not one immediately associated with fundamentalism or the Religious Right. Whether their political stance will actually amount to a position distinct from the Religious Right remains to be seen.

Evangelical studies must continue to move beyond the focus solely on what evangelicals believe or what their political positions are. This investigation of evangelical sentimentality offers new roads to think about evangelical practice. Relatively few studies have examined evangelical practice, although those studies have provided important contribution to the scholarly understanding of evangelicals and American religion in general. Marie Griffith's *God's Daughters*, John Corrigan's *Business of the Heart*, Aaron Ketchell's *Holy Hills of the Ozarks*, James Bielo's *Emerging Evangelicals*, Lynn Neal's *Romancing God*, and T. M. Luhrmann's *When God Talks Back* are a few of the recent works that accept the importance of evangelical belief but move beyond simply focusing on belief or politics.[51] These studies take evangelical practice seriously and provide examples of the plethora of observations awaiting scholars who move beyond these categories. Studies of belief and politics are important and should not be abandoned, but attention to practice and how it is related to belief and politics would fill gaps in the historiography and offer a richer picture of evangelicalism in the United States, past and present. Emotion will be a key avenue to developing this new historiography. It is time for scholars of evangelicalism to drop the burden of describing evangelicals through their beliefs and begin to travel...well...at least a *little* lighter.

ENDNOTES

INTRODUCTION

1. "OHC Year in Review," available online at http://issuu.com/ohchurch/docs/ yearinreview.singles/13, accessed February 6, 2012 (now discontinued).
2. Cindy Crosby, "America's Pastor," *Christianity Today* (March 2004): 58–63.
3. "America's 100 Best: Connections," *Reader's Digest* (May 2005): 158.
4. "Thomas Nelson Inc. Releases Results of Lucado Market Research Project," available online at http://www.mmpublicrelations.com/recent-comethirsty-research.html, accessed January 18, 2013.
5. Max Lucado, *In the Grip of Grace* (Nashville, TN: W Publishing Group, 1996), 174.
6. Joel Osteen, *Your Best Life Now: 7 Steps to Living at Your Full Potential* (New York: Warner Faith, 2004), 58–59.
7. Rick Warren, *The Purpose-Driven Life: What on Earth Am I Here For?* (Grand Rapids, MI: Zondervan, 2002), 70, emphasis in original.
8. For an overview of the media outlets and message of these ministers and others see Shayne Lee and Phillip Luke Sinitiere, *Holy Mavericks: Evangelical Innovators and the Spiritual Marketplace* (New York: New York University Press, 2009).
9. Jonathan Edwards, *A Treatise Concerning Religious Affections: In Three Parts* (Whitefish, MT: Kessinger Publishing, 2004).
10. Robert I. Levy, "Emotion, Knowing, and Culture," in *Culture Theory: Essays on Mind, Self, and Emotion*, ed. Robert A. Shweder and Robert A. LeVine (Cambridge: Cambridge University Press, 1984), 214–237.
11. Joyce Warren, "Sentimentalism," in *American History through Literature*, vol. 3, ed. Janet Gabler-Hover and Robert Sattlemeyer (Detroit: Charles Scribner's Sons, 2006), 1059–1065; June Howard, "Sentiment," *Keywords for American Cultural Studies* (New York: New York University Press, 2007). *Credo Reference*, available online at http://www.credoreference.com, accessed February 20, 2012.
12. Robert C. Solomon, *In Defense of Sentimentality* (Oxford: Oxford University Press, 2004,) 4.

13. Ibid., 4–10.
14. Ibid., 18.
15. Julia A. Stern, *The Plight of Feeling: Sympathy and Dissent in the Early American Novel* (Chicago: University of Chicago Press, 1997), 2.
16. Ibid.
17. Ibid., 4.
18. Ann Douglas, *The Feminization of American Culture* (New York: Anchor Press, 1977; reprint, 1988), 77.
19. Jane Tompkins, *Sensational Designs: The Cultural Work of American Fiction, 1790–1860* (New York: Oxford University Press, 1985), 130.
20. Ibid., particularly 126–142.
21. Tracy Fessenden, *Culture and Redemption: Religion, the Secular, and American Literature* (Princeton, NJ: Princeton University Press, 2007), 84–107, noted, however, that sentimental authors in the nineteenth century attempted to pass off middle-class, white, feminine values as universals, applicable to all of society.
22. John Corrigan, "'Habits from the Heart': The American Enlightenment and Religious Ideas about Emotion and Habit," *Journal of Religion 73* (April 1993): 188.
23. Ibid., 190
24. Philip Greven, *The Protestant Temperament: Patterns of Child-Rearing, Religious Experience, and the Self in Early America* (New York: Alfred A. Knopf, 1977), 151.
25. Corrigan, "Habits from the Heart," 194–199; Also see Jacqueline S. Reinier, *From Virtue to Character: American Childhood, 1775–1850* (New York: Twayne Publishers, 1996).
26. Susan Friend Harding, *The Book of Jerry Falwell: Fundamentalist Language and Politics* (Princeton, NJ: Princeton University Press, 2000), x
27. Ibid., 12.
28. Kathryn Lofton, *Oprah: The Gospel of an Icon* (Berkeley: University of California Press, 2010), 15–17, takes a similar approach. She emphasizes that, although individual agency is important, consumers' continual returning to substantially similar products demonstrates that important observations can be derived from the product and not necessarily what people do with that product.
29. A classic example of this is Mark Noll, *The Scandal of the Evangelical Mind* (Grand Rapids, MI: Eerdmans, 1994).
30. See Levy, "Emotion, Knowing, and Culture," 214–237.
31. Lauren Berlant, *The Female Complaint: The Unfinished Business of Sentimentality in American Culture* (Durham, NC: Duke University Press, 2008), viii.
32. Ibid., 2
33. Ibid., 5.
34. Ibid., 7.

35. Harriet Beecher Stowe, *Uncle Tom's Cabin; or, Life Among the Lowly*, in *The Oxford Harriet Beecher Stowe Reader*, ed Joan D. Hedrick (New York: Oxford University Press, 1999) 402.

36. Alternatively, I refer to the members of their various audiences as readers because more people connect to such ministers through reading what they have written rather than through sermons or personal contact. In some places I do refer to the audience as consumers to emphasize the commercial aspects of such interactions.

37. Religious studies scholar Lynn Neal, *Romancing God: Evangelical Women and Inspirational Fiction* (Chapel Hill: University of North Carolina Press, 2006), demonstrates the prevalence of sentimental tropes in her study of evangelical romance novels and the women who read them. Nor should we necessarily limit the presence of sentimentality to the United States. Both Max Lucado and Rick Warren especially have made attempts to spread their messages beyond American borders by having their works translated into other languages. They both have also been active globally, particularly in Africa, encouraging and participating in various missionary and relief efforts. Although I cannot speak to the global impact of evangelical sentimentality, there is certainly an attempt to give it global presence.

CHAPTER I

1. Max Lucado, *God Came Near* (Nashville, TN: W Publishing Group, 2004).

2. R. Marie Griffith, *God's Daughters: Evangelical Women and the Power of Submission* (Berkeley: University of California Press, 1997), 36–39; Philip Rieff, *The Triumph of the Therapeutic: Uses of Faith after Freud* (New York: Harper & Row, 1966); Louise Woodstock, "Vying Constructions of Reality: Religion, Science, and 'Positive Thinking' in Self-Help Literature," *Journal of Media and Religion 4* (July 2005): 155–178.

3. George Marsden, *Fundamentalism and American Culture, New Edition* (Oxford: Oxford University Press, 2006), 72–80.

4. Douglas Frank, *Less Than Conquerors: How Evangelicals Entered the Twentieth Century* (Grand Rapids, MI: Eerdmans, 1986), 103–66; Charles H. Lippy, *Being Religious, American Style: A History of Popular Religiosity in the United States* (Westport: Praeger, 1994), 132–134. Betty DeBerg, *Ungodly Women: Gender and the First Wave of American Fundamentalism* (Minneapolis: Fortress Press, 1990), 9, 145–47, challenges Frank for not including gender in his analysis of the Keswick movement but acknowledges the impact Keswick had on evangelicalism and fundamentalism.

5. Frank, *Less Than Conquerors*, 193.

6. Robert F. Martin, *Hero of the Heartland: Billy Sunday and the Transformation of American Society, 1862–1935* (Bloomington: Indiana University Press), 106.

7. Many scholars have focused on Sunday's promulgation of *muscular Christianity*. While it is true that Sunday targeted men and couched his message in masculine terms, he was also very appealing to women as well and often held women-only meetings during his revivals. See Margaret Bendroth, "Why Women Loved Billy Sunday: Urban Revivalism and Popular Entertainment in Early Twentieth-Century American Culture," *Religion and American Culture 14* (Summer 2004): 251–271.

8. Louise Woodstock, "Vying Constructions of Reality: Religion, Science and 'Positive Thinking' in Self-Help Literature," *Journal of Media and Religion* 4(3): 2005, 164; Philip Rieff, *The Triumph of Therapeutic: Uses of Faith After Freud* (New York: Harper & Row, 1966), 38; Robert N. Bellah et al., *Habits of the Heart: Individualism and Commitment in American Life* (Berkeley: University of California Press, 1996), 224–225.

8. Wade Clark Roof, *Spiritual Marketplace: Baby Boomers and the Remaking of American Religion* (Princeton, NJ: Princeton University Press, 1999), 39–41. See also Christopher Lasch, *The Culture of Narcissism: American Life in an Age of Diminishing Expectations* (New York: W.W. Norton & Company, 1978), for a more contemporary critique of this cultural shift.

10. Norman Vincent Peale, *The Power of Positive Thinking* (New York: Prentice Hall, 1987; original publication 1952).

11. Charles H. Lippy, *Being Religious, American Style: A History of Popular Religiosity in the United States* (Westport, CT: Praeger, 1994), 201.

12. Carol V. R. George, *God's Salesman: Norman Vincent Peale & the Power of Positive Thinking* (New York: Oxford University Press, 1993), 128–159.

13. Woodstock, "Vying Constructions of Reality," 168–171.

14. Bellah et al., *Habits of the Heart*, xvii.

15. Ibid., 231–232. Sociologist James Davison Hunter, *American Evangelicalism: Conservative Religion and the Quandary of Modernity* (New Brunswick, NJ: Rutgers University Press, 1983), 91–101, explores this individualism as well, noting how it combined with therapeutic concerns in the late 1970s.

16. Hunter, *American Evangelicalism*, 95–96.

17. Roof, *Spiritual Marketplace*, 130.

18. Max Lucado, *On the Anvil* (Wheaton: Tyndale House, 1985).

19. "America's 100 Best: Connections," *Reader's Digest* (May 2005): 158; "Party's Schedule," *New York Times*, August 30, 2004, Late Edition (East Coast), available online at http://www.nytimes.com/2004/08/30/us/the-republicans-the-convention-in-new-york-party-s-schedule.html, accessed March 16, 2006; Hanna Rosin and Hamil R. Harris, "President, at Prayer Breakfast, Calls for Reconciliation," *Washington Post*, February 5, 1999, available online at http://www.highbeam.com/doc/1P2-575416.html, accessed March 16, 2006; HR 1737, 79(R) Texas House of Representatives, May, 26, 2005, available online at http://

www.capitol.state.tx.us/tlodocs/79R/billtext/html/HR01737F.htm, accessed November 14, 2005.

20. Rick Warren, *The Purpose Driven Church.* (Grand Rapids, MI: Zondervan, 1995), and The Purpose-Driven Life (Zondervan, 2002).

21. Shayne Lee and Phillip Luke Sinitiere, *Holy Mavericks: Evangelical Innovators and the Spiritual Marketplace* (New York: New York University Press, 2009, 129–148; Randall Balmer, *Mine Eyes Have Seen the Glory: A Journey into the Evangelical Subculture in America*, 4th ed. (Oxford: Oxford University Press, 2006), 322–334.

22. Joel Osteen, *Your Best Life Now: 7 Steps to Living at Your Full Potential* (New York: Warner Faith, 2004); idem, *Become a Better You: 7 Keys to Improving Your Life Every Day* (New York: Free Press, 2007); Marcia Z. Nelson, "Purpose-Driven Marketing," *Publishers Weekly* (August 13, 2007), available online at http://www.publishersweekly.com/pw/print/20070813/6806-purpose-driven-marketing.html, accessed May 20, 2013.

23. Lee and Sinitiere, *Holy Mavericks*, 25–51.

24. For an excellent overview of the themes of romanticism and sentimentality in American Protestantism, see Amanda Porterfield, *The Protestant Experience in America* (Westport, CT: Greenwood Press, 2006), 93–134.

25. Max Lucado, *The Great House of God: A Home for Your Heart* (Nashville, TN: Word Publishing, 1997).

26. Ibid., 59.

27. Ibid., 95.

28. Ibid., 2–3.

29. Max Lucado, *In the Grip of Grace* (Nashville, TN: W Publishing Group, 1996), 174. Picturing heaven as a divine home is not unique in sentimental literature. Elizabeth Stuart Phelps wrote several popular novels in the post–Civil War era, including *Gates Ajar* (Boston: Fields, Osgood, & Co, 1869) and *Beyond the Gates* (Boston: Houghton Mifflin, 1883), that envisioned the world beyond as several Victorian homes. See Ann Douglas, *The Feminization of American Culture* (New York: Anchor Press, 1977; reprint, 1988), 223–226; Porterfield, *Protestant Experience*, 115.

30. Osteen, *Your Best Life Now*, 6.

31. Ibid., 8.

32. Ibid., 12.

33.. Ibid., 4–6.

34. Ibid., 39.

35. Ibid., 38.

36. Warren, *Purpose-Driven Life*, 22.

37. Ibid.

38. Ibid., 22–23.

39. Ibid., 23.

40. Ibid., 24.

41. Ibid.

42. "Bruce Wilkinson," available online at http://www.brucewilkinson.com/about/bruce-wilkinson,accessed November 19, 2012; Bruce H. Wilkinson with David Kopp, *The Prayer of Jabez: Breaking through to the Blessed Life* (Sisters, OR: Multnomah, 2000).

43 Wilkinson, *Prayer of Jabez*, 27.

44. Ibid., 28–29.

45. Ibid., 51.

46. Ibid., 52–53.

47. Warren, *Purpose-Driven Life*, 17.

48. Warren, *Purpose-Driven Life*, 118, makes a distinction between human beings, who are all created by God, and Christians, who are children of God.

49. Max Lucado, *The Applause of Heaven* (Dallas, TX: Word Publishing, 1990), 58.

50. Ibid., 59.

51. Lynn S. Neal, *Romancing God: Evangelical Women and Inspirational Fiction* (Chapel Hill: University of North Carolina Press, 2006), 100–104.

52. Lucado, *Great House of God*, 137.

53. Warren, *Purpose-Driven Life*, 117.

54. Ibid., 119.

55. Osteen, *Become a Better You*, 34.

56. Ibid., 38.

57. Ibid., 39.

58. Ibid.

59. Randall Balmer, *Mine Eyes Have Seen the Glory: A Journey into the Evangelical Subculture in America*, 4th ed. (Oxford: Oxford University Press, 2006),160.

60. Warren, *Purpose-Driven Life*, 118.

61. Ibid.

62. Ibid.

63. Osteen, *Become a Better You*, 290.

64. Ibid.

65. Ibid., 293.

66. Ibid., 287.

67. Lucado, *God Came Near*, 116.

68. Ibid.

69. Max Lucado, *Come Thirsty* (Nashville, TN: W Publishing Group, 2004), 47–51.

70. Ibid., 48.

71. Jerome D. Frank and Julia B. Frank, *Persuasion and Healing: A Comparative Study of Psychotherapy*, 3d ed. (Baltimore: Johns Hopkins University Press, 1991), xiii–xiv.

72. Ibid., 132.

73. Ibid., 133.

74. Ibid.

75. Ibid., 134.

76. Ibid.

77. Ibid., 152.

78. Again, this is not to suggest there is something duplicitous about the production of a "Max Lucado" that is marketed or to insinuate that the marketed "Max Lucado" is inherently different from Max Lucado himself. I am, however, drawing here on ideas from Erving Goffman, *The Presentation of Self in Everyday Life* (Garden City, NY: Doubleday, 1959), that much of how we present ourselves to others (even when such interaction is face to face) is performative. It matters not whether "Max Lucado" and Max Lucado are one in the same, but I do not want to claim that even if disparity exists it is necessary devious.

79. Julia A. Stern, *The Plight of Feeling: Sympathy and Dissent in the Early American Novel* (Chicago: University of Chicago Press, 1997), 18.

80. Lucado, *Great House of God*, ix.

81. Lucado, *In the Grip of Grace*, viii. Colossians 4:3–4 (NRSV) reads, "Pray for us as well that God will open to us a door for the word, that we may declare the mystery of Christ, for which I am in prison, so that I may reveal it clearly, as I should."

82. Max Lucado, *When God Whispers Your Name* (Nashville, TN: W Publishing Group, 1994), 3.

83. Ibid.

84. Ibid., 4.

85. Ibid.

86. Joyce Meyer, *Beauty for Ashes: Receiving Emotional Healing*, rev. and exp. edition (New York: Warner Faith, 2003).

87 Ibid., 3.

88. Warren, *Purpose-Driven Life*, 5. Like Lucado, Warren also tells his readers that he has been praying for them while preparing *Purpose-Driven Life*: "As I wrote this book, I often prayed that you would experience the incredible hope, energy, and joy that comes from discovering what God put you on this planet to do....I am excited because I know all the great things that are going to happen to you" (11–12).

89. Cindy Crosby, "America's Pastor," *Christianity Today* (March 2004), 60; Crosby, "Nice Guys Finish First," *Publishers Weekly* (September 8, 2003), available online at http://www.publishersweekly.com/pw/print/20030908/32901-nice-guys-finish-first.html, accessed January 29, 2013. See also Hallmark Press Room, "Many Americans Have Found a Voice in Max Lucado," available online at http://pressroom.hallmark.com/lucado_cards.html, accessed November 10, 2005 (now discontinued).

90. See Mara Einstein, *Brands of Faith: Marketing Religion in a Commercial Age* (London: Routledge, 2008), 100, 124–125.

91. Frank, *Persuasion and Healing*, 195.

92. Ibid.

93. Ibid., 194–195.

94. Ibid., 195–196.

95. Meyer, *Beauty for Ashes*, 32.

96. Ibid., 36.

97. Ibid., 43.

98. Warren, *Purpose-Driven Life*, 312–319.

99. Max Lucado, *Facing Your Giants: A David and Goliath Story for Everyday People* (Nashville, TN: Thomas Nelson, 2006), 101–102.

100. Lucado, *God Came Near*, 39

101. Ibid.

102. Ibid., 40.

103. Max Lucado, *A Love Worth Giving: Living in the Overflow of God's Love* (Nashville, TN: W Publishing Group, 2002), 93.

104. Ibid., 92

105. Ibid.

106. Wilkinson, *Prayer of Jabez*, 11.

107. Susan Friend Harding, *The Book of Jerry Falwell: Fundamentalist Language and Politics* (Princeton, NJ: Princeton University Press, 2000), 88.

108. Lucado, *Facing Your Giants*, 166.

109. Max Lucado, *Cure for the Common Life: Living in Your Sweet Spot* (Nashville, TN: W Publishing Group, 2005).

110. Ibid., 2.

111. Ibid.

112. Ibid., 4.

113. Ibid., 26–27.

114. Ibid., 115.

115. Osteen, *Best Life Now*, 76..

116. Ibid., 34.

117. Warren, *Purpose-Driven Life*, 173.

118. Ibid., 9.

119. Hunter, *American Evangelicalism*, 99–101.

120. Christian Smith, *American Evangelicalism: Embattled and Thriving* (Chicago: University of Chicago Press, 1998), 210–217, noted that individualism has created a cognitive dissonance in evangelicalism in that evangelicals emphasize the importance of individuals freely choosing to pursue a relationship with God while also supporting legislation of Christian morality. He pointed to the *personal influence strategy* of evangelicals as part of this dissonance. I suggest that part of this dissonance has been exacerbated by the narcissism of therapeutic approaches to evangelicalism.

121. Balmer, *Mine Eyes Have Seen the Glory*, 8.

CHPTER 2

1. Frank E. Peretti, *This Present Darkness* (Westchester, IL: Crossway Books, 1986); Tim LaHaye and Jerry B. Jenkins, *Left Behind: A Novel of the Earth's Last Days* (Wheaton, IL: Tyndale House Publishers, Inc., 1995).
2. Mark A. Noll, *The Scandal of the Evangelical Mind* (Grand Rapids, MI: Eerdmans, 1994).
3. Ibid., 12.
4. Ibid., 23.
5. The Editors, "The Top 50 Books That Have Shaped Evangelicals," *Christianity Today 50* (October 2006): 52.
6. See, for example, E. Brooks Holifield, *Theology in America: Christian Thought from the Age of the Puritans to the Civil War* (New Haven, CT: Yale University Press, 2003), a comprehensive survey of the variety of American Christian theology.
7. Lisa Jardine, "Introduction" in Francis Bacon, *The New Organon*, ed. Lisa Jardine and Michael Silverthorne (Cambridge, UK: Cambridge University Press, 2000), vii–xxvii.
8. Charles Webster, *The Great Instauration: Science, Medicine and Reform, 1626–1660* (New York: Holmes and Meier Publishers, 1975), 367.
9. Ibid., 506.
10. Ibid., 514.
11. Theodore Dwight Bozeman, *Protestants in an Age of Science: The Baconian Ideal and Antebellum Religious Thought* (Chapel Hill: University of North Carolina Press, 1977), 21.
12. C. Leonard Allen, "Baconianism and the Bible in the Disciples of Christ: James S. Lamar and 'The Organon of Scripture,'" *Church History 55* (March 1986): 66.
13. Mark A. Noll, "Common Sense Traditions and American Evangelical Thought," *American Quarterly 37* (Summer 1985): 224–225; See also Bozeman, *Protestants in the Age of Science*, 132–159; and Allen, "Baconianism and the Bible," 65–80.
14. John D. Woodbridge, Mark A. Noll, and Nathan O. Hatch, *The Gospel in America: Themes in the Story of America's Evangelicals* (Grand Rapids, MI: Zondervan, 1979), 110–113. For an examination of the acceptance of organic evolution among Protestants see Jon H. Roberts, *Darwinism and the Divine in America: Protestant Intellectuals and Organic Evolution, 1859–1900* (Madison: University of Wisconsin Press, 1988; reprint, Notre Dame: University of Notre Dame Press, 2001).
15. It is questionable whether Darwin actually followed Bacon's inductive method or its opposite—hypothesis and deduction. See Ernst Mayr, "The Philosophical Foundations of Darwinism," *Proceedings of the American Philosophical Society 145* (December 2001): 488–495.

16. Particularly insightful about the origins of fundamentalism is Michael Lienesch, *In the Beginning: Fundamentalism, the Scopes Trial, and the Making of the Antievolution Movement* (Chapel Hill: University of North Carolina Press, 2007). Lienesch applied social theory to fundamentalism to detail how fundamentalists self-consciously created fundamentalism particularly around the issue of evolution by how they framed the ideas that challenged Baconian Common Sense philosophies of science. Noll, *Scandal of the Evangelical Mind*, 24, commented that "fundamentalism, dispensational premillennialism, the Higher Life movement, and Pentecostalism were all evangelical strategies of survival in response to the religious crises of the late nineteenth century. In different ways each preserved something essential of the Christian faith. But together they were a disaster for the life of the mind." For an example of opposition to modernism, see J. Gresham Machen, *Christianity and Liberalism* (Grand Rapids, MI: Eerdmans, 1923). For an intellectual survey of the rise and acceptance of liberal theology see William R. Hutchison, *The Modernist Impulse in American Protestantism* (Durham: Duke University Press, 1992).

17. George Marsden, *Fundamentalism and American Culture, New Edition* (Oxford: Oxford University Press, 2006), 111.

18. Ibid.,114.

19. Ibid.

20. Hutchison, *Modernist Impulse*, 196–206; Marsden, *Fundamentalism and American Culture*, 118–123.

21. Edward J. Larson, *Summer for the Gods: The Scopes Trial and America's Continuing Debate over Science and Religion* (New York: Basic Books, 1997), 7. This is the now standard text on the controversy.

22. For the impact of the Scopes Trial on fundamentalism see Marsden, *Fundamentalism and American Culture*, 184–195.

23. Randall Balmer, *Mine Eyes Have Seen the Glory: A Journey into the Evangelical Subculture in America*, 4th ed. (Oxford: Oxford University Press, 2006), 132.

24. George M. Marsden, *Reforming Fundamentalism: Fuller Seminary and the New Evangelicalism* (Grand Rapids, MI: Eerdmans, 1987), uses the creation of Fuller Seminary as a self-consciously evangelical institution to demonstrate that despite the intent of neo-evangelicals to create an identity separate from fundamentalism, neo-evangelicalism arose from the foundation of fundamentalist theology and is heavily indebted to it.

25. For a comprehensive survey of the changes and challenges of creationisms, see Ronald L. Numbers, *The Creationists: From Scientific Creationism to Intelligent Design*, expanded ed. (Cambridge, MA: Harvard University Press, 2006).

26. Ibid., 268–285.

27. Ibid., 373–398. A good overview of the legal challenges of creationism, intelligent design, and evolution is Edward J. Larson, *Trial and Error: The American Controversy over Creation and Evolution*, 3d ed. (Oxford: Oxford University

Press, 2003). For a critique about whether intelligent design is scientific or not, see Matt Young and Taner Edis, eds., *Why Intelligent Design Fails: A Scientific Critique of the New Creationism* (New Brunswick, NJ: Rutgers University Press, 2004).

28. Henry M. Morris, *Creation and the Modern Christian* (El Cajon, CA: Master Book Publishers, 1985), 145.

29. Ibid.

30. Ibid., 147, emphasis in original.

31. Ibid.

32. Ibid.

33. Charles Colson and Anne Morse, "Verdict That Demands Evidence: It Is Darwinists, not Christians, Who Are Stonewalling the Facts," *Christianity Today* 49 (April 2005): 112, available at http://www.ebscohost.com, accessed May 20, 2013.

34. Ibid.

35. Ibid.

36. Ibid.

37. Marsden, *Fundamentalism and American Culture*, 32–39; Robert F. Martin, *Hero of the Heartland: Billy Sunday and the Transformation of American Society, 1862–1935* (Bloomington: Indiana University Press, 2002), 83–85, 106–109; Joel A. Carpenter, *Revive Us Again: The Reawakening of American Fundamentalism* (New York: Oxford University Press, 1997), 221–223. John G. Turner, *Bill Bright & Campus Crusade for Christ: The Renewal of Evangelicalism in Postwar America* (Chapel Hill: University of North Carolina Press, 2008), 36–37, tells a similar narrative of Bill Bright, who founded the popular college ministry Campus Crusade for Christ. Bright, a student at Fuller Seminary, decided that education and evangelism were incompatible. He was failing several courses at the time.

38. Max Lucado, *In the Grip of Grace* (Nashville, TN: W Publishing Group, 1996), 26.

39. Ibid.

40. Ibid., 32

41. Warren, *Purpose-Driven Life*, 25.

42. Ibid., 23.

43. Ibid., 25.

44. Ibid., 24.

45. Ibid., 24–25.

46. Ibid., 290–291.

47. Ibid.

48. For the combination of anti-elitism and anti-intellectualism in nineteenth-century evangelicalism, see Nathan O. Hatch, *The Democratization of American Christianity* (New Haven, CT: Yale University Press, 1989).

49. Cindy Crosby, "America's Pastor," 58; Crosby, "Nice Guys Finish First," 48.

50. Max Lucado, *Just Like Jesus* (Nashville, TN: Word Publishing, 1998), 71 (Mother Teresa); Lucado, *Cure for the Common Life*, 11 (Carver), 25 (Graham); Lucado, *In the Eye of the Storm* (Dallas, TX: Word Publishing, 1991), 35 (appendectomy), 205 (Newton); Lucado, *3:16: The Numbers of Hope* (Nashville: Thomas Nelson, 2007), 25 (fibrodysplasia ossificans progressiva), 35 (Matheson); Lucado, *And the Angels Were Silent* (Dallas, TX: Word Publishing, 1992), 5 (Eisenhower); Lucado, *He Chose the Nails: What God Did to Win Your Heart* (Nashville, TN: W Publishing Group, 2000), 51–52 (Booth); Max Lucado, *Come Thirsty* (Nashville, TN: W Publishing Group, 2004), 133–134 (Hitchcock); Lucado, *A Love Worth Giving: Living in the Overflow of God's Love* (Nashville, TN: W Publishing Group, 2002), 87–88 (garbage barge); Max Lucado, *A Gentle Thunder: Hearing God through the Storm* (Nashville, TN: W Publishing Group, 1995), 15–16 (seagull); Lucado, *In the Grip of Grace*, 149–150 ($1 a week).

51. Lucado, *Come Thirsty*, 108.

52. Rick Reilly, "The Play of the Year," *Sports Illustrated* 97(20), November 18, 2002), 108, available online at http://find.galegroup.com, accessed January 7, 2009.

53. Ibid.

54. Harding, *Book of Jerry Falwell*, 59–60.

55. Osteen, *Best Life Now*, 44.

56. Ibid., 44–47.

57. Osteen, *Become a Better You*, 72.

58. Ibid., 79.

59. Ibid., 80.

60. Warren, *Purpose-Driven Life*, 272.

61. Ibid., 274.

62. Ibid., 277

63. Wilkinson, *Prayer of Jabez*, 9.

64. Ibid., 55.

65. Ibid., 61.

66. T. D. Jakes, *From the Cross to Pentecost: God's Passionate Love for Us Revealed* (New York: Howard Books, 2010), 124–125.

67. Philip N. Mulder, *A Controversial Spirit: Evangelical Awakenings in the South* (Oxford: Oxford University Press, 2002), 8.

68. Ibid., 170.

69. Lucado, *In the Grip of Grace*, 160.

70. Ibid.

71. Ibid., 161.

72. Ibid.

73. Ibid.

74. Ibid., 161–162.

75. Ibid., 162

76. Ibid., 165.

77. Ibid., 166–167.

78. Colleen McDannell, "Beyond Dr. Dobson: Women, Girls, and Focus on the Family," in *Women and Twentieth-Century Protestantism*, ed. Margaret Lamberts Bendroth and Virginia Lieson Brereton (Urbana: University of Illinois Press, 2002), 128.

79. Warren, *Purpose-Driven Life*, 34.

80. Ibid., 183.

81. Ibid., 161. Warren summarizes the message of God in the following way: "God has never made a person he didn't love. Everybody matters to him. When Jesus stretched his arms out wide on the cross, he was saying, "I love you *this* much!" (294).

82. Ibid., 87.

83. Jakes, *From the Cross to Pentecost*, 64.

84. Ibid., 63

85. Max Lucado, *No Wonder They Call Him the Savior* (Multnomah Press, 1986), 125.

86. Ibid., 126.

87. Ibid.

88. Ibid., 127.

89. Ibid.

90. Max Lucado, *When Christ Comes* (Dallas, TX: Word Publishing, 1999), 117.

91. Ibid., 118.

92. Lucado, *3:16*, 96.

93. Ibid., 97

94. Ibid., 100.

95. Lucado, *When Christ Comes*, 122–123.

96. Ibid., 121.

97. Ibid., 124.

98. Lucado, *3:16*, 99.

99. Jonathan Edwards, "Sinners in the Hands of an Angry God," in *The Sermons of Jonathan Edwards: A Reader*, ed. Wilson H. Kimnach, Kenneth P. Minkema, and Douglas A. Sweeney (New Haven, CT: Yale University Press, 1999), 57.

100. Lucado, *When Christ Comes*, 125.

101. Rob Bell, *Love Wins: A Book about Heaven, Hell, and the Fate of Every Person Who Ever Lived* (New York: HarperOne, 2011).

102. Eric Marrapodi, "Christian Author's Book Sparks Charges of Heresy," *CNN Belief Blog*, March 1, 2011, available online at http://religion.blogs.cnn.com/2011/03/01/what-is-a-heretic-exactly-in-the-evangelical-church, accessed June 29, 2011; Marrapodi, "Firestorm Grows over 'Christian Heresy' Book," *CNN Belief Blog*, March 8, 2011, available online at http://religion.blogs.cnn.com/2011/03/08/firestorm-over-bell-book-continues, accessed June 29, 2011;

Marrapodi, "Rob Bell Punches Back against Claims of Heresy," *CNN Belief Blog*, March 19, 2011, available online at http://religion. blogs.cnn.com/2011/03/19/rob-bell-punches-back-against-claims-of-heresy, accessed June 29, 2011.

103. Bell, *Love Wins*, 31.
104. Ibid., 32.
105. Ibid.,,107. See also, ibid.,110.
106. Ibid., 44.
107. Ibid., 59.
108. Ibid., 109–110.
109. Ibid., 46.
110. Ibid., 93.
111. Ibid., 92–93.
112. Ibid., 99.
113. Ibid., 107.
114. Interestingly, in Bell's chapter on hell, the people who experience hell the most are those who deserve it the least. Bell suggests that children who have been mutilated, women who have been raped, wives who have experienced spousal infidelity, and parents who have lost children all experience some form of hell, which for Bell suggests that hell is real.
115. Peter J. Thuesen, *Predestination: The American Career of a Contentious Doctrine* (Oxford: Oxford University Press, 2009).
116. Ibid., 215.

CHAPTER 3

1. In using the dichotomy of "presence" and "purity," I am drawing on Candy Gunther Brown, *The Word in the World: Evangelical Writing, Publishing, and Reading in America, 1789–1880* (Chapel Hill: University of North Carolina Press, 2004).
2. Scholars usually refer to these changes as the *market revolution*, but in recent historiography some scholars have questioned the accuracy of this terminology. Daniel Walker Howe, *What Hath God Wrought: The Transformation of America, 1815–1848* (Oxford: Oxford University Press, 2007), 5, argues that it would be more appropriate to speak of a *market evolution* because these changes were more of a process than a spontaneous occurrence. See also R. Laurence Moore, *Selling God: American Religion in the Marketplace of Culture* (New York: Oxford University Press, 1994), 7.
3. Frank Lambert, *"Pedlar in Divinity": George Whitefield and the Transatlantic Revivals, 1737–1770* (Princeton, NJ: Princeton University Press, 1994), 8.
4. See Brown, *Word in the World*.
5. David Paul Nord, *Faith in Reading: Religious Publishing and the Birth of Mass Media in America* (Oxford: Oxford University Press, 2004). Although Daniel

Walker Howe has challenged the utility of the market revolution hypothesis for understanding changes in the eighteenth century, he does put forth a *communications revolution* hypothesis for changes in the way American communicated ideas with each other. See Howe, *What Hath God Wrought*, 5–7, 690–698.

6. Amanda Porterfield, *The Protestant Experience in America* (Westport, CT: Greenwood Press, 2006), 125–126; Colleen McDannell, *The Christian Home in Victorian America, 1840–1900* (Bloomington: Indiana University Press, 1986), 38.

7. Bruce Evensen, *God's Man for the Gilded Age: D. L. Moody and the Rise of Modern Mass Evangelism* (Oxford: Oxford University Press, 2003).

8. George Marsden, *Fundamentalism and American Culture, New Edition* (Oxford: Oxford University Press, 2006), 39.

9. Ibid., 35–39.

10. Robert F. Martin, *Hero of the Heartland: Billy Sunday and the Transformation of American Society, 1862–1935* (Bloomington: Indiana University Press), 45–65.

11. Douglas Carl Adams, *Selling the Old-Time Religion: American Fundamentalists and Mass Culture, 1920–1940* (Athens: University of Georgia Press, 2001), 11–39.

12. Colleen McDannell, *Material Christianity: Religion and Popular Culture in America* (New Haven, CT: Yale University Press, 1995), 222–269.

13. Mara Einstein, *Brands of Faith: Marketing Religion in a Commercial Age* (London: Routledge, 2008), 6.

14. "Thomas Nelson Inc. Releases Results of Lucado Market Research Project," available online at http://www.mmpublicrelations.com/recent-comethirsty-research.html, accessed January 18, 2013.

15. Ibid.

16. Ibid.

17. Ibid.

18. Ibid.

19. Ibid.

20. Kevin Lane Keller, "Conceptualizing, Measuring, and Managing Customer-Based Brand Equity," *Journal of Marketing 57* (January 1993): 1.

21. Ibid.

22. Kevin Lane Keller, "Brand Synthesis: The Multidimensionality of Brand Knowledge," *Journal of Consumer Research 29* (March 2003): 596.

23. See Einstein, *Brands of Faith*, chapters 5 and 6 for examinations of Warren's and Osteen's brands. Einstein also discusses other aspects of the marketing of these two ministers throughout her book.

24. A search on Amazon.com and the websites of purposedrivenlife.com and joelosteen.com demonstrates the wide range of products under these brand names.

25. Einstein, *Brands of Faith, 60–65, for example.*

26. Ibid., 65.

27. Ibid.

28. June Hadden Hobbs, *"I Sing for I Cannot Silent": The Feminization of American Hymnody, 1870–1920* (Pittsburgh: University of Pittsburgh Press, 1997).

29. Ibid., 10; see also Brown, *Word in the World*, 190–208.

30. Hobbs, *"I Sing for I Cannot Be Silent"*, 34–69; Charles H. Lippy, *Being Religious, American Style: A History of Popular Religiosity in the United States* (Westport: Praeger, 1994), 98.

31. Joseph Scriven, "What a Friend We Have in Jesus," in *The Worship Hymnal* (Nashville, TN: LifeWay Worship, 2008; written c. 1855).

32. Hobbs, *"I Sing,"* 10–11, 146–147. Hobbs claimed that Crosby used at least 204 pseudonyms in her writing.

33. Fanny J. Crosby, "Tell Me the Story of Jesus," *Worship Hymnal*, written 1880. Dates for Crosby's hymns come from Stephen Marini's list of frequent Protestant hymns, which is an appendix to Richard J. Mouw and Mark A. Noll, eds., *Wonderful Words of Life: Hymns in American Protestant History and Theology* (Grand Rapids, MI: Eerdmans, 2004), 251–264.

34. Crosby, "Tell Me the Story of Jesus."

35. Ibid.

36. Ibid.

37. Ibid.

38. Ibid.

39. Fanny J. Crosby, "Jesus Is Tenderly Calling," *Worship Hymnal* (written 1869).

40. Ibid.

41. Ibid.

42. Ibid.

43. Hobbs, *"I Sing,"* 78. Will L. Thompson evokes similar imagery in his 1880 hymn "Softly and Tenderly": "Softly and tenderly/Jesus is calling/Calling for you and for me/See, on the portals/He's waiting and watching/Watching for you and for me." Jesus is "Calling, O sinner, come home."

44. Fanny J. Crosby, "I Am Thine, O Lord," *Worship Hymnal* (written 1875).

45. Ibid.

46. Ibid.

47. Ibid.

48. Ibid. See also Hobbs, *"I Sing,"* 85–91, for examples of other hymns that evoke sexual surrender of the believer to God.

49. Lippy, *Being Religious*, 109–110; see also Kevin Kee, "Marketing the Gospel: Music in English-Canadian Protestant Revivalism, 1884–1957," in Mouw and Nolls, *Wonderful Words of Life*, 99–100; and David W. Stowe, *How Sweet the Sound: Music in the Spiritual Lives of Americans* (Cambridge, MA: Harvard University Press, 2004), 105.

50. Stephen Prothero, *American Jesus: How the Son of God Became a National Icon* (New York: Farrar, Straus, and Giroux, 2003), 76.

51. Ibid., 77.

52. Hobbs, "*I Sing*," 144.

53. Fanny J. Crosby, "Blessed Assurance," *Worship Hymnal* (written 1873); see Hobbs, "*I Sing*," 144–145.

54. Thomas E. Bergler, "'I Found My Thrill': The Youth for Christ Movement and American Congregational Singing, 1940–1970," in Mouw and Noll, *Wonderful Words of Life*, 129.

55. Ibid., 143–147.

56. David W. Stowe, *No Sympathy for the Devil: Christian Pop Music and the Transformation of American Evangelicalism* (Chapel Hill: University of North Carolina Press, 2011), 26.

57. Ibid., 200.

58. For an overview of the issues surrounding *sacred* and *secular* in the realm of CCM (as well as the question of the utility of those categories), see Shaun Horton, "Redemptive Media: The Professionalization of the Contemporary Christian Music Industry" (MA thesis, Florida State University, 2007).

59. For a historical overview of the rise of *Jesus rock* and CCM, see Heather Hendershot, *Shaking the World for Jesus: Media and Conservative Evangelical Culture* (Chicago: University of Chicago Press, 2004), 55–57; Prothero, *American Jesus*, 136–139, 151–153; Randall Balmer, *Mine Eyes Have Seen the Glory: A Journey into the Evangelical Subculture in America*, 4th ed. (Oxford: Oxford University Press, 2006), 297–300.

60. Hendershot, *Shaking the World*, 64–73.

61. Kevin Max, Mark Heimermann, Michael Tait, and Toby McKeehan, "Consume Me" *Supernatural* (Achtober Songs/Out of Twisted Roots Music/Blind Thief Publishing/Fun Attic Music, 1998).

62. Ibid.

63. Ibid.

64. "The dc Talk Story," available online at http://www.dctalk.com/story.html, accessed May 19, 2009.

65. Ibid.

66. Ibid.

67. Ibid.

68. Ibid.

69. Mac Powell, "Love Song, " *Third Day* (Provident Music Group, 1996). Third Day recorded this song for its first album (a self-titled release), but it also appears on *3:16: Songs of Hope*, a CCM companion album to Max Lucado, Lucado, *3:16: The Numbers of Hope* (Nashville: Thomas Nelson, 2007).

70. Ibid.

71. Ibid.

72. Ibid.

73. Ibid.

74. Ibid.
75. Jason Gray and Jason Ingram, "More Like Falling in Love" *Everything Sad is Coming Untrue* (Centricity Music, 2010).
76. Ibid.
77. Ibid.
78. Ibid.
79. Aaron Sprinkle, James Mead, Jon Micah Sumrall, Kyle Mitchell, and Ryan Shrout, "Sea of Faces" *Sea of Faces* (BEC Recordings, 2004).
80. Ibid.
81. Ibid.
82. I am not suggesting *The Worship Hymnal* is the most popular or most used hymnal in evangelicalism, but I am asserting that the songs included are representative of the kinds of songs used in evangelical worship.
83. Lifeway Christian Resources, "Who We Are," available online at http://www.lifeway.com/Article/Who-we-are, accessed January 29, 2013.
84. To make sure that I was getting at music that was widely used among evangelicals, I supplemented songs from *The Worship Hymnal* (Nashville, TN: LifeWay Worship, 2008), with information from CCLI, a copyright license clearinghouse that allows churches to distribute and perform songs that may not be in their hymnals. Two of the songs I examine—"Breathe" and "Beautiful One"—were CCLI's Top 25 royalty payout songs for February 2009 (covering April–September 2008). This means that these two songs were among the 25 songs most copied by churches enrolled at CCLI during this period. "CCLI Top 25 Songs (February 2009)," available online at http://www.ccli.com/LicenseHolder/Top25Lists.aspx, accessed May 23, 2009.
85. Kelly Carpenter, "Draw Me Close" (Mercy/Vineyard Publishing, 1994); *Worship Hymnal*.
86. Ibid.
87. Marie Barnett, "Breathe" (Mercy/Vineyard Publishing, 1995); *Worship Hymnal*.
88. Ibid.
89. Ibid.
90. Tim Hughes, "Beautiful One" (Thankyou Music, 2002); *Worship Hymnal*.
91. Ibid.
92. Ibid.
93. Ibid.
94. McDannell, *Christian Home in Victorian America*, xiii.
95. Ibid., 49.
96. Ibid., 48.
97. Jacqueline S. Reinier, *From Virtue to Character: American Childhood, 1775–1850* (New York: Twayne Publishers, 1996).
98. See ibid., chapter 4.
99. For Little Eva as spiritual guide, see Jane Tompkins, *Sensational Designs: The Cultural Work of American Fiction, 1790–1860* (New York: Oxford University

Press, 1985), 122–146. For the ways changing conceptions of children were reflected in religious movements developing in the nineteenth century see Todd M. Brenneman, "A Child Shall Lead Them: Children and New Religious Groups in the Early Republic," in *Children and Youth in a New Nation* ed. James Marten (New York: New York University Press, 2009), 108–126.

100. Tompkins, *Sensational Designs*, 128; J. B. McClure, ed., *D. L. Moody's Child Stories Related by Him in His Revival Work in Europe and America, with Pictorial Illustrations* (Chicago: Rhodes & McClure, 1877), 41–44; Hathi Trust Digital Library, available online at http://babel.hathitrust. org/cgi/pt?id=mdp.39015063595683#page/7/mode/1up, accessed January 29, 2013.

101. Marsden, *Fundamentalism and American Culture*, 37.

102. Ibid., 35–37.

103. Charles Fuller, "The Spirit Filled Christian Home" 50 min. 9 sec., *Old Fashioned Revival Hour Broadcast-Biblebelievers.com*, available through https://itunes. apple.com/us/itunes-u/old-fashioned-revival-hour/id380160034, accessed July 28, 2009.

104. Betty A. DeBerg, *Ungodly Women: Gender and the First Wave of American Fundamentalism* (Minneapolis: Fortress Press, 1990), 59–74; Margaret Lamberts Bendroth, *Fundamentalism & Gender, 1875 to the Present* (New Haven, CT: Yale University Press, 1993), 97–117. See also Thomas E. Bergler, *The Juvenilization of American Christianity* (Grand Rapids, MI: Eerdmans, 2012).

105. Max Lucado, *Just In Case You Ever Wonder* (Nashville, TN: Tommy Nelson, 1992; reprint, 2000).

106. Ibid., [8]

107. Ibid., [12]

108. Ibid., [27]

109. Ibid., [28–29]

110. Ibid. [31]

111. Max Lucado, *You Are Special* (Wheaton, IL: Crossway Books, 1997).

112. Ibid., 29.

113. Ibid., 32.

114. Ann M. Trousdale, "'And What Do the Children Say?' Children's Reponses to Books about Spiritual Matters," in *Spiritual Education: Literary, Empirical and Pedagogical Approaches*, ed. Cathy Ota and Clive Erricker (Brighton, UK: Sussex Academic Press, 2005), 33–36.

115. *VeggieTales: Rack, Shack, and Benny*, VHS (Nashville, TN: Big Idea Entertainment, 1995).

116. Ibid.

117. Ibid.

118. Ibid.

119. Ibid.

120. Ibid.

121. Ibid.

122. Ibid.
123. Ibid.
124. Ibid.
125. Ibid.
126. Hendershot, *Shaking the World for Jesus*, 42
127. See *VeggieTales: Rack, Shack, and Benny* as but one example..
128. Keller, "Brand Synthesis," 595–599.
129. McDannell, *Material Christianity*, 274.
130. Hendershot, *Shaking the World for Jesus*, makes a similar argument about evangelical popular culture.
131. Ibid.
132. Aaron K. Ketchell, *Holy Hills of the Ozarks: Religion and Tourism in Branson, Missouri* (Baltimore, MD: Johns Hopkins University Press, 2007).
133. Ibid., xvii.
134. Catherine Bell, *Ritual Theory, Ritual Practice* (New York: Oxford University Press, 1992), 108.

CHAPTER 4

1. J[ack] T. C[hick], *"Somebody Loves Me"* (Ontario, CA: Chick Publications, 2005).
2. Ibid., [19].
3. Ibid.
4. Ibid., [22].
5. The issue of whether or not fundamentalists retreated from American society is one that is currently being contended in evangelical historiography. According to the thesis advanced by historians like George Marsden, Randall Balmer, and Joel Carpenter, fundamentalists largely retreated from the public sphere only to be reawakened (in Carpenter's phrase) in the latter part of the twentieth century due to a variety of reasons. Recent works by Darren Dochuk and Daniel Williams challenge this thesis and suggest that fundamentalists did not retreat from public life but sought other avenues to shape American life. In general I side with Marsden and Balmer but think that the retreat was never a complete one and that fundamentalists were always seeking opportunities to return to public prominence, accounting for what Dochuk and Williams have observed.
6. Christian Smith et al., *American Evangelicalism: Embattled and Thriving* (Chicago: University of Chicago Press, 1998), 9–10. See also Joel A. Carpenter, *Revive Us Again: The Reawakening of American Fundamentalism* (New York: Oxford University Press, 1997), 206–10.
7. Smith et al., *American Evangelicalism*, 11; Sydney Ahlstrom, *A Religious History of the American People* (New Haven, CT: Yale University Press, 1972), 957–958;

George M. Marsden, *Reforming Fundamentalism: Fuller Seminary and the New Evangelicalism* (Grand Rapids, MI: Eerdmans, 1987), 47–50.

8. Marsden, *Reforming Fundamentalism*, 24.

9. See Chapter 1 and Chapter 2.

10. Carpenter, *Revive Us Again*, 161–165; John G. Turner, *Bill Bright & Campus Crusade for Christ: The Renewal of Evangelicalism in Postwar America* (Chapel Hill: University of North Carolina Press, 2008), 22–23. See also Thomas E. Bergler, *The Juvenilization of American Christianity* (Grand Rapids, MI: Eerdmans, 2012), which examines the attitudes toward adolescents among evangelicals and other Christians in the middle of the twentieth century.

11. Carpenter, *Revive Us Again*, 217–226.

12. Turner, *Bill Bright*, 24.

13. Ibid., 13–68.

14. Marsden, *Reforming Fundamentalism*, 153–171; Turner, *Bill Bright*, 76–92.

15. Michael G. Long, *Billy Graham and the Beloved Community* (New York: Palgrave Macmillan, 2006); D. Michael Lindsay, *Faith in the Halls of Power: How Evangelicals Joined the American Elite* (Oxford: Oxford University Press, 2007), 53–54, 66;

16. Turner, *Bill Bright*, 87.

17. Gary Dorrien, *The Remaking of Evangelical Theology* (Louisville, KY: Westminster John Knox, 1998), 103–152.

18. See, for example, Sara Diamond, *Not by Politics Alone: The Enduring Influence of the Christian Right* (New York: Guilford Press, 1998); Lindsay, *Faith in the Halls of Power*; Jon A. Shields, *The Democratic Virtues of the Christian Right* (Princeton, NJ: Princeton University Press, 2009); Christian Smith, *Christian America?: What Evangelicals Really Want* (Berkeley: University of California Press, 2000).

19. David John Marley, *Pat Robertson: An American Life* (Lanham, MD: Rowman & Littlefield Publishers, 2007), chronicles not only Pat Robertson's life but also Robertson's interactions with other televangelists like Jimmy Swaggart, Jerry Falwell, and Jim Bakker.

20. Daniel K. Williams, *God's Own Party: The Making of the Christian Right* (Oxford: Oxford University Press, 2010), focuses on showing how the development of the Christian Right was not simply a product of the 1970s but one that stretched back to the 1920s and 1930s. Another monograph that outlines the early twentieth-century roots of political evangelicalism is Darren Dochuk, *From Bible Belt to Sun Belt: Plain Folk Religion, Grassroots Politics, and the Rise of Evangelical Conservatism* (New York: W.W. Norton and Company, 2011).

21. Smith, *Christian America*, 99. See Mara Einstein, *Brands of Faith: Marketing Religion in a Commercial Age* (London: Routledge, 2008), 179–180, for references to Warren and Osteen's "apolitical" statements.

22. Smith, *Christian America*, 119.

23. Smith, *Christian America*, 37–49.
24. Lindsay, *Faith in the Halls of Power*, 24.
25. See Smith, *Christian America*, 92–128.
26. Max Lucado, *Turn: Remembering Our Foundations* (Sisters, OR: Multnomah, 2005).
27. Ibid., 23–24.
28. Ibid., 26.
29. Ibid., 29.
30. Ibid., 31.
31. Ibid., 51.
32. Ibid., 81.
33. Ibid., 82.
34. Ibid., 93.
35. Smith, *Christian America*, 37.
36. Ibid.
37. Max Lucado, "What God Says about Gay Marriage," July 18, 2004, available online at http://www.maxlucado.com/pdf/marriage, accessed July 11, 2011 (now discontinued).
38. Ibid., 2.
39. Ibid., 3.
40. Ibid., 4.
41. Ibid., 7.
42. Ibid.
43. Ibid.
44. Ibid., 9.
45. "Rick Warren's Controversial Comments on Gay Marriage," *beliefnet.com*, available online at http://blog.beliefnet.com/stevenwaldman/2008/12/rick-warrens-controversial-com.html, accessed July 13, 2011; Transcript for *Larry King Live*, April 6, 2009, available online at http://transcripts.cnn.com/TRANSCRIPTS/0904/06/lkl.01.html, accessed July 13, 2011; Sarah Pulliam, Q&A: Rick Warren, April 8, 2009, available online at http://www.christianitytoday.com/ct/2009/aprilweb-only/114-31.0.html?start=1, accessed July 13, 2011; Sarah Pulliam Bailey, "Rick Warren Clarifies Same-Sex Marriage Remarks," April 9, 2009, available online at http://blog.christianitytoday.com/ctpolitics/2009/04/rick_warren_cla.html, accessed July 13, 2011.
46. "Rick Warren's Controversial Comments," *beliefnet.com*.
47. Bailey, "Rick Warren Clarifies."
48. Transcript for *Larry King Live*.
49. Julia A. Stern, *The Plight of Feeling: Sympathy and Dissent in the Early American Novel* (Chicago: University of Chicago Press, 1997), 31.
50. Jane Tompkins, *Sensational Designs: The Cultural Work of American Fiction, 1790–1860* (New York: Oxford University Press, 1985), 124

51. Ibid., 122–146.

52. Ann Douglas, *The Feminization of American Culture* (New York: Anchor Press, 1977; reprint, 1988), 9.

53. Ibid.

54. Ibid., 32.

55. Jon Butler, *Awash in a Sea of Faith: Christianizing the American People* (Cambridge, MA: Harvard University Press, 1990).

56. See Colleen McDannell, *The Christian Home in Victorian America, 1840–1900* (Bloomington: Indiana University Press, 1986).

57. Amanda Porterfield, *The Protestant Experience in America* (Westport, CT: Greenwood Press, 2006), 127–130; Randall Balmer, *Blessed Assurance: A History of Evangelicalism in America* (Boston, MA: Beacon Press, 1999), 94–110. For an example of this type of rhetoric see Jerry Falwell, "An Agenda for the 1980s," in *Piety and Politics: Evangelicals and Fundamentalists Confront the World*, ed. Richard John Neuhaus and Michael Cromartie (Washington, DC: Ethics and Public Policy Center, 1987), 109–123.

58. Einstein, *Brands of Faith*, 100. See also Lucado, *Turn*.

59. George Marsden, *Fundamentalism and American Culture, New Edition* (Oxford: Oxford University Press, 2006), 7; Smith et al., *American Evangelicalism*, 136–143; Lindsay, *Faith in the Halls of Power*, 15, all point to an intriguing paradox in evangelicalism. As Marsden puts it, there is an "establishment-or-outsider paradox" that allows evangelicals to claim both that they represent authentic American culture and that they are an "embattled" constituency. Lindsay notes that this rhetoric of marginalization persists even when evangelicals sit in the White House or other positions of power. Whether or not audiences make the connection between this rhetoric of the apolitical or seek sentimentality as a consolation for political marginalization, the historical development of sentimentality as a trope of ministers has brought us to this point.

60. Jason C. Bivins, *Religion of Fear: The Politics of Horror in Conservative Evangelicalism* (Oxford: Oxford University Press, 2008).

61. Ibid., 15–17.

62. Ibid., 41, 47; "Complete list of Chick cartoon gospel tracts," available online at http://www.chick.com/catalog/tractlist.asp, accessed May 27, 2009. The tracts are also available for online reading.

63. Chick, "Somebody Loves Me."

64. Bivins, *Religion of Fear*, 56–66; Mark S. Massa, *Anti-Catholicism in America: The Last Acceptable Prejudice* (New York: Crossroad Publishing Company, 2003), 100–120.

65. J[ack] T. C[hick], *"The Present"* (Ontario, CA: Chick Publications, 1993).

66. Ibid., [6].

67. Ibid., [9].

68. Ibid., [11].

69. Ibid.
70. Ibid., [19].
71. Ibid., [21].
72. Ibid., [22].
73. See Amy Johnson Frykohlm, *Rapture Culture: Left Behind in Evangelical America* (Oxford: Oxford University Press, 2002); Hendershot, *Shaking the World*, 176–209. Hendershot appears to question whether the creation of media by evangelicals can actually reach nonevangelical audiences; quite often the product comes across as "confused in that it wants to convert outsiders, but ultimately only preaches to the choir" (214); and Bivins, *Religion of Fear*, 169–211.
74. Frykohlm, *Rapture Culture*, 97–101; Bivins, *Religion of Fear*, 193–197.
75. See Tim LaHaye and Jerry B. Jenkins, *Left Behind: A Novel of the Earth's Last Days* (Wheaton, IL: Tyndale House Publishers, Inc., 1995), 48, 75, 125; Bivins, *Religion of Fear*, 194.
76. LaHaye and Jenkins, *Left Behind*, 216.
77. Ibid., 37.
78. Ibid., 47.
79. Ibid., 211.
80. Ibid.
81. Ibid., 62.
82. Ibid., 103.
83. Ibid.
84. See ibid., 97–98, 144.
85. Ibid., 89
86. See ibid., 66–68, 73–76
87. Ibid., 165.
88. Ibid.
89. Ibid., 166.
90. Ibid., 212. See also 200–201,where God's love is discussed as well as the relationship someone can have with God once converted..
91. Grant Wacker, "Searching for Norman Rockwell," in Neuhaus and Cromartie, *Piety and Politics* (see note 30), 345–347.
92. Randall Balmer, *Mine Eyes Have Seen the Glory: A Journey into the Evangelical Subculture in America*, 4th ed. (Oxford: Oxford University Press, 2006), 159.
93. Diamond, *Not by Politics Alone*, 131–155. For examples of this rhetoric of children, spirituality, and innocence, see the National Right to Life Committee's mission statement: "NRLC Mission Statement," available online at http://www.nrlc.org/missionstatement.htm, accessed January 29, 2013; articles on the American Family Association's website: Pat Centner, "Life: A Miraculous Gift," *AFA Journal*, January 2003, available online at http://www.afajournal.org/2003/january/prolife_issues.asp, accessed January 29, 2013; Ed Vitagliano, "Murder: So What?"

AFA Journal, November–December 2004, available online at http://afajournal.
org/2004/nov-dec/11-1204pro-life.asp, accessed May 28, 2009.

94. See, for example, Jenny Tyree, "Mom and Dad: Kids Need Both," *CitizenLink*, available online at http://www.citizenlink.com/2010/06/15/mom-and-dad-kids-need-both, accessed January 30, 2013; Tyree, "Woven Together," *CitizenLink*, available online at http://www.citizenlink.com/2010/06/15/woven-together, accessed January 30, 2013; Carrie Gordon Earll, "Talking Points to Protect Marriage," *CitizenLink*, available online at http://www.citizenlink.com/2012/06/21/talking-points-to-protect-marriage, accessed January 30, 2013; Diamond, *Not by Politics Alone*, 168–171.

95. Randall Balmer, *Thy Kingdom Come: How the Religious Right Distorts the Faith and Threatens America, An Evangelical's Lament* (New York: Basic Books, 2006), 71–108. For examples of *school choice* rhetoric, see Candi Cushman, "Focus on the Family Policy Statement on Homeschooling," *CitizenLink*, available online at http://www.citizenlink.com/2010/06/10/focus-on-the-family-policy-statement-on-homeschooling, accessed January 30, 2013; Cushman, "Capturing Children's Minds," *CitizenLink*, available online at http://www.citizenlink.com/2011/09/20/capturing-childrens-minds, accessed January 30, 2013; Cushman, "School Choice: What Exactly Are My Choices?" *CitizenLink*, available online at http://www.citizenlink.com/2010/06/14/school-choice-what-exactly-are-my-choices, accessed January 30, 2013; Cushman, "Dig Deeper: Why This Week's Supreme Court Ruling Matters to Families," *CitizenLink*, available online at http://www.citizenlink.com/2011/04/05/dig-deeper-why-this-weeks-supreme-court-ruling-matters-to-families, accessed January 30, 2013; Cushman, "Focus on the Family's Parental Rights Statement," *CitizenLink*, available online at http://www.citizenlink.com/2010/06/10/focus-on-the-familys-parental-rights-statement, accessed January 30, 2013.

96. Linda Kintz, *Between Jesus and the Market: The Emotions That Matter in Right-Wing America* (Durham, NC: Duke University Press, 1997), noted the importance of domestic emotion (particularly concerning ideals of motherhood) to understanding evangelical political rhetoric but did not connect this to larger trends in evangelicalism.

97. "Chick-fil-A: Who We Are," CFA Properties, Inc., available online at http://www.chick-fil-a.com/Media/PDF/who-we-are.pdf, accessed November 26, 2012.

98. K. Allan Blume, "'Guilty as Charged,' Dan Cathy Says of Chick-fil-A's Stand on Faith," *Biblical Recorder*, available online at http://www.brnow.org/News/July-2012/%E2%80%98Guilty-as-charged,%E2%80%99-Dan-Cathy-says-of-Chick-fil-A, accessed November 28, 2012.

99. See, for example, Tiffany Hsu, "Is Chick-fil-A Anti-Gay Marriage? 'Guilty as Charged,' Leader Says," *Los Angeles Times*, available online at http://www.latimes.com/business/money/la-fi-mo-chick-fil-a-gay-20120718,0,3020372.

story, accessed January 25, 2013; Rene Lynch, "Chick-fil-A Appreciation Day Draws Crowds, Company Gratitude," *Los Angeles Times*, available online at http://articles.latimes. com/2012/aug/01/nation/la-na-nn-chick-fil-a-appreciation-day-20120801, accessed Janaury 25, 2013; Susana Kim, "Chick-fil-A Benefited from Summer's Gay Marriage Flap with More Customer Visits," *ABC News*, available online at http://abcnews.go.com/Business/chick-fil-benefited-summers-gay-marriage-debate/story?id=17562204, accessed January 25, 2013.

100. The intersection between gender and politics in evangelicalism is a rich field to explore. Several excellent works provide important contributions to evangelical historiography. See, for example, Diamond, *Not by Politics Alone*; Kintz, *Between Jesus and the Market*; R. Marie Griffith, *God's Daughters: Evangelical Women and the Power of Submission* (Berkeley: University of California Press, 1997); Griffith, *Born Again Bodies: Flesh and Spirit in American Christianity* (Berkeley: University of California Press, 2004).

101. Max Lucado, *Outlive Your Life: You Were Made to Make a Difference* (Nashville, TN: Thomas Nelson, 2010).

102. Ibid., 12.

103. Ibid., 46.

104. Ibid.

105. Ibid., v.

106. Ibid., 123.

107. Ibid., 124.

108. Ibid.

109. Ibid., 127–130.

110. Texas Youth Commission, "Who Are TYC Offenders?" available online at http://www.tyc.state.tx.us/research/youth_stats.html, accessed July 18, 2011.

111. Ibid.

112. "What We Do," available online at http://thepeaceplan.com/what-we-do, accessed May 20, 2013.

113. "Rick Warren-About the PEACE Plan," available online at http://www. saddleback.com/betarw/about/thepeaceplan/, accessed May 20, 2013.

114. Ibid.

115. "The PEACE Plan," available online at http://www.revivecommunity.org/about/signature-ministries/the-peace-plan.html, accessed May 20, 2013. Revive is a "Saddleback Network Church." Saddleback refers to the church that Warren pastors.

116. "The PEACE Plan," available online at http://thepeaceplan.com, accessed July 20, 2011. The homepage has since changed, but the video on the homepage expresses similar sentiments.

117. "About The PEACE Plan," available online at http://thepeaceplan.com/AboutUs, accessed July 20, 2011 (now discontinued).

118. See "What We Do."

119. Michael O. Emerson and Christian Smith, *Divided by Faith: Evangelical Religion and the Problem of Race in America* (Oxford: Oxford University Press, 2000), 117, describe this mind-set of individual change effecting structural change as the *miracle motif.* Although their focus is on how this way of thinking prevents changes in racial situations, their conclusions are certainly analogous to other social issues. They are also adamant (and rightly so) that the hopes of individual Christian conversion creating mass social conversion are unfounded and ineffective (130–133).

120. Joyce Meyer, *Beauty for Ashes: Receiving Emotional Healing*, rev. and exp. edition (New York: Warner Faith, 2003), 4–5.

CONCLUSION

1. Evangelical Manifesto Steering Committee, "An Evangelical Manifesto: A Declaration of Evangelical Identity and Public Commitment," available online at http://www.anevangelicalmanifesto.com/docs/Evangelical_Manifesto.pdf, accessed June 8, 2009.

2. Ibid., 6

3. Ibid., 19.

4. Ibid., 19–20.

5. The Steering Committee list is available online at http://www.anevangelicalmanifesto.com, accessed June 8, 2009. The Charter Signatories list is available online at http://www.anevangelicalmanifesto.com/sign.php, accessed June 8, 2009. On that page, there is a list of other people who have signed the manifesto as well as the opportunity for website visitors to sign.

6. Evangelical Manifesto Steering Committee, "Evangelical Manifesto," 11.

7. Ibid., 12.

8. Ibid.

9. Ibid., 13.

10. Ibid., 12.

11. Ibid.

12. Richard Hofstadter, *Anti-Intellectualism in American Life* (New York: Knopf, 1963).

13. I need to thank one of the anonymous readers from Oxford University Press for making this salient observation.

14. Evangelical Manifesto Steering Committee, "Evangelical Manifesto", 15.

15. Ibid., 15, 13–14.

16. Ibid., 14–15, 17.

17. Ibid., 17.

18. Ibid., 15.

19. Ibid.

20. Comments on the manifesto are available online at http://www. anevangelicalmanifesto. com/talk.php, accessed June 8, 2009.

21. Evangelical Manifesto Steering Committee, "Evangelical Manifesto," 13.

22. Ibid., 15.

23. This is an area where it remains to be seen whether the generational divide between evangelicals over same-sex marriage will have a substantial impact politically.

24. See Mark A. Noll, "Common Sense Traditions and American Evangelical Thought," *American Quarterly 37* (Summer 1985): 220–223; Sydney E. Ahlstrom, "Scottish Philosophy and American Theology," *Church History 24* (September 1955): 257–272.

25. Evangelical Manifesto Steering Committee, "Evangelical Manifesto," 4. It is interesting that the authors want the right of self-definition but deny it to others. They make a clear distinction between Christians and Mormons (17); however, Latter-Day Saints self-identify as Christians. These "evangelicals" evidently do not view Mormons as Christians, probably due to both the history of the movement and its Christology. If scholars should accept the self-definition of evangelicals, should the authors of this document not do the same? Evidently they believe that there are other "true" or "real" aspects behind Mormonism to distinguish it from Christianity.

26. Mark A. Noll, *America's God: From Jonathan Edwards to Abraham Lincoln* (Oxford: Oxford University Press, 2002).

27. Ibid., 9.

28. This is not to suggest that Noll was wrong. Instead it is to affirm that often religious subjects (and in fact all subjects) are willfully or unwillfully aware of other forces acting upon them. Scholars can never take what is said by subjects solely at face value if they are to understand those they are studying.

29. See, for example, R. Marie Griffith, *God's Daughters: Evangelical Women and the Power of Submission* (Berkeley: University of California Press, 1997), and Lynn Neal, *Romancing God: Evangelical Women and Inspirational Fiction* (Chapel Hill: University of North Carolina Press, 2006).

30. William R. Hutchison, *The Modernist Impulse in American Protestantism* (Durham, NC: Duke University Press, 1992; originally publication 1976).

31. Ibid., 3–4.

32. See, for example, Christian Smith with Patricia Snell, *Souls in Transition: The Religious and Spiritual Lives of Emerging Adults* (Oxford: Oxford University Press, 2009).

33. Justin Farrell, "The Young and the Restless? The Liberalization of Young Evangelicals," *Journal for the Scientific Study of Religion 50* (September 2011): 517–532.

34. Farrell, "Young and the Restless," 519–521.

35. Smith with Snell, *Souls in Transition*, 45–53.

36. Randall Balmer, *Mine Eyes Have Seen the Glory: A Journey into the Evangelical Subculture in America*, exp. ed. (New York: Oxford University Press, 1993), xiii.

37. George Marsden, "The Evangelical Denomination," in *Evangelicalism and Modern America*, ed. George Marsden (Grand Rapids, MI: Eerdmans, 1984), ix–x.

38. D. W. Bebbington, *Evangelicalism in Modern Britain: A History from the 1730s to the 1980s* (London: Unwin Hyman, 1989).

39. See Noll, *America's God*, 5; Mark A. Noll, David Bebbington, and George A. Rawlyk, eds., *Evangelicalism: Comparative Studies of Popular Protestantism in North America, the British Isles, and Beyond, 1700–1990* (New York: Oxford University Press, 1994), 6.

40. Bebbington, *Evangelicalism in Modern Britain*, 6.

41. Ibid., 12.

42. Ibid., 14.

43. Ibid., 15.

44. Amy Johnson Frykohlm, *Rapture Culture: Left Behind in Evangelical America* (Oxford: Oxford University Press, 2002).

45. Lynn S. Neal, *Romancing God: Evangelical Women and Inspirational Fiction* (Chapel Hill: University of North Carolina Press, 2006), 10.

46. Douglas A. Sweeney, "The Essential Evangelicalism Dialectic: The Historiography of Neo-Evangelicalism and the Observer-Participant Dilemma," *Church History* 60 (March 1991): 70–84.

47. Ibid., 73.

48. Donald W. Dayton, "Some Doubts about the Usefulness of the Category 'Evangelical,'" in *The Variety of American Evangelicalism*, ed. Donald W. Dayton and Robert K. Johnston (Knoxville: University of Tennessee Press, 1991; reprint, 2001), 245–251.

49. Balmer, *Mine Eyes Have Seen the Glory*, 112; George M. Marsden, *Fundamentalism and American Culture*, new ed. (Oxford: Oxford University Press, 2006), 234.

50. Neal, *Romancing God*, 194.

51. Griffiths, *God's Daughters*; John Corrigan, *Business of the Heart: Religion and Emotion in the Nineteenth Century* (Berkeley: University of California Press, 2002); Aaron K. Ketchell, *Holy Hills of the Ozarks: Religion and Tourism in Branson, Missouri* (Baltimore, MD: Johns Hopkins University Press, 2007); James S. Bielo, *Emerging Evangelicals: Faith, Modernity, and the Desire for Authenticity* (New York: NYU Press, 2011); Neal, *Romancing God*; T. M. Luhrman, *When God Talks Back: Understanding the American Evangelical Relationship with God* (New York: Alfred A. Knopf, 2012).

INDEX